YOU CAN'T PLAY THE GAME IF YOU DON'T KNOW THE RULES

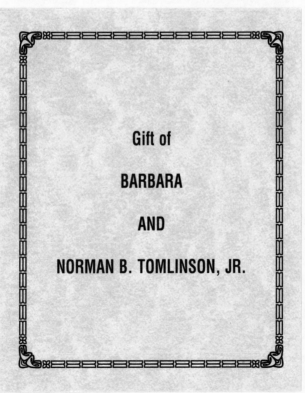

YOU CAN'T PLAY THE GAME IF YOU DON'T KNOW THE RULES

Career Opportunities in Sports Management

David M. Carter

IMPACT PUBLICATIONS
Manassas Park, VA

YOU CAN'T PLAY THE GAME
IF YOU DON'T KNOW THE RULES

Copyright © 1994 by David M. Carter

Library of Congress Cataloguing-in-Publication Data

Carter, David M., 1964—
    You can't play the game if you don't know the rules : uncovering career opportunities in sports management / David M. Carter.
        p. cm.
    Includes bibliographical references and index.
    ISBN 1-57023-005-6 : $14.95
    1. Sports—Management—Vocational guidance—United States.
I. Title.
GV716.C37 1994
796'.06'9—dc20   93-47435
                                                                       CIP

For information on distribution or quantity discount rates, Tel. 703/361-7300, FAX 703/335-9486, or write to: Sales Department, IMPACT PUBLICATIONS, 9104-N Manassas Drive, Manassas Park, VA 22111-5211. Distributed to the trade by National Book Network, 4720 Boston Way, Suite A, Lanham, MD 20706, Tel. 301/459-8696 or 800/462-6420.

CONTENTS

PART II

The Athletic Department

PART III

Athletic Representation Firms

PART VI

Sports Management Companies

PART VII
Conclusion

Dedication

TO VICKIE,

whose love, encouragement,

and never ending support

made this all possible.

ACKNOWLEDGEMENTS

A number of very special people helped me with this book—providing enormous encouragement and guidance. Had either of these been lacking, there is little doubt that this project would have remained nothing more than a hazy idea, never to be completed.

Foremost among those responsible for this effort were my family and close professional friends. Each family member participated in the process either directly by critiquing the work-in-progress or passively, by simply staying out of the way. In either event, I thank each one for their support during yet another episode of what has been a fascinating journey in the sports management business.

Among my close professional friends, I would like to personally thank each of the contributing writers.

Frank Stephens, the Assistant Athletic Director at UCLA, provided immeasurable direction regarding collegiate athletics—despite the fact that he graduated from, and works for, that "other school" in town.

Steve Freyer, the 'Boston Brahmin' whose learned vernacular kept me constantly scurrying to the dictionary, provided extraordinary insight into the world of personal representation. His experiences have not only enriched this book but have also had a lasting impact on my career.

The lone Warrior among us (of the Golden State variety), Bryan Deierling, provided the necessary comic relief throughout the process. But, with his franchise finishing an injury plagued season with a meager

34-48 record, did he ever really have a choice? Moreover, with the birth of his first son, I was honored Bryan made the time and found the energy to complete his contribution!

No discussion of sports could ever be considered complete without including one's college roommate. Lonnie White's accounting of the media's impact on sports was poignant and fostered many intriguing discussions about the topic. I wish to thank him again for his friendship and congratulate him on his recent marriage.

Bert Geiger's knowledge and understanding of the financial world as it relates to servicing professional athletes may be unparalleled. His knack for accomplishing this level of professional success while interspersing humorous anecdotes made for an excellent working relationship.

Everyone should be fortunate enough to have a friend like Greg Bunker, especially when it comes to discussing sports over a couple of ice cold beers. He is one of the truly eminent attorneys in this country, whose reputation for fairness and practicality are beyond reproach. While it did not seem possible, my respect for him has grown to new heights after working on this book together.

The final contributor, Jon Grossman, was an absolute pleasure to work with. His dedication and passion for this project (as well as our other joint efforts) will always be appreciated. And while his input was pragmatic from start to finish, I must add that Jon's most endearing contribution was his unequalled wit (carefully and generously laced with cynicism) about the business. Jon, who will ever forget Knoxville, Tennessee?

While it would not be possible to construct an exhaustive list of all those who were helpful in the writing of this book, I would like to acknowledge the efforts of the following: Jim Edgeworth, David Geyer, Don Klosterman, Jack Mills, Mark Griege, Graham Pope, Marty Rodick, Mark Levin, Inoh Choi, Duane Knopke, and, of course, my close personal friends who constantly egged me on.

And, finally, special thanks to Ron Krannich of Impact Publications, for without his trust and hard work, this book would not have been possible.

FOREWORD

Greg Bunker, a sports and business attorney, has represented both professional athletes, including Indy Race Car Champion, Arie Luyendyk and professional sports organizations such as the Los Angeles Raiders. Additionally, he has represented such international business concerns as Anheuser-Busch and Mercedes Benz.

In addition to his Juris Doctor from the University of the Pacific's McGeorge School of Law, Bunker also holds Bachelor and Master Degrees in political science from the University of Northern Colorado and the University of Kansas, respectively. Through his memberships in the Sports Lawyers Association and the Sports & Entertainment Section of the American Bar Association, he is able to remain abreast of the legal, business, and regulatory issues confronting collegiate and professional athletics.

So you think you want a career in sports? Why read this particular book on the subject? It's really quite simple: knowledge is power. Specifically, *You Can't Play the Game If You Don't Know the Rules* provides commentary and first person analysis of five different, but intricately intertwined areas within the sports business. The more knowledge you possess regarding these interworkings including the

xi

structure and business philosophies inherent in the various aspects of the sports industry, the more control you will have in determining your employment destiny within the industry. This book will make you think; in short, it will help you gain the power necessary to enhance your entry and potential success in a career in the sports business.

Until you fully appreciate and comprehend the dependant relationships which exist among intercollegiate athletics, personal representation, professional franchises, the media, and sports management companies, you will always be on the outside looking in. If nothing else, this book will create food for thought regarding these relationships and shed some light on your ability to integrate personal expertise, knowledge and interest in each of these areas.

If you are truly interested in the business side of sports, you are well aware of the scarcity of analytical and introspective literature on the subject. The obvious value of this work is its comprehensive analysis of the various interrelated aspects of the sports management industry and related employment opportunities. Consider that, like many professionals or scholars, it is often difficult to find information sources or the time to learn about other subjects which, at first glance, appear unrelated to your discipline. As this book will demonstrate, this first glance is commonly quite deceiving.

For a single all encompassing example, consider the relationship created by basketball's "March Madness," the NCAA's National Championship Tournament. An institution's invitation to the "Dance" means thousands (and often hundreds of thousands) of dollars to the athletic department in addition to favorable publicity for the institution in a national forum. This translates to increased alumni contributions, job security for the coaching and administrative staffs, and exposure for the student-athletes to national audiences—and, eventually, the NBA.

But the school is not the only one to benefit from this tournament bid. The agent for the coach or future professional athlete is thrilled by this national coverage. He can utilize these appearances to prolong a coaching career (or perhaps begin lobbying for another) and maximize potential endorsements. The agent's star hoop prospect enjoys the interaction with NBA scouts, the media, and sports management companies. In short, the tournament begins 'making' tomorrow's basketball stars—much to the agent's delight.

Professional sports franchises view the tourney as an opportunity to solidify mutually beneficial relationships with universities and their coaches. These healthy relationships make it easier for pro teams to gain access to a university's players and coaches—those transient teachers that are always considering that coaching opportunity at the next level. Also, these cozy relationships can help franchises minimize recruiting costs as ease of information and access to players surely makes the scouting process more efficient.

And don't forget the media. They paid over a billion dollars to showcase the tournament on national television, leaving no angle, on or off the court, uncovered. They, too, must continue to establish and maintain strong relationships with the universities, coaches and players, and, of course, the rest of the media, professional franchises, and sports management companies. For without a smooth and professionally orchestrated event, the network would lose millions and end up in the same financial disarray as major league baseball's network relationships; the media can ill afford to have the other factions in sports crack the golden egg that they took such pains to lay.

Finally, sports management companies use this time to network, obtain new clients, and promote existing clientele to universities, professional franchises and the media. As we will see, these national sports venues make for captive corporate and consumer audiences —audiences which regularly seek added exposure, additional goodwill and increased sales.

This over-simplified account of how the five disciplines discussed throughout this book interact in a specific context should serve to begin the thought process, a process that will help you discover your niche or career interest in the world of sports.

Additionally, a working knowledge of the different components within the sports industry will enable you to better comprehend sports' *total* employment picture—essentially allowing you to position yourself to seize that first career opportunity, as an employee of a large sports-oriented corporation, member of a mid-sized sports management company, athletic department specialist, franchise front officer, member of the media, or even as a sports agent.

Over the last five years, David Carter and I have spent hours discussing endless athletic contests, sparkling individual performances, and the diverse personalities throughout 'Big Time Sports'—not unlike any other hard-core sports fans! Undoubtedly, you have similar discussions with friends, business acquaintances, or even the guy sitting next to you at the local sports bar. However, we each brought something else to the table: the insatiable desire to combine our education and professional expertise in the type of business that was our true passion—sports.

As a business and sports lawyer, the relationship between business and sports was readily apparent. Professional and intercollegiate athletics are *Big Business*—a multi-billion dollar industry—which is constantly facing complex business and legal issues such as collective bargaining agreements, the licensing of sports-related products, antitrust issues, the negotiation of television contracts, salary caps, free agency, league-wide revenue sharing, drug testing, expansion, etc. Furthermore, let's not forget the business and legal issues confronted by the 21 year old multi-millionaire athlete who generally lacks the business sophistication to match the dollars in his investment portfolio. Obviously, having a clear understanding of these current issues is critical. Perhaps more important, however, is the ability to forecast future issues which are destined to have a similar and major impact on the sports industry. Again, this book will help you uncover these issues within this ever-evolving business.

The contributing authors will provide first person accounts that reflect their experiences and unique ability to intertwine their professional expertise with the business side of sports, especially the five areas mentioned in this book. Needless to say, we all encounter trials and tribulations in our chosen careers. It is the intention of the contributors to help you through these experiences by providing a road map and/or an occasional short cut that will make your venture into a career in sports a much more fulfilling one.

Many individuals who are gainfully employed in sports hold neither a J.D., M.B.A. nor other related professional degree. Every industry has its own requirements which need to be considered and understood long before seeking a career—and sports is no different. Depending on personal interests, your educational level and work experience, the requirements typically range from a specific degree or professional license to even an occasional non-paying internship. As you will notice upon your review of the contributors' chapters, there is no single, correct way to obtain the requisite experience for a career in this industry but proper timing, creativity and hard work appear to play a major role in each contributor's success in the business.

Nonetheless, as an attorney, I would assert that a competent business lawyer, one who understands the business side of sports and is familiar with the intricacies of the particular sport in question, is a very hard combination to beat. An attorney (and, in particular, a business and sports attorney) generally has the requisite education, communication skills, extensive knowledge and experience with contracts and other related legal issues. This background regularly brings creativity to the bargaining table as innovative concepts and complex issues are raised throughout the personal representation process.

For example, the qualified agent must understand the entire "playing field." This comprehensive understanding begins with the terms included in the league-approved form contract, a contract which has evolved and been refined over the years. It also incorporates the relative financial strength of the specific team with whom you are negotiating as well as the financial stability of the league in general. All of this must be accomplished while remaining cognizant of the league's collective bargaining agreement (C.B.A.).

Simultaneously, the agent is forced to ask himself, as well as the client, how many years should the contract last? How large should the signing bonus be? What about deferments? What other bonuses or performance-based incentives are available? If the player is a rookie, where does his salary fit into the "slotting" process? Can you improve the team's offer by suggesting a different structuring of the terms and incentives? Do you understand the philosophy of team ownership and management regarding player relations? This abbreviated laundry list barely scratches the surface of the issues which must be addressed by the competent agent during contract negotiations.

From the perspective of a sports and business lawyer, an understanding of the complexities of all the ancillary sports business industries is critical when negotiating a player's contract, a shoe endorsement for a coach, a television or radio sponsorship for a franchise, or an employment contract for a media personality. This understanding is imperative because the contract creates a legal obligation between the parties. But, what about the ancillary issues created by a contract? Does the player contract anger teammates or upset team or league contract parity? Does the coach's shoe endorsement contract create a conflict of interest with the league or his franchise? Is the television contract with the league, franchise, academic institution or event so "out of line" that it creates an economic ripple effect which influences all aspects of that sport or all sports? Again, complex inter-relationships do exist and significantly impact all areas of sports.

The other disciplines discussed in this book face similarly pertinent issues. For example, intercollegiate athletic departments may be concerned about graduation rates, the revenue generated by fielding a competitive squad, student-athlete eligibility issues and high school recruiting. All of which must be accomplished without sacrificing the overall agenda of the school.

Continuing to turn our focus toward the other areas of sports management, remember the importance of networking in each of the areas discussed in this book. Experiencing each of these areas will add to your overall level of expertise. Bear in mind, however, that networking alone usually will not result in landing a job. Without sufficient knowledge and experience your sports career could be short and relatively uneventful. Armed with a solid resume, networking can enhance your career mobility and create additional opportunities.

In closing, consider the athlete that fails to appreciate the business side of sports. During the week leading up to a recent East-West Shrine Game, I was sitting in the lobby of the hotel where the players, coaches, scouts and agents were lodging. I noticed a player approaching a certain part of the lobby—that area frequented by NFL scouts. Wearing socks but no shoes, a pair of faded gym shorts, a t-shirt marked by numerous holes and a baseball cap *worn sideways*, the player presented a number of sheets of paper to a man I recognized as the West Coast scout for a perennial NFL play-off team. The player said, "Here's your question-naire," turned and walked back toward the elevator.

The very next day I happened to talk to this scout during practice. Naturally, the conversation turned toward his analysis of the skills demonstrated by various players. In response to a question regarding his organization's philosophy concerning drafting players, the scout noted that while each of the participants at the all-star bowls possesses tremendous athletic ability, many do not maintain the character, intellect and mental toughness required to play in the NFL. In fact, his organization was so serious about the character and psychological make-up of its players that even the head coach reviewed every potential draftee's psychological profile report.

Interestingly, the scout mentioned the previously described player without knowing that I witnessed the entire incident in the hotel lobby. The scout described the player, his poor attire, the failure to be person-able and a general lack of interest in the process. The scout's notes reflected all of this and concluded that particular player would not likely fit the team's needs, noting, "That young man doesn't realize that he just flunked his job interview."

Once you have acquired a basic understanding of the five inter-relationships discussed in this book, you will be better armed to avoid flunking your job interview. Your view of the sports world already has a business slant and readily explains why you are reading this text. The issues and the personalities continue to change and, as your knowledge grows, so does your power to control your career destiny.

You Can't Play the Game avoids candy-coating the hard work and patience which was demonstrated by each of the contributing authors in this book. Their first opportunity did not arise simply because they wanted to work in the sports industry. Rather, they worked hard, persevered—and, yes, had a little luck and proper timing. The one common thread among the contributors, however, is their understanding of the strong inter-relationship between and among our diverse chosen (and respective) areas of expertise. Once you have acquired a similar understanding and professional experience, doors previously closed will become wide open. Enjoy your new knowledge—and power.

Gregory E. Bunker

****

PART I:
Getting into the Game

****

1

THE INDUSTRY AND ITS PLAYERS

*I*n order to find a job, any job, one must be creative, persistent and thorough. Consequently, this book is not going to hand you a great job on a platter, but will serve as a tool to make you think. Additionally, I do not consider this writing to be a listing of all of the varied sports careers. I do, however, believe there are certain classifications that encompass the vast majority of sports opportunities. It is my sincere hope that this book assists you in determining your strengths and areas of interest, as well as discover those unique opportunities in the sports industry.

Much like the medical or engineering professions, not everyone is ready for a career in sports. Winning the rotisserie league or hosting a tailgate party does not guarantee preparation for this competitive and often frustrating profession. Instead, the same analytical rigor applied to other industries should be applied to the sports business, with special attention to economic trends.

Even if you firmly believe you are ready for a career in sports, you may not have a fully developed focus or direction. The Sports Industry must be viewed not solely as leisure and entertainment, but as the *Leisure and Entertainment Industry*—one that generates billions of dollars annually and employs tens of thousands of professionals. It has its own economic structure (Gross National Sports Product, or GNSP) encompassing labor unions, professional organizations, rules and regulations, and governing bodies. Sports is an industry that overwhelms us as consumers, and thrills as well as frustrates us as fans and participants.

There are many reasons why I chose, and continue to choose to work in this industry. I will briefly address these now, and provide greater detail later in this manuscript.

As is the case with many of us, I maintain more than a passing interest in sports. I found enormous satisfaction through collegiate athletics as a student spectator at the University of Southern California. My interests were further piqued by attending professional athletic events around the country, as well as actively participating in a wide variety of sports activities, either as an "armchair quarterback" or "weekend warrior." The allure of sports and perceived excitement of working in the industry were most compelling. The notion of being able to make a living in such an inviting manner was inconceivable—perhaps too good to be true.

I also believed there were numerous financial opportunities available for those willing to persevere and work diligently—against significant odds. It was one thing to 'get a job' in sports and quite another to actually have a position that paid the bills. "Jobs" in sports traditionally do not pay well, but a "career in sports management" appeared to be lucrative. The difference between 'the job' and 'the career' was two-fold. One's ability to sacrifice most short term gains was necessary. These gains are most often associated with more traditional professions, and include the ability to save, settle down or obtain graduate level credentials.

In addition to these sacrifices, it is strongly suggested that a keen entrepreneurial spirit be present. If everyone wants to work in this industry, what makes you or your idea unique? What skills or experiences differentiate you from the pack?

Next, the fascinating dynamics of the sports management industry are both intriguing and challenging. They include: an industry in financial disarray (where spiraling salaries and corporate overhead seriously threaten the well-being of the business) and a massive unbundling of the financial services offered to both athletes and their interests. Furthermore, the merging of traditionally mutually exclusive groups—athletes and corporate America, and an overwhelming need for conservative financial management (in an environment frequented by risk takers) have also contributed to the fascination and allure of the industry. Each of these relationships will be thoroughly examined throughout this book in an effort to uncover and/or discover where employment opportunities exist—not only today but well into the 21st Century.

Finally, sports can be tremendously fun and extremely rewarding—not all the time and not as often as you would like, but frequently and with great satisfaction. Whenever an industry or profession is glorified, certain myths within that industry surface. Sports is no exception. Many of these common perceptions are true while others are baseless.

I cannot count the number times that I have heard the following: "I know sports—am a big fan—I should do well." Unfortunately, it is not that simple. After all, it is one thing to know an industry or topic and quite another to transform that knowledge into a revenue-generating activity. Many of the professionals I associate with believe they know and understand the stock market; in reality, very few of them actually make a living trading securities (and even fewer make a *good* living). To be proficient at an activity, one must be dedicated to it and persistent enough to develop a successful track record. Few who know sports have actually taken the time to explore the complexities of the business.

Another common myth is that one must be an attorney to enjoy most of the employment opportunities in sports. While I believe attending law school and passing the Bar Exam are worthwhile endeavors, they are not necessarily prerequisites for handling most sports related transactions.

For example, what do you need to represent an athlete? A law degree? How about experience? Maybe a license? The answer to all of these is basically "no." The truth is that the only prerequisite needed to represent an athlete is *the client himself.*

Many years before sports was a multi-billion dollar industry, players looked for advice from those professionals who had experienced a wide variety of business relationships in complex situations. Because lawyers were most capable of trouble-shooting these issues for their clients, athletes began using them in broader applications of their personal transactions. No transaction was more personal than the personal services contract the athlete had with his professional team. Consequently, most agents were attorneys who were able to comprehend and explain the intricacies of a player's contract. This, in part, explains why most of the established agents who have negotiated contracts for decades are attorneys.

More recently, however, business schools have begun to produce sports agents. This is largely the case as sports becomes an even bigger business with finance, marketing and accounting disciplines becoming at least as important to the athlete as the negotiation of his contract. Over the next several years, I believe the percentage of agents who are attorneys will decline while those with business and business-related backgrounds will increase.

The above addresses only the athlete representation process and does not take into account those services involving athletes which do not require legal expertise such as athletic departments, the media, etc. It is certainly beneficial to have a law degree when assisting athletes and working in sports, but there are numerous opportunities available to those who have comparable education and training.

"I must have deep pockets to break into the sports business." While I understand the reasoning behind this remark, I have a hard time believing it. A great idea is much more important than money, as a unique product or service will attract any necessary funds. Currently, the sports industry is becoming more service-oriented. This allows those attempting to build a career through entrepreneurship a chance to do so with little overhead. No need to be discouraged just because your bank account is small!

The single most frustrating myth I hear is, "It can't be *that* hard." Perhaps the actual transaction or service to be provided is not a difficult one to complete or provide. However, maneuvering into a position to land the account **can** be very difficult. Executing an endorsement contract with a Fortune 500 company may not be hard (although it is), but the months of phone calls, preliminary meetings and detail work is exhausting. As with most things, people only see and judge the final product, forgetting or disregarding what may have led to the accomplishment.

Finally, sports is "always fun." This simply isn't true. Success in any endeavor requires the ability to solve problems, battle deadlines, and resolve delicate situations with conflicting personalities. Losing clients, breaking contracts, sacrificing eligibility and/or trading players is certainly not "always fun." The guest contributors to this book will address specific situations in which they were having anything *but* fun.

Years of personal experiences have enabled me to gain a balanced perspective on the sports community. Along the way, I have received numerous inquiries from individuals interested in learning more about breaking into the world of sports management. It is this combination of experience and overwhelming industry interest that has led to the composition of *You Can't Play the Game*.

I began my career in sports management, where I now serve in a consulting capacity, by gaining work experience in the five categories that comprise this book: Collegiate Athletic Departments, Athlete Representation Firms, Professional Franchises, the Media, and Sports Management Companies. I believed that participation in these areas, whether directly—as an employee, or more passively—as a consultant, was critical to gaining a proper understanding and perspective of the entire industry. While pursuing these five areas, I was able to determine which areas I found appealing and those in which I was less interested. This process has enabled me to build a consulting business over the years and concentrate on business strengths and personal interests.

Throughout this journey, I have witnessed an unbundling of the services provided and products offered to athletes. These products and services include, but are not limited to: financial services—for athletes, management firms and franchises; marketing—including endorsements, promotions and publicity; and management—of franchises, athletes and events. It appears as though this trend will continue well into the next decade, providing many of us with numerous career opportunities. These possibilities will be available to those who are creative, persistent, and poised to seize the opportunity. In addition to these characteristics, an individual must also be able to interface with the diverse and sometimes maddening personal and corporate cultures pertinent to this industry.

When contemplating sports opportunities in the 1990's, it is necessary to think globally. Jobs within most disciplines are likely to experience growth abroad as the new century approaches. Sports is no different, as we have witnessed the popularity of basketball in Europe (and beyond), the founding of the fledgling World League of American Football (WLAF) and the unprecedented potential for increased international competitions arising from the fall of Communism in Eastern Europe. How will you carve out your piece of the pie?

You Can't Play the Game is divided into five major parts, each addressing a different aspect of the sports management industry. Each of these parts includes a chapter contributed by a noted industry professional who has either worked in or is currently employed by the discipline discussed.

The sequence of the parts may appear a little peculiar, but there is a method to the madness. This book examines the life cycle of the star athlete and highlights the various aspects of the sports industry that profit from his participation. This life cycle addresses the athlete from high school stardom until the time he enters the hall of fame. Where there is a profit to made, there are jobs to be found.

ATHLETIC DEPARTMENTS

This first of five major parts to be examined in this book deals with collegiate athletic departments. Specifically examined in this part is the national framework of the athletic departments, as well as their intended purposes and functions. Following this is a detailed look at the relationship between the athletic department and the university, with specific attention to financial considerations. Since no discussion of collegiate athletics would be complete without addressing the NCAA, part of chapter two is devoted to this association. Finally, as is the case in each of these parts, employment opportunities are summarized.

ATHLETE REPRESENTATION FIRMS

Part II reviews athlete representation firms. Chapter four traces the growth of this flourishing business, beginning with a historical perspective and then focusing on both the representation process and the negative perceptions associated with the agency business. Given the structure of the athlete representation process, this portion of the book is especially intriguing.

FRANCHISES, UNIONS AND LEAGUES

Professional franchises and associations comprise Part III. Working for a team, union or league presents a number of interesting issues (for example, chapter six will describe front office politics and evaluate managerial positions available within a franchise). Additionally, support-type positions and their long-term pay prospects are evaluated. Other issues within these factions include racial discrimination, player relations, and drug abuse.

MEDIA

The next part observes the complex world of the media. The massive increases in network contracts and their effects on the sports economy is scrutinized. The future of radio and print in the world of sports, coupled with the prospects for international growth as sports becomes even more of a global community into the year 2000 is also highlighted.

SPORTS MANAGEMENT COMPANIES

Finally, Part V examines sports management companies, observing the many types of organizations and their diversities and specialties. A comparison and discussion of the "Big 3" (International Management Group, ProServ, and Advantage International) to smaller and regional firms will also be made. Also incorporated in this part is a review of the basic foundation of sports management companies, as well as an analysis of employment opportunities and compensation issues.

You Can't Play the Game is designed to provide you with the insight necessary to discover or uncover employment opportunities in the world of sports. This is not a "how to" book in the traditional sense; it is, however, an analytical and creative approach to examining the business side of sports.

2

SKILLS FOR
SUCCESS

*Y*ou can't play the game if you don't know the rules. And the rules for preparing for a career in sports revolve around several critical criteria. These include a mastery of certain personal skills, the realization of one's abilities and limitations, an *adequate* education, and a strategic plan for providing a value-added idea or service. A combination of these 'rules', which are fairly universal, and a little good luck and proper timing will often lead to "getting into the game."

PERSONAL

Since the personal skills required are almost too numerous to mention, I will highlight those that appear most critical in developing a career and successful track record in sports. Salesmanship is everything. *Everything.* Selling encyclopedias, asking someone for a date, being accepted into the university of your choice, and working on the business side of sports each requires salesmanship. In the sports industry, salesmanship is synonymous with personality. Personal chemistry and the power of persuasion are perhaps more critical in sports and other entertainment related businesses because of the diversity of it's participants. Interacting with individuals of varied educational backgrounds, diverse values, and competing financial interests will inevitably force one to be more flexible and open-minded while simultaneously managing one's personal agenda. This delicate balancing act requires continual adjustments.

This ability to interact professionally with such a wide cross-section of society is further complicated by the increasingly stringent requirement that business be conducted ethically. In the unlikely event that ethics is not a personal priority, realize that sports is a very small, very closed fraternal community where everyone knows what everyone else is up to. Break the rules, either legally or morally, and you will no doubt be a short timer.

Intense scrutiny tends to follow those who are either extremely successful or fatally short-sighted. Maintaining absolute honesty and integrity may make the journey a little longer, but bear in mind that you will at least have the opportunity to complete the trip. Many who have begun a career in sports management with the "quick kill" are either in prison, out of work, or essentially banished from the industry. While this is not intended to be a sermon, I do feel it extremely important to stress that without integrity, long term success is virtually unattainable.

There is never a substitute for hard work—just ask Larry Bird, Nolan Ryan, or Joe Montana. Hard work as it relates to preparing for and building a career in sports requires discipline, persistence, patience, and extraordinary self-confidence. Every time you turn around, someone will tell you that you will not be one of the minority that can actually earn a comfortable living in sports. This must serve as the 'fuel' that flames your 'fire'. Of the attributes previously mentioned, patience will probably be the most difficult to muster.

Why? Consider that while learning the business you will likely be in a position to make a noteworthy contribution, only to learn that no one wants to hear it. And if that isn't enough, you'll also feel a sense of aggravation at the lack of managerial competence within the business side of sports; just read the transactions column in the newspaper or listen to the frequent horror stories from athletes. This, too, should serve to further motivate you. Remain confident, maintain a positive attitude, and disregard the nay-sayers. After all, you'll have the last laugh.

SELF-REALIZATION

Closely related to personal skills is the ability to "know yourself." Self-realization requires being truthful with oneself; about personal strengths and weaknesses, interests, and motivations. Concentrating on your primary areas of expertise while simultaneously improving weaknesses will allow you to experience sports from your perspective and at your own pace.

It has taken me several years to even begin to determine my primary areas of interest—and they continue to develop and change as I meet people and learn more about the industry. You will find that your career in sports will evolve over time as you experience the five components of the sports management industry described in this book. While you may already have established a keen interest in a particular area, do not disregard the others. The more you learn about the other disciplines, the more you will realize that they are inter-related.

Are you motivated by money? Are you seeking prestige or status in pursuing a career in sports? What about self-fulfillment? Does the challenge or mystique of the business side of sports motivate you? Whatever your motivations, recognize them and incorporate them into your overall strategy and goals.

EDUCATION

Educational requirements are perhaps the most widely misunderstood element in sports management. An education has always been preferred and respected, but has not always contributed in the scope of "real world" applications. Nonetheless, as the business of sports becomes increasingly competitive and greater attention is given to specialization, higher education will be necessary for both advancement and exposure to the premium opportunities. Many businesses and sports organizations have used the college degree as a minimal benchmark, signifying some basic level of competence within a certain discipline. Recently, however, that benchmark has been changing with the new minimal acceptance level being graduate school—either law, business or management. While attending graduate school does not necessarily contribute in the scope of the "real world," it commonly signifies a sincere interest in pursuing a career in sports management.

As previously mentioned, education was not always as much of a requirement as it is today. Since the late eighties, graduation rates of athletes have been published, Proposition 48 has been enacted and a new breed of business manager has been born. This is not to say that our predecessors were not educated or qualified. It only reflects an ever-changing marketplace and society's influence upon it.

Receiving a graduate or post-graduate degree reminds me of getting a ticket punched—you may seldom use it, but without it you are destined for a much more difficult time obtaining employment in sports. Graduate school, like *You Can't Play the Game*, should be used as a vehicle to make you think and reflect upon your strengths, weaknesses, and personal interests.

One final note regarding education: if you are contemplating attending graduate school, apply sooner rather than later, as with every day you wait it becomes increasingly difficult to begin (and complete) the process.

VISION AND PLANNING

All endeavors require vision and sound strategic planning. Preparing for a career in sports is no different, as one needs to set short term goals and objectives, devise medium term plans, and develop a final long term game plan.

Short term goals can be both basic and productive. When attempting to learn more about a specific field, one can begin by attending seminars. Seminars in sports management pop up periodically in the major sports markets around the country. These seminars typically address such issues as sports marketing, law (as it relates to athlete representation), and even general sports management topics. Combining research and extensive reading are a great way to complement these seminars and workshops. Studies in sports can be found in most libraries and deal with very broad sports issues; the local bookstore, and especially those stores with a sports theme, can provide the essential works that comprise the foundation of sports management.

With respect to reading and research, it is important to focus on both analytical and creative (diaries and journals) works in order to observe how the business is reflected in every day sports lifestyles.

Another short term priority may encompass the honest self-evaluation previously mentioned. It is critical to begin to build an idea of what you hope to gain from a career in sports during the early stages. This will enable you to strategically plan exactly how you will fulfill this dream. While there are numerous additional aspects to developing a short term plan, I will mention just one more: education. Early in the planning phase, it is necessary to determine whether you are comfortable with your existing education level. Chances are you will be. However, in the event that you elect to further this pursuit, begin planning now since adequate schooling takes time to complete.

Medium term planning is a little more complicated. Assuming you have proceeded through most of the early stages and goal setting period, it is time to focus on other issues. For example, does the industry still interest you or do you feel as though you are merely spinning your wheels? Have you received positive feedback from your experiences and inquiries?

At this point, it is suggested that gaining work experience in one of the five areas described in detail throughout this book is required. It really does not matter in which area(s) or in what capacity. What is important is that you begin to get a flavor for what the industry is really like from a participant's perspective. It is understood that most people cannot just donate their time or resources without reason. But at the same time, don't be too proud or too busy to help someone in the industry for nothing. You will likely find that it is most appreciated—and appreciation can often lead to referrals, additional introductions, and potentially that first paying position.

BUILD RELATIONSHIPS

Continuing to meet people in the industry and scheduling information-oriented interviews in those areas in which you are primarily interested should become and remain a priority. Sharing ideas with those who are further along than you in this journey will be most helpful. They can advise you of potential pitfalls and perhaps provide you with valuable guidance. Never be afraid to ask for an individual's time and insights—all he can say is no and, if approached professionally, he will usually be willing to share his experiences.

At this point you will have established a track record even if it has been only on a volunteer or academic level. You have begun an important phase of positioning yourself for the future. This positioning is both internal—developing interests and motivations, and external—extending practical applications in the sports management business. At this time it would be worthwhile to evaluate your progress. Are you satisfied with your progress? In which areas will you require improvement? How are you going about laying the foundation to learning about the other four areas? Are you on a pace or track that is satisfactory for you or are you becoming disillusioned and questioning whether this business still interests you? How profitable do you believe your activities can be?

This line of questioning should assist you to further develop your long range strategic plan. But first, another look back. In addition, consider the following questions. Are you fulfilling the objectives previously deemed important? Have you made steady, methodical progress, moving from the tailgate party to the draft-day party and/or corporate hospitality tent? Throughout all of this, it will be necessary to have begun completing the "work experience gathering." Hopefully you will need experience in only one or two more of the five areas and have been able to focus on specific personal interests—those that have developed as a direct result of broad industry experience.

Another key to continuing the momentum is establishing, encouraging, and enhancing quality relationships within the industry. Are you still in touch with those who may have served as mentors in the early stages? Have you been successful in avoiding "bridge burning?" Do you have an identity and reputation that will serve to propel your activities?

With any luck, you have been able to accomplish this while simultaneously working on any remaining weaknesses. If so, you will have a fairly good notion of whether participation in this business is right for you both personally and financially. You have established a value-added idea, haven't you?

Very few employers are content these days with managers that merely "punch the clock." The current trend in business is to manage an operation that is both 'lean and mean' with little waste and even fewer employees. The decadent 1980's produced inefficient corporations that amassed millions of dollars of debt. The mid-1990's and beyond will be quite different, as this era will be dominated by those with value-added ideas and contributions.

ADD VALUE

Sports management in the nineties and beyond will be no different, with the industry managed by those few who have found a valued idea or service. This value-added concept applies to the self-employed as well as the corporate employee.

Basically, there are two ways to "add value." The first is to create a job or perform a function that increases revenue. This must be accomplished while minimizing the burden on the employer. The other way to add value is to develop and/or implement a plan or program wherein the business entity can reduce expenses. It's that simple: either increase revenue or reduce costs.

The individual who is capable of this and whose contribution can be easily measured, as in increased attendance at a sporting event or dollars saved by creating a more efficient computer software system, will be the most marketable in the sports management community.

Now take this concept and apply it to the service-oriented world of sports. There are numerous ways to add value or reduce cost as this industry heads toward the 21st century. For example, negotiate favorable terms for an individual or firm. The athlete views his agent's value by the favorable terms negotiated and dollars added to a personal services contract; a team may witness its attorney and marketing staff complete a contract that requires additional services or contributions from corporate sponsors. Generating what is considered to be more favorable terms is easily quantifiable.

Another way to participate in this value added concept is to be compensated through commission. Receiving compensation for securing new accounts or being paid for reducing a firm's expenses are great ways to display your value while not significantly adding to the firm's traditional expense items. This type of business development is similarly easy to quantify.

The point should now be obvious: create or add value for the entity without significantly increasing overhead and fixed costs. Minimize burden to the employer and maximize potential revenue to you.

In the event that you are interested in starting your own business, it is still necessary to consider similar issues. The major difference to self-employment, however, is that you must be concerned with both sides of the equation. That is, you are the employee, the boss, and the firm. Are you the self-starter type or do you need some form of external motivation? What about creating a service that, at least in the early stages, only requires working part time. This would enable you to grow slowly and without considerable expense.

In either case, certain elements apply as you are forced to wear the hats of both labor and management. Self-employment has tremendous upside and an equally treacherous downside. Fear of failure is the basic motivating factor. Fixed and variable costs, including rent and other overhead, continue to draw attention to the need to produce revenue and eliminate extraneous expenses. The time frame for producing this revenue, and hopefully a profit, is accelerated. Ideally, these revenue generating activities will lead to a retainer or a steady income-producing relationship. At this point, attention must be given to both servicing existing clients and expanding the client base.

Perhaps I have over-simplified this complex course of events; but the idea here is to begin the thought process of what needs to be accomplished to build a successful career in sports management.

This first section was intended to acquaint you with the primary issues and opportunities in the sports management business. Perhaps it has made you think about sports from a different perspective.

There have been many critical points addressed in this section. First, be prepared to work diligently, creatively, and persistently. Next, view sports as a business, not a hobby. Third, have a series of strategic plans. Fourth, learn by participation—attend sports related conferences and seminars, read industry publications, and meet people. Finally, match these experiences with your primary areas of interest and create a service that adds value.

****

PART II:
The Athletic Department

****

3

POLITICS, PERKS, AND STUDENT-ATHLETES

*U*niversity settings for sports often witness the athletic departments in a continual battle for respect and profit. Focusing on the roles associated with "student-athletics," this chapter examines the structure, bureaucracy, and politics of collegiate athletic departments.

Athletic departments have been established over a very long period of time and for a number of very good reasons. One would assume that the primary role of an athletic department is to assist in the academic process by matriculating student-athletes. Unfortunately, this is a rather naive view.

Organizational handbooks and mission statements do not exist in the traditional sense for most athletic departments. They evolve over time, depending on how and why the athletic department is operating and what its specific needs may be.

The first, and most obvious reason for establishing a department, is the need to provide a structure in which intercollegiate athletics can take place. Once this has been established, swirling economic and political conditions intercede and begin to control its progress and philosophy.

An additional reason for the development of an athletic department is simply revenue generation. It is not unusual for intercollegiate athletics to effectively subsidize other areas of the university. These areas, which are not cost effective to operate such as libraries, rely on successful sports programs in order to provide a full range of academic services. Without sports-generated revenue, many important services would either be reduced or eliminated entirely.

A third reason for the formation of these departments is marketing related. That is, the athletic department is responsible for garnering support for the wide variety of athletic events held at the university and within the conference. Once established, the athletic department partially serves as a publicity machine, ensuring appropriate coverage of the activities hosted and participated in by the institution.

The ability to provide "checks and balances" is clearly an ancillary reason for continuing the existence of the department. The athletic department can troubleshoot between the athlete and the NCAA and provide invaluable compliance and enforcement information.

The final reason is to establish and maintain a sports program that assists student-athletes in their academic pursuits. This was not the initial or primary reason for their foundation, but has become a rather hot topic over the last few years. The reason for this will be addressed, in detail, below.

TALK ABOUT A BUREAUCRACY!

An incredible and often times suffocating bureaucracy exists between the university and its very own athletic department. Competing agendas, differing academic pursuits, and profit margins all contribute to this tenuous relationship. For the purposes of this discussion, consider them to be separate education and profit centers whose interests are at odds.

Let us first examine the conflicting educational issues. The university, as an institution of higher education, has a set of criteria from which it evaluates prospective students. These include grade point average, entrance exam scores such as the Scholastic Aptitude Test (SAT), extra curricular activities, and academic specialties. The athletic department also has its set of criteria: athletic ability. This may sound somewhat cynical, but realize that the academic entrance requirements for student-athletes are infinitely different than those for the remainder of the student body.

Specifically, Proposition 48 does not exist for the everyday student. If the average student does not qualify academically, he is relegated to considering another university or college to attend. The athlete, on the other hand, can be admitted under Prop 48 which was implemented to help combat functional illiteracy (*NCAA Manual*: 130).

Simply stated, this proposition originally required that in order to qualify for an athletic scholarship, incoming athletes must have a cumulative GPA of 2.00 ("C" average) in eleven core curriculum classes as well as a minimum score of 700 on the SAT, or 15 on the American College Testing (ACT) exam. And, while minimal standards continue to increase, a glaring double standard still exists.

Think about this for a moment. A 700 on the SAT requires that only 25 percent of the questions be answered correctly. The maximum score available for each of the math and verbal sections is 800; a student is given 200 points per section automatically—just for putting his name on the exam. This leaves the student in need of 300 of the remaining 1200 possible points, or 25 percent. It must also be noted that not all universities accept Proposition 48 athletes, citing a higher moral and educational code.

For most student applicants, a 700 on the SAT is utterly abysmal—for the athlete, however, it can be a ticket to a blue-chip Division 1 academic institution! Is it any surprise that the true academicians—a dying breed—at the universities are angered and frustrated by this blatant favoritism?

Recently, the long awaited publishing of student-athlete graduation rates began. In order to demonstrate to the university administration, the community and, most importantly, the parents of prospective athletes, athletic departments assumed an active role in assisting athletes with their academics. Unfortunately, however, this assistance has not only resulted in the abuse of graduation rate information as colleges and universities manipulate data, but has also led to athletes graduating in academic disciplines in which there is little substance—or career opportunity.

Perhaps the most pessimistic view of this is that if athletes are in fact pursuing and receiving college degrees, they are likely to do so not for their own well-being and prosperity, but rather to remain eligible in an effort to continue to raise revenue for the athletic department and prepare for the elusive career as a professional athlete. These types of situations serve to further exasperate the university as a whole. In many cases it boils down to the universities' academic reputation versus the athletic departments' desire to win national championships and remain "in the black."

The other remaining critical academic issue, assuming an athlete is interested in academics, is whether there is even time for student-athletes to study. Think about the number of classes missed due to participation in amateur athletics. What about the sheer number of hours required to perfect an athletic pursuit such as football or basketball? The NCAA bylaws state that 20 hours a week is the maximum during the playing season that student-athletes can devote to various forms of practice.[2] But this is the maximum *organized* number of hours and does not include extra personal training and game preparation.

Perhaps we should just scratch the whole idea of the "student-athlete" and allow athletes to major in "hoping for a career in professional athletics and putting all my eggs in that basket while disregarding education." This would enable us to eliminate the charade, and actually assist those who place importance on their studies.

This is an example of how the universities and their respective athletic departments are at odds. Now analyze the situation a bit further. Might opportunities for employment arise from such conflicts?

The design of a program or service that would actually accomplish the agendas of both factions would be well received. Is there some way to eliminate the obvious conflicts of educational interest without sacrificing winning percentage? How much is it worth, in terms of dollars, to a prominent Division 1 school to have achieved both an outstanding academic program and a comparably successful athletic department? This type of flagrant breakdown in the system is precisely what creates entrepreneurial opportunities.

THE FINANCIAL STRANGLEHOLD

In addition to conflicting educational issues, financial concerns also permeate the arena of collegiate athletics. The relationship between the athletic department and the university was once viewed as somewhat vertically integrated, with the various departments and schools eventually accountable to a higher authority. Now it is horizontally integrated, wherein both factions are attempting to turn a profit by "producing" a different product—educated students, or a service—athletic entertainment. Athletic pursuits used to be a subset of the larger institution; now they are becoming "the" institution.

The general perception that academic institutions were founded to educate society is a fairly accurate one. By the same notion, one would tend to believe that collegiate athletics enrich the overall academic experience. Unfortunately, however, both entities have compromised their principles with *athletics* playing a far more prominent and widely publicized role.

Generally speaking, universities and athletic departments raise funds in the same ways. Schools raise funds by charging tuition and other fees to students, receiving contributions such as government tax revenue and grant allocations, successfully soliciting various alumni groups, etc. Athletic departments approach this process with even more vigor and intensity. Murray Sperber, in writing *College Sports Inc.*, summarizes athletic department revenue sources very accurately, breaking revenue into two categories: earned and unearned.

Earned revenue, states Sperber, includes ticket sales, guarantees (in which small schools are willingly trounced by a national powerhouse in order to share a portion of the receipts), bowl game and tournament payouts, television, and corporate sponsorships. Unearned revenue includes booster and alumni club donations, student fees, and state/government support.

Even from this abbreviated review, it is apparent that athletic departments wield an incredible amount of power and influence. This influence is not always appreciated by the university as a whole, as purists submit the argument that "the tail is now wagging the dog."

Many financial issues exist between the university and the athletic department; issues which continue to generate animosity, internal struggles, and conflict. The university is comprised of numerous schools and organizations that produce Nobel Laureates, philanthropists, and industry leaders in the fields of medicine, law, and business. Yet, these schools and academic disciplines are constantly struggling for their financial survival. The university would love to know what motivates alumni and boosters to contribute to athletics while disregarding the heart and soul of the learning institution—as it was this heart and soul that enabled these now powerful and affluent alumni to become leaders in their respective professions.

Universities continue to remain frustrated that their athletic departments, as competition breeds contempt, are in a position to sustain this type of growth. However, as long as the team wins on the field, both entities are successful in increasing revenue, with the athletic department showing a more marked improvement.

An increasing source of frustration is now observed between the Athletic Director's office and the President of the University, including the Board of Regents or other governing body. The goal of the athletic department is to increase revenue from athletic competition. Consequently, the athletic director commonly assumes the role of public relations specialist, lobbying the university for support that leads to this goal. Unfortunately, the university's position is quite different. It hopes to establish and maintain some basic level of academic integrity, including the development of minimum grade point averages for student-athletes, as well as creating an overall atmosphere that is conducive to the simultaneous pursuit of academics and athletics. Accordingly, a strategic conflict exists between the two as one employs a push approach while the other attempts to succeed using the pull philosophy.

While the university may not be pleased by these developments, it needs to appreciate the impact of a successful athletic program on the entire school.

For example, the 1990 national championship in football was shared by Colorado and Georgia Tech. This increased exposure and success of Georgia Tech was evident university-wide the following year as athletic donations rose more than 12 percent, the school's general fund donations were up a dramatic 18 percent, and freshman applications increased 22 percent. The University of Colorado also displayed impressive results. General fundraising was up nearly 30 percent, while trademark/logo licensing witnessed an incredible 184 percent increase.

A similar licensing phenomenon can be seen in basketball. For instance, fans of the two-time NCAA Champion Duke Blue Devils purchased nearly $40 million worth of souvenirs during (and shortly after) their successful seasons. In fact, on-campus sales of merchandise reached approximately $2 million during the twelve month period from July 1, 1991 through June 30, 1992 (*USA Today*, August 3, 1992).

Naturally, the success of the sports programs was not responsible for the entire increase, as each university was already engaged in other revenue producing activities. Nonetheless, success on the field often translates to success in other areas.

The massive athletic department budgets and perceived waste within the department budget also draw attention from the university. No other department(s) on campus have the exorbitant budgets and overhead enjoyed by the sports programs. As a rule, the salary of the head football coach is considerably higher than that of a tenured faculty member. This immediately stirs debate as to which one is more productive, the Coach or the Teacher? By and large, the coach is responsible for generating millions of dollars of revenue for both his department and the university. The tenured faculty member, while providing a much more valuable service to society, is essentially a drain on the system. Who makes more money, the guy raising the funds or the one who spends them?

A final point to consider for the university is whether academic success, in terms of quality graduates and breakthrough research, is worth sacrificing in order to chase the almighty sports dollar. In some instances, the revenue generated from television appearances and/or bowl participation is forwarded to the "General Scholarship Fund", a fund which can finance such ventures as the building of a new library or research facility. In these cases, the athletic department is likely to enjoy only a small percentage of these total dollars. Again, a very obvious potential conflict arises: would the university rather have academically average student-athletes and millions of dollars from playing in the Orange Bowl or have academically outstanding student-athletes who might be incapable of raising substantial revenue for the university as a whole? This dilemma often forces athletic departments and universities to choose between winning on the field and excelling in the classroom.

Is it acceptable for a university to produce lower quality gradu-ates—athletes with meaningless degrees—while pursuing economic gain? The answer lies in the comparison between the major university student-athlete graduation rates and the efforts of the athletic department, but not necessarily their actual success, to be profitable. This is discussed at greater length below. But, in the meantime, it does not appear to be a very tough call, does it?

The competing financial interests within the athletic department can be as fierce as those with the university. Many athletic departments have the ability to show either an economic profit or loss, depending on which is preferable. As with many corporations, athletic departments use a somewhat "creative" accounting system, which has the effect of showing a profit or loss—whichever is preferred. While there may not be anything wrong with this practice, it makes it very difficult to determine whether a program is actually in the black. However, many universities prefer to believe that they are in the red. Black or red, how can an athletic department or any business operate over long periods of time without some measure of financial feasibility?

Realizing that blue-chip team sports subsidize all other amateur collegiate athletics creates interesting internal dynamics. The reason the financially successful sports in the program are willing to tolerate paying the expenses of non-revenue producing sports is simple: the NCAA requires that colleges and universities field a certain number of men's and women's sports—both team and individual.

For example, Bylaw 20.9.3 in the NCAA Manual states:

> Division 1 institutions must offer six Varsity intercolle-
> giate sports, including at least two team sports, based on
> minimum requirements and involving *all-male teams or
> mixed teams of males and females*, and six varsity
> intercollegiate sports, including at least two team sports,
> based on minimum requirements and involving
> *all-female teams*.

Any failure to comply with these basic criteria would result in a school losing its Division 1 membership—and an opportunity at the millions of dollars available to this elite classification of membership. This serves as sufficient motivation to retain those team and/or individual sports that are incurring expenses but providing little revenue.

This criteria, among others, significantly affects the overall financial stability of the department. This, along with Title IX, discussed below, and the provision of adequate academic support, will have serious implications on the financial stability of athletic departments. As we approach the 21st century, accurate financial forecasts will become increasingly important.

Another very important and somewhat cynical financial issue now needs to be addressed. While it is widely believed that athletes are not graduating at an "acceptable" rate from their institutions, it is also fair to state that athletic departments are in business to make a profit. If one believes these assumptions, the implications are distressing. If this situation were to be applied in business terms, it would mean that these corporations—athletic departments—like most, are depreciating their assets. In this case, unfortunately, the assets are athletes, whose eligibility expires over time. At the conclusion of this eligibility, many of the athletes—assets—have no value remaining, as they have no degree, no marketable skills, and were not among the one-in-one-hundred who made it into professional athletics. Think about this when attending "Senior Day"—or creating a job in sports management.

While there are certainly other interesting and conflicting financial dealings within the athletic department, there is one more that receives incredible attention: shoes. Yes, shoes! College basketball coaches, especially those from major Division 1 programs, can earn more than $250,000 annually for endorsing athletic shoes. The deal is simple: the shoe company pays the coach to have his players wear its brand of sneakers. Perhaps the best example of this practice can be found at Duke University where Head Coach Mike Krzyzewski recently signed a new shoe contract with Nike; the agreement will reportedly pay Krzyzewski $6.6 million over the next fifteen years (*Sports Illustrated,* August 26, 1993: 76)!

L.A. Gear, Adidas, Nike, and Converse believe this is cost effective, especially if the team wearing their shoes makes it to the Final Four. One 30 second commercial alone during the Final Four can cost more than this type of endorsement. A forty minute commercial, consisting of two twenty minute halves during as many as 30 games, sure beats one 30 second spot—an advertisement missed by many arm chair hoopsters who are already half way to the fridge by air time!

Additionally, it is the intent of the shoe manufacturer to establish a close relationship with each of the university's rising stars. This enables them to position themselves favorably for a future relationship with these athletes as they become NBA stars. In fact, the collegiate coach often serves as the go-between—personally promoting the shoe company that is paying him this astronomical sum of money. In the end, the players' experience with the manufacturers and the "advice" of the coaches lead to a more formal and lucrative future relationship for all parties involved.

This obviously places a strain on relations within the athletic department office and on the court. Fellow administrators feel slighted as perhaps the revenue should be available for the entire department while players again feel used by the very system that gives them a mere 2.7 percent chance of playing professional basketball (*NCAA News* November 19, 1990: 16).

ACADEMIC POLITICKING AND OTHER PERKS

All of this culminates into the frenzied politicking and positioning that takes place in athletic departments. For years, the general student body and alumni have believed that athletes receive preferential treatment and perks generally unavailable to the non student-athlete. The student *sees* the student-athlete as the privileged elite.

For example, most athletes are provided summer jobs through the athletic department. These jobs typically require minimal effort and yield premium compensation. The liberal arts student is essentially on his own to pursue summer employment opportunities. To the general student body, it is insignificant that student-athletes are restricted from working during the season and that they are not directly compensated by the athletic department for the revenue they generate. The bottom line is that animosity exists as a result of these perceptions and realities of preferential treatment.

Additionally, study tables and available tutorials also create tension. Once again, these services are provided for the student-athlete whereas the general student body must independently search out and pay for these services. Even with this academic support, the graduation rates of team sports participants is atrocious.

In a survey published by the NCAA and reported in *USA Today* (May 20, 1993: C, 1, 10), there were many interesting and disturbing findings. The positive findings noted that the six-year graduation rate for all Division 1 student-athletes was 52 percent. This trailed the 54 percent rate for all students. The major reason for these similar percentages is financial. The majority of the general student body that fails to graduate has experienced financial difficulties. College is expensive and students and their families often struggle, unsuccessfully, to remain in school. The graduation rate would no doubt soar if expenses were paid by the university—as they are for the student-athlete.

More disturbing findings were the following racial graduation rates. Division 1A black football players graduated at a rate of 34 percent whereas the graduation rate of the white football players at the Division 1A level was 58 percent. The graduation rate for black Division 1 basketball players is only 33 percent, compared to 62 percent for the white basketball player. As a general rule, the greater the "sports power," the lower the graduation rate. What this suggests is that schools are more concerned with the financial success of their sports programs than they are with the critical matter of educating their student-athletes—especially the minority student-athlete.

Other student-athlete "perks" have included loans with either a deferred payback or no payback at all, grade changing, and complimentary tickets. With respect to loans and financial corruption in collegiate football, *A Payroll to Meet*, written by David Whitford, examined the issue most candidly. *Payroll* evaluated the Southern Methodist University Football Program of the 1980's and revealed the massive corruption and win at any cost philosophy prevalent in college football.

In this work, Whitford demonstrated what many already believed: athletes are pursued, pampered, and catered to during their eligibility while the general student body is left to struggle on its own.

Many also believe that athletes receive preferential treatment in the classroom. Accusations of grade changing in order to keep athletes eligible is rampant. Jan Kemp, an English professor from the University of Georgia, refused to play this grade-changing game. She was ultimately fired for refusing to bow to the pressures. The result was a trial in which she prevailed and received $2.57 million in both damages and back pay. The airing of this dirty laundry such as at the University of Georgia is quite rare, but the damages were intended to send a message to other institutions. In the years to come, we will learn whether this ruling actually had any effect, or if educationally disadvantaged student-athletes are still passing courses for the sole purpose of remaining athletically eligible.

Complimentary tickets to athletic events are also a sore subject. Student-athletes receive these tickets and then often sell them for a hefty profit to boosters and other associated groups. The general student body is not capable of scalping its tickets in the same fashion as the athlete because it does not have the name recognition. A major athletic booster is more willing to pay $500 under the table for tickets purchased from the quarterback than spend $50 and buy a similar ticket from a dentistry student. The result, the well known "hundred dollar handshake," serves as supplementary income to the athletic scholarship.

Boosters also receive perks at the expense of the student body. For example, it is not unusual for boosters to monopolize the tickets to a particular event or for an entire season. When this occurs, the general student body is relegated to sitting in the "cheap seats" as the most influential boosters enjoy the game "courtside."

These examples only begin to scratch the surface of the preferential treatment given many student-athletes. Not all schools, and certainly not all student-athletes, participate in these activities. However, the numerous and well publicized cases which have highlighted the abuse continue to draw the skepticism of the general student body and alumni groups. The athletic departments constantly attempt to position themselves in a favorable light, while politicking university-wide for increased positive publicity.

Throughout this process, the athletic department is also concerned about its relationship with the student-athletes. Many athletes are uncertain about the department's motives, often viewing them as the

"Big Brother." Strained relations have evolved from this lack of trust, and athletes are unsure of the department's role in the larger scope of things. Are the departments attempting to shelter and insulate their assets (athletes) from such outside influences as agents? Do they attempt to persuade their athletes to remain in school instead of foregoing their remaining eligibility and entering a professional draft?

In addition to the lack of trust mentioned above, an additional issue may exist that affects the athlete's perception of amateur competition and the collegiate experience. Sociological concerns, such as an inner-city minority athlete's ability to adjust to a potentially more conservative academic institution, play a role in the continued alienation of many student-athletes. The general student body is likely to encounter less of a "culture shock" when transitioning from high school to college. The scholarship athlete, on the other hand, may have difficulty adjusting to this new environment since he may not have a similar academic and socioeconomic foundation. While this is not the fault or responsibility of the athletic department, it may, in fact, be best suited to assist the athletes during this difficult transition. Taking a more active role in this awkward transition may serve to endear the athlete to the university, effectively reducing some of the "Big Brother" effect.

The reasoning used by the athletic department often conflicts with the individual athlete's needs, desires, and attitudes. This results in an ongoing strain in which athletes question whether the athletic department has their best interests in mind—or just the overall welfare of the program.

ON THE HORIZON

As with any business or industry, over time, trends develop that ultimately present opportunities. Athletic departments are not different, as they are constantly evolving to meet the needs of universities, the NCAA, and their own student-athletes. Specifically, there are academic, financial, marketing, and other changes occurring as athletic departments prepare for a fiercely competitive 21st century.

With respect to the academic trends, we are seeing athletic departments slowly change their personnel. Years ago, administrators within the department were largely drawn directly from coaching or athletics. As we head into the mid-1990's, a transformation is taking place where educators and scholars are playing prominent roles in the development of these programs. One reason for this transformation is the fact that academicians are better suited to devise and implement programs that balance athletics and academics.

It is also a matter of priorities. As previously mentioned, graduation rates are becoming a benchmark from which student-athlete prospects and their families are judging schools. Athletic department motives include the ability to market their services more effectively to this group, while maximizing the relationship between graduation rates and potential revenue.

Trends are also evident in the categories of revenue and expense. Fund development is a rapidly increasing function handled internally by the athletic department. Instead of relying on the occasional alumni contribution for support, athletic departments are becoming much more creative and proactive. A few are even financed primarily by booster groups and/or wealthy professionals who have no connection to the school save their financial support of collegiate athletics.

Many schools, including the University of Southern California (USC), have implemented football endowment programs. In USC's program, each position on the team is endowed with a *minimum* gift of $250,000. This money is then invested to provide grants-in-aid funds for the student-athletes who play the sponsored position.

Mike McGee, then Athletic Director at USC, appreciated the impact of this, "The endowment program is the key to the competitive viability in college athletics for private institutions—and therefore important to USC's ability to compete successfully in future years."

In addition to increasing revenue, athletic departments are also extremely interested in finding new ways to reduce costs. Many programs have begun "trimming" unnecessary "fat" in order to compete more efficiently—reflecting the present attitude in American business.

Marketing and public relations are also becoming a priority. In the entertainment industry, service, reputation, and goodwill are critical. Athletic departments appreciate this and are concentrating more efforts on generating positive publicity, i.e., the timely release of favorable graduation rates and marketing materials designed to lure recruits to the institution. "Image is everything"—or so we've heard.

One final trend receiving a tremendous amount of attention is Title IX. Title IX is a federal law that essentially guarantees equal access to sports opportunities for both sexes in the nation's schools and universities. While the law has been in effect for 20 years, it has only recently become a critical issue. The implications are extraordinary when

one considers how significantly football teams influence this gender
equality issue. What financial implications arise if athletic departments
are required to balance their participation in athletics based on gender?

Many believe that the impact will be a polarization of amateur
athletic competition whereby a few super conferences exist. These
conferences would operate as business units and be required to follow
traditional business and legal practices. The other, a less likely
alternative, is to de-emphasize athletics as revenue creating activities and
leave the big stakes to newly created minor leagues (*Roberts*).

THE OLD BOY NETWORK

The existing employment structure within athletic departments does
not allow for many employment opportunities. Granted, while there are
hundreds of colleges and universities around the country, most have very
few professional and administrative positions available within their
respective athletic departments. The positions that may actually be
available are likely to be in lower division schools in non-metropolitan
areas which provide little compensation.

While this may not sound very appealing, consider the unspoken
pecking order in collegiate athletics. Unless you are a powerful alumni
with major name recognition, there is little chance of attaining a real job
in a renowned Division 1 athletic department. More than likely, the first
opportunity will arise from either a volunteer activity or proving oneself
at a lower level, say Division 3. A pecking order is generally present and
requires working your way to the more prestigious universities by
mastering similar positions at less competitive levels. This "leapfrog-
ging", from a small school to a medium sized college, and eventually to
a university, resembles the process coaches experience when pursuing
their dreams.

And as if this isn't discouraging enough, the "Old Boy Network" is
heavily utilized. Many qualified professionals have been passed over for
promotions because athletic directors either return favors or hire their old
buddies for the job. Experience, in this case, may be secondary to
intangibles over which you have no control.

As a university offers a greater number of sports, employment
opportunities increase. This is an obvious observation but there is more
to it than meets the eye. Even at the major Division 1 institutions, only
about 12-15 full time business-oriented professional and administrative

positions exist. Can you imagine how few positions exist at lower division schools? How many resumes do you think the Universities of Michigan or Notre Dame might receive for one quality position?

With only 106 Division 1A institutions, fewer than 1,500 professional, full time positions exist. If you have to send a resume as a means of introduction, you can forget it! By the time the help wanted sign is seen, the job has more than likely already been given to an insider.

Assuming an elusive position is actually found, chances are it is in a non-revenue generating position. These positions typically deal with smaller sports and seldom involve any team sports activities. The pecking order, previously referenced when changing schools, also applies here. Mastering such areas as intramurals or small individual sports are required before one is exposed to revenue producing sports such as football or basketball. Particular staff responsibilities at lower levels encompass the most menial of tasks—and you will be compensated commensurately!

Again, the financial opportunities exist only in those key positions that either increase revenue or reduce cost—sound familiar? It is very difficult to substantially affect either when employed at a small school where athletics are not a major money maker. The same is true when relegated to organizing the intramural co-ed volleyball tournament.

Moreover, additional duties such as helping with alumni and other extra-curricular activities are mandatory. This leads to long and often times unappreciated days for everyone. The difference is that at least the athletic director is getting paid for this overtime.

While we are on the subject of compensation, let us consider supply and demand. Approximately 1,500 business and management related jobs exist nationally within these collegiate athletic departments with tens of thousands of people interested in these positions. This results in low salaries; mid-twenty thousand dollar a year range for entry level managers and mid-thirty to low-forty thousand dollar a year range for middle managers. Only top echelon administrators command salaries approaching six figures. Exceptions do exist for those unique individuals who possess either exceptional work experience or unequalled name recognition such as the former All-American returning to campus to begin a special program.

THE ATHLETIC DEPARTMENT VS. THE NCAA

Any discussion of the Collegiate Athletic Department must include an examination of its relationship to the National Collegiate Athletic Association, or NCAA.

College football in the early 1900's was a dangerous sport whose image was suffering immensely. As the severity of football-related injuries increased, pressure to reform the game was voiced by many—including U.S. President Theodore Roosevelt. However, the Intercollegiate Football Rules Committee, formed in 1894 by the dominant Ivy League schools, met to consider the alternatives and propose potential solutions in order to restore the sport's credibility. Unfortunately, these larger schools, whose football programs generated hundreds of thousands of dollars for their universities, were not interested in any rule changes that would jeopardize their revenue.

Frustrated by the lack of commitment displayed by larger schools, presidents from other football playing schools met on December 9, 1905, to discuss how they would facilitate the necessary changes in college football. A subsequent meeting was attended by representatives of more than 60 universities. It was this meeting, on December 28, 1905, that led to the beginning of the Intercollegiate Athletic Association of the United States which was formally founded in 1906; in 1910 this organization became the NCAA. Now, more than eighty years later, the NCAA has fully defined its purposes, principles, and bylaws in exhaustive detail in its own operating manual. These rules and regulations are intended to service its member institutions and amateur participants—essentially monitoring and updating the previously agreed upon reforms in collegiate athletics.

The NCAA defines its basic purpose (*Bylaw 1.31*) as follows:

The competitive athletics programs of member institutions are designed to be a vital part of the educational system. A basic purpose of this Association is to maintain intercollegiate athletics as an integral part of the educational program and the athlete as an integral part of the student body and, by doing so, retain a clear line of demarcation between intercollegiate athletics and professional sports.

The two primary 'General Purposes' of the Association are (*Bylaw 1.2*):

a) To initiate, stimulate and improve intercollegiate athletics programs for student-athletes and to promote and develop educational leadership, physical fitness, athletics excellence and athletics participation as a recreational pursuit;

b) To uphold the principle of institutional control of, and responsibility for, all intercollegiate sports to conformity with the constitution and bylaws of this Association;

In addition to these purposes, the NCAA has both general and specific principles as follows.

General Principle (*Bylaw 2.01*):

Legislation enacted by the Association governing the conduct of intercollegiate athletics shall be designed to advance one or more basic principles, including the following, to which the members are committed. In some instances, a delicate balance of these principles is necessary to help achieve the objectives of the Association.

Specific principles (*Bylaws 2.1 through 2.13*):
1) The Principle of Institutional Control and Responsibility
2) The Principle of Student-Athlete Welfare
3) The Principle of Ethical Conduct
4) The Principle of Sound Academic Standards
5) The Principle of Rules Compliance
6) The Principle of Amateurism
7) The Principle of Competitive Equity
8) The Principle Governing Recruiting
9) The Principle Governing Eligibility
10) The Principle Governing Financial Aid
11) The Principle Governing Playing and Practice Seasons
12) The Principle Governing Postseason Competition
    and Contests Sponsored By Noncollegiate Organizations
13) The Principle Governing the Economy of Athletics Program
    Operation

Given the purposes and principles, now consider the NCAA as a governing body. The Association is located in Overland Park, Kansas, home of the NCAA's first Executive Director, Walter Byers. Byers was responsible for the growth and well being of the organization, serving in a management capacity from 1951 until 1990. Toward the end of Byers reign, Dick Schultz assumed the post of Executive Director, essentially becoming the most powerful person in amateur athletics.

Schultz, viewed as the ideal professional, resigned in May of 1993 after it was determined that he was involved in a controversial student-athlete loan program during his tenure as Athletic Director at the University of Virginia. Schultz's successor, Cedric Dempsey, steps up from his current position of Secretary-Treasurer. Dempsey's impressive qualifications include his serving as Athletic Director at both the Universities of Arizona and Houston as well as Chairman of the NCAA Division 1 Men's Basketball Committee.

This Overland Park location houses all of the approximately 230 employees who perform functions that include Administration, Business, Championships, Communications, Compliance Services, Enforcement, Legislative Services, Publishing, and Special Projects. All employees, even at the lower level management positions, have at least a bachelor's degree. In fact, many have completed master's degrees in various disciplines. Additionally, the NCAA is often characterized as an Association where employees work long hours for relatively low pay.

These functions are performed by the NCAA for its 1,051 entities which comprise four membership groups. The first membership group is the Active Membership, 847 colleges and universities. The Conference Membership group includes 108 members of the various regional conferences. An even smaller group, the Affiliated Membership, is comprised of 58 officiating, coaching, and other related organizations. Finally, there are 38 Corresponding Members which are primarily of a non-profit nature.

Since more than 80 percent of the membership is made up of colleges and universities, it is important to further examine this classification. Specifically, there are 106 members from Division 1A, 89 members from Division 1AA, 103 members from 1AAA, 218 members from Division 2, and 331 members at the Division 3 level. Forty percent (331 out of 847) of the Active Membership comes from very small schools that generally receive very little national attention. Nonetheless, these colleges should not be overlooked with respect to potential employment opportunities, as they are located throughout the country and may offer excellent opportunities at many levels.

The relationship between the NCAA and its member universities has been a very volatile one over the years. They keep a keenly trained eye on one another in order to protect their various interests. Recall that the NCAA is preoccupied with maintaining competitive equity, increasing the graduation rates of student athletes, and *making money*. Collegiate athletic departments have slightly different priorities which reflect their microcosmic approach to amateur sports issues, including winning championships, or at the very least, remaining competitive regionally and nationally; manipulating graduation rates, if necessary, in order to remain competitive in revenue producing sports; and *making money*.

For all practical purposes, the generation of revenue is the only common thread shared. Consequently, they compete to a certain degree for the same dollar. The dollar each is pursuing in revenue raised, expenses reduced, or other in-kind benefits can be somewhat hidden to the novice fan or booster.

For example, the NCAA has rules for operations, actually entitled bylaws, that address such issues as an athlete's eligibility and athletic department compliance requirements. Any violation of these bylaws inevitably results in the transfer of funds from one body to the other. The obvious circumstances for this occurrence is when athletes are declared ineligible according to the rules. If this occurs, the NCAA can demand repayment of any revenue earned during this ineligible athlete's participation such as revenue earned in the NCAA Basketball Tournament. Should this violation lead to more extreme sanctions such as probation, the university will surely suffer as prize recruits may elect to attend other institutions.

As these student-athletes, in order to better market their athletic skills, enroll in competing programs that have similar national exposure, the result is often more powerful competition. Perhaps the Southwest Conference in the 1980's best exemplifies this as its members lost top in-state recruits to schools which were not on probation.

As a team's performance falls, so too does the amount of revenue it is able to generate. Declining attendance, sub-par recruiting classes, reduced booster contributions, and foregone television revenue all contribute to this downward spiral. Conversely, competing schools that reap the benefit of transferring athletes and bowl berths (gained by default) are certain to witness the reverse of this spiral. In this scenario, the university has lost actual revenue and has been forced to forego even greater benefits.

The major problem with this process is the NCAA's selective enforcement. After all, it needs to be concerned with enforcement, but at the same time it does not want to bite the hand that feeds it. A disincentive to punish may actually exist with the most elite programs. Elite, in this case, is defined by an institution's ability to raise funds for collegiate athletics and promote the NCAA. A major violation typically has to take place in order for a top Division 1 school to be placed on probation. This is not necessarily true of the smaller schools which, in the overall financial scheme of things, do not contribute as significantly. The saying goes something like this, "The NCAA is so angry at the University of Texas that it is likely to punish Texas State."

The previously mentioned NCAA purposes and principles have been the source of many conflicts and confrontations between the Association and collegiate athletic departments. As one might imagine, this friction has created numerous employment opportunities.

For example, those NCAA staff members who have gained invaluable experience in areas such as compliance and institutional control are valuable assets to athletic departments. Ex-NCAA staffers provide universities with insights as to how to better handle Association inquiries and deal with eligibility issues. Conversely, former athletic department personnel can play important roles at the NCAA. By providing pertinent information and relaying first hand experiences, these individuals are in a position to analyze the real world trials and tribulations faced by athletic departments. It is this analysis that enables the NCAA to better understand and communicate with its members.

Law firms have even begun specializing in the representation and defense of athletic departments. These professional niches did not exist a few years ago—lending credence to the notion that developing a value added idea and applying it to a specific portion of the sports management industry can be lucrative; more lucrative, in fact, than a traditional position within an athletic department or the NCAA.

CAUSE AND EFFECT

The five areas discussed throughout this book are interrelated. Industry guidelines, changing regulatory environments, and economic influences that affect one group will more than likely alter the opportunities available to the remaining four. While the number and degree of the opportunities may change for either the better or worse, this "cause and effect" section of each chapter traces the positive relationship each category has on the other.

For starters, athletic departments enhance the personal interests of the agents desiring to represent the schools' athletic elite. In the past, poor regulation has permitted the agent to have "free reign" over the collegiate stars—thus allowing agents to entice athlete's with whatever inducements they wanted to provide in the hopes of negotiating the star's contract. Further, the student-athlete's sometimes skeptical relationship with the athletic department has led to numerous openings for the player representative.

Professional franchises also derive many advantages from athletic departments, including the fact that colleges and universities essentially serve as a minor league system for the team sports of football and basketball. This enables the franchises to minimize many player development costs while simultaneously benefiting from the athletic department's marketing efforts. The publicity and exposure bestowed upon a star athlete while participating at the amateur level helps build fan interest in the careers of these players as they begin playing professionally. Again, this free marketing enhances the credibility of the professional product.

As one might expect, the media participates in this process very actively and directly. Collegiate sports and the activities of athletic departments create many new jobs in the media, ranging from print beat reporters to network broadcasters. In general, these jobs are the result of America's interest in college athletics, an interest which is contributing billions of dollars to the sports economy as a whole.

Athletic departments are also in a position to assist those members of the sports management community. Simply stated, without much of the free publicity and marketing efforts contributed at the amateur level, sports management companies would have to spend more time, money, and resources developing a player's identity and name recognition.

It is important to bear in mind that the actions of any one industry participant can significantly affect the others.

4

IN THE TRENCHES

*F*rank Stephens, Acting Director for Academic and Student Services for the University of California, Los Angeles, has been associated with collegiate athletics for more than fifteen years. A three year starter at outside linebacker for the Bruins, Stephens completed his professional football career in 1982 and returned to UCLA as a volunteer coach, the first of two college coaching positions.

Maintaining a strong desire to return to collegiate athletics, Stephens left a successful five year career in restaurant management to rejoin the UCLA staff in 1990, serving as the Assistant Athletic Director for Student Services. As the current Acting Director for Academic and Student Services, Stephens is responsible for managing the delicate balance between athletics and academics.

My father was an uneducated sharecropper from Oklahoma. He worked every day as a trash collector in order to provide for his wife and seven children. You always knew where you stood with him; education was a privilege—not a right. I remember him telling me, at the ripe old age of five, "If you're not going to get an education, then quit school and begin helping out around here." Face it, at five years of age, no little kid wants to go to school or work for a living, especially

40

under those circumstances. It was this experience, along with many others, that led me to understand and appreciate just how important education was; a privilege my father was never afforded.

Throughout all this, I was introduced to Pop Warner football—it was the perfect outlet for me because it helped me gain the respect of family and friends, not to mention reducing my work load around the house. Organized athletics also kept me out of trouble, taught me personal discipline and presented me with my first role model: Deacon Jones, the awesome defensive lineman for the Los Angeles Rams. I emulated Jones by playing his position, wearing the #75—and patterning my game day routine after his.

Without knowing it, this was my first experience with the business side of sports. Jones' presence on and off the field affected me greatly; the image of Jones (largely created by those in the sports business), attracted me beyond belief. I not only wanted to play high school and college football, but wanted a career as a professional athlete. Then again, who didn't?

My discipline and motivation on the field lead to enormous confusion in my personal life as I began to be recruited by colleges and universities. Since my father had no concept of the athletic scholarship and no one else in my family had ever attended college, it was largely up to me to screen potential universities—and I ultimately chose UCLA, believing it offered the best balance between athletics and academics. UCLA also had a tremendous reputation around the country and maintained a strong alumni.

The first thing I noticed during my very first practice was that football was no longer a game, it had become a business—*a big business*. The fierce competition for playing time, the attitude of the coaching staff and the demeanor of the athletic department all confirmed this initial perception. Nonetheless, I continued to love football even as this transition from sport to business was taking place.

Throughout college, I did not want to believe that, as a 6'2", 198 pound linebacker, I was too small for the NFL. But, as one might expect, I was too small to play linebacker and too slow to play safety at the next level. Still, no one could convince me that I would not play at least ten years in the NFL (hopefully for the Raiders).

Even as a marginal prospect, the agents were all over me, telling me that I would be drafted no later than the seventh round. "Begin thinking about investments and marketing opportunities," they said. "Get ready for the big time," they told me. Well, the draft came and went and my name was never called. After all the work and subsequent hype, I was a free agent!

During this period, I did nothing, *nothing*, to prepare for a career after football. I was devastated and scared, wondering, "What's next?"

I decided to sign a free agent contract with the Seattle Seahawks which included a signing bonus of $1,000; I knew the dream was fading fast. They wanted me to play strong safety; I knew my best 40 yard dash time was 4.7 seconds. They wanted me to compete against other top strong safeties; I had no previous experience at the position. Just before the final cut, I was told that the coach wanted to see me—and that I should bring my play book. Needless to say, I had been cut.

After a short stint in a semi-pro league and two seasons with the Toronto Argonauts of the Canadian Football League, it dawned on me that professional athletics was nothing more than high priced slavery. I was supposed to do everything I was told, keep my mouth shut and make sure management was happy. It was sickening. I wasn't about to sacrifice my identity but, as a second tier player, it was required.

I decided to return to Los Angeles and begin my career after football. I was still determined to be the one in my family that received a college degree—I wanted to help them out, I wanted them to know that I cared.

On a whim, I called Terry Donahue, UCLA's Head Football Coach, to see if it would be possible to return to school. Terry found a way to bring me back as a volunteer coach, basically working with the staff and the scout team. It was a start. I enjoyed the work and was able to finish my degree in sociology. In order to make this situation work, I had to take a job pumping gas during the grave yard shift at a service station in a less than desirable part of Los Angeles. Thinking back, I must have really wanted to work in sports because I had no money, no leisure time and virtually no personal life.

On the brighter side, I was really hitting it off with the players. Their athletic and academic performances were improving and, more important, they trusted and confided in me. It was at this point that I realized that this would be my calling; I could work with athletes, contribute to their academic experience and feel physically and emotionally involved in big-time sports.

The only problem was that it was not possible to make a living, especially when you're engaged to be married and need a basic level of financial security. After five years in a financially secure position in management with an up-scale restaurant chain, I was ready to get back into football.

Five years had passed before another opportunity arose at UCLA. I quickly accepted a position as the Assistant Athletic Director for Student Affairs, a position I felt was well suited to my interests and capabilities. This was especially the case since, when I played for UCLA, there was no such professional on the staff to help assist the student-athletes in the wide variety of academic and personal issues typically facing a student-athlete.

On the one hand, I have been pleasantly surprised at UCLA's efforts and commitment to these programs, and equally pleased by the accomplishments of the athletic department. On the other hand, however, I remain genuinely puzzled by many of the NCAA's specific actions and further confused by their inactions in other situations. In short, do we have the same goals when it comes to educating student-athletes? Sometimes I wonder.

Universities have well defined rules and regulations designed to assist athletic directors, head coaches, administrators and, last but not least, student-athletes accomplish this delicate balancing act between academics and athletics. Working for an athletic department as one of its many administrators, my eyes have certainly been opened to the various applications of these rules; rules which are sometimes applied selectively, thus confusing both the student-athletes and collegiate administrators nation wide.

Specifically, I am referring to the term "student-athlete." In some cases, it is the "student" in 'student-athlete' which is emphasized, while in other instances (and for other reasons) the "athlete" takes precedence in this unique and combined role. So, should it be 'student' first and 'athlete' second, or the other way around? Often, that depends on the needs and desires of the athletic department.

At UCLA, for example, the 'student' always comes first. In fact, UCLA expects its student-athletes to be students first, athletes second. This philosophy, which reflects my personal beliefs, helped reinforce my desire to work in this capacity. It has also helped me to realize that I have been (unknowingly) preparing myself for this position for quite some time, believing that administrators like myself are critically needed in athletic departments of all sizes and levels of competition.

As the acting Assistant Athletic Director for Academic and Student Services, I am responsible for a variety of areas over and above the on campus recruiting of prospective student-athletes. For example, I administer our tutorial and study hall program where student-athletes are encouraged to meet with learning specialists who assist the players in their academic endeavors. Additionally, I am responsible for the monitoring of class attendance and academic progress; personal counseling; and career planning.

And, if this does not keep me busy enough, I am the liaison for the Bruin Athletic Counsel, a panel consisting of 21 representatives of the various athletic teams. This counsel meets quarterly to discuss issues pertaining to improving the relationship between the athletic department and its student-athletes. Somewhat related to this, I also participate on a panel which assists student-athletes in their search for credible personal representation.

Finally, I manage a program called "Final Score," designed to assist those student-athletes who have left the university prior to receiving their degrees. In many cases, these athletes have pursued careers in professional athletics and, consequently, have left UCLA a few units short of achieving their degree. "Final Score" encourages these athletes to return to campus, earn the remaining credits and complete their undergraduate education.

When a student-athlete is being recruited by the institution, he or she spends 80 percent of the visit discussing academic issues, meeting professors, counselors and other faculty members who have a sincere interest in his or her success after graduation. The remaining time is spent on such non-academic issues as meeting other players and touring the athletic facilities. Having said this, I strongly believe that if you sell a prospect on academic achievement and post-graduation opportunities, you must deliver on these promises upon his or her arrival—or you breech the fundamental duty of the athletic department.

Once an athlete signs a letter of intent to attend a university and actually reports to the institution, he or she faces a demanding academic orientation and endless workshops which are established to aid in the transition from high school academics to the rigors of university studies. It is at this time that many universities begin positioning the delicate balance between academics and athletics. I find it encouraging that most major universities take the time and devote the necessary resources to build these academic programs, for without them, some athletes would simply exhaust their athletic eligibility without regard to any tangible academic progress. Nonetheless, athletic departments must focus on financial issues as a simple matter of survival. Not surprisingly, then, athletic departments are often torn between bottom line financial success to the department and the overall welfare of its student-athletes.

While I could easily continue to describe athletic department programs and philosophies, I would like to turn my focus to the NCAA and some of the issues they have addressed, to varying degrees of success, over the past few years.

To begin, the NCAA makes the university responsible for the student-athlete **before** he enters the university, perhaps burdening the institution unfairly. I mention this because it is apparent that many communities place significant importance on high school athletics—sometimes an even greater importance than collegiate or professional athletics. When this occurs, the opportunity for academic fraud and deceit commonly follows as high school coaches and administrators posture to keep their star athletes eligible for that big, cross-town rivalry. I am reminded of the starting quarterback who is a marginal student but happens to have his head football coach as his algebra teacher. With the big game just around the corner and players' participation tied to academic eligibility, might it be possible for that teacher (coach) to cut the better athlete a little slack on an upcoming exam? In certain prep circles, it is "athlete" first and "student" second.

In the event that the community (or society in general) is willing to tolerate these injustices, why shouldn't athletic departments and/or the NCAA? And, if we do tolerate them, we are faced with the uphill battle of educating student-athletes who enter our institutions with artificially inflated grade point averages—student-athletes who begin the collegiate process highly disadvantaged. When we, as institutions of higher learning, are unable to assist this group, we must answer to the NCAA. Shouldn't the high schools committing these atrocities be held accountable? In my opinion, all they are doing is passing the player through the system. It just doesn't seem fair.

The bottom line is that many universities recruit potential student-athletes that look good on paper but, in reality, are truly under-prepared for the rigors of university life. Personally, I remember taking the Scholastic Aptitude Test (SAT) the morning after an extremely long night of partying.

Moreover, I was required to take a bus to the exam, over an hour away from our house. No preparation for the exam whatsoever—not even breakfast the morning of the test. Nothing. The odds were heavily stacked against me. Where were the high school counselors who should have, at the very least, informed me of the importance and consequences of a good test score? Even my family could not have helped me as I was the first one in my family to ever register for the exam. I was lost and had no real support system, either at home or at school, to help me through this overwhelming academic process.

Unfortunately, the NCAA can't help as they do not presently address these issues; however, they should consider getting involved as this type of issue clearly affects student-athletes at the collegiate level. When will the NCAA begin focusing on the core issues affecting the integrity and well being of the very people it was designed to assist? The NCAA desperately needs to begin holding the high schools responsible to some degree for preparing their students for the demands and requirements of competitive college sports.

Why don't the universities (and possibly even the high schools) create a community relations-type of position for ex-student-athletes? These battle tested young athletes could prepare the incoming stars for the rigors of college life, including acquainting them with the many difficulties associated with transitioning from high school to college. After all, there is nothing more valuable to these big-eyed high school stars than the ability to relate to the real life experiences shared by this type of mentor. This may sound like a great concept but, knowing the budget limitations inherent at all levels of education, this would be practically impossible to finance.

The other issue that affects prospects arriving at the universities via scholarship is that different schools have different requirements. How can it be that a prospective student-athlete gets admitted to one Pac-10 institution but not another? A large part of the answer lies in the fact that many schools offer special programs to help assist the marginal student gain admittance, including the ability of institutions to accept the Proposition 48 student. Remember, not all schools permit these academically challenged athletes to attend their universities. Couldn't this create an undo recruiting advantage? What signal does it send to the prospect's parents when their child is admitted not because of his ability as a student, but based on his ability to raise revenue for the university?

How much longer will we, as educators and parents, allow our student-athletes to be used as pawns, essentially turning them back onto the streets in many cases simply because we have breached our fundamental duty to educate? The NCAA, not the individual member institutions, have the resources to begin solving this problem.

Assume, for the moment, that the athlete actually gets through all of these obstacles and signs a letter of intent to attend a university. He or she is then often faced with having to make major adjustments in both academic and social circles. The athletic departments, in some cases, become no more than glorified baby sitters. It is time for all of us educators, families, coaches and the NCAA to begin taking full responsibility, and blame, if appropriate, for our actions and/or inactions.

Occasionally, universities are faced with the interesting dilemma of dealing with a potential high first round draft pick who is considering foregoing his senior year and making himself available for either the NFL or NBA draft. What position should the university take when counseling this student? Should it stress the importance of education and recommend that the student-athlete stay in school? Should it tell the prospect to turn pro, earn millions, and return for the degree in the off season? Or, finally, should the school offer no advice at all?

The NCAA tells us, at the university level, to allow the athletes and their parents or guardians to consult with agents, coaches and scouts. Where is the value of academics in this procedure? Also, be reminded that the agents, coaches and scouts all have their own agendas; the agent trying to derive a commission, the coach trying to better his team and the scout attempting to fill a positional void on the roster. Who's watching out for the best interest of the *student*-athlete?

NCAA rules and regulations become confusing at this point because they say it's okay for that athlete to turn pro. However, in the event that a football playing student-athlete doesn't get drafted, the NCAA simply says that the player made a bad decision; one beyond its control. Nonetheless, the NCAA refuses to reinstate the eligibility of this underclassman. So much for the education process.

I bring these involved issues up for debate in an effort to facilitate further discussion about them and let the reader know the types of issues we, as collegiate athletic department administrators, must face on a daily basis. There are, of course, no easy answers or quick fixes. But, at the very least, we all must think about solving these problems when we discuss future employment opportunities in the world of collegiate athletics.

On a more personal level, I became an assistant athletic director to help address these issues and make the lives of student-athletes more complete—I certainly am not doing it for the money (remember the passage about budget limitations?). In fact, very few of those associated with collegiate athletics, at least at the athletic department level, ever earn the "big bucks," especially when these modest salaries are compared to the lifestyles of professional athletes. Most of us work in this business because we enjoy it and are able to make a comfortable living.

It is very possible that my current position will allow me to become either an Athletic Director at some point or an administrator with an NFL team. In the event that I choose to pursue a career in an NFL front office, it would likely be in a community service, public relations or player personnel capacity.

This next level, whether at the collegiate or professional franchise level, will bring with it enormous competition. This competition becomes much more fierce as the stakes are raised to a new and unbelievable level, full of added pressure and stress. The focus on winning becomes so intense that the experience changes from that of athletics to big business—a change I'm preparing for.

From where I'm sitting, I don't necessarily see the hypocrisy in collegiate sports improving any time soon. How can education ever become a priority to those student-athletes capable of pursuing the riches of professional athletics? It becomes increasingly more difficult for me to persuade talented student-athletes to stay in school and bypass the immediate financial return of a career in professional sports, even though a college degree is the only form of long term security in this competitive society of ours.

Sometimes, I feel as though the deck is stacked against the education process. The many challenges facing those hoping to educate student-athletes will continue to provide opportunities of all types in the 21st century, and I am excited about being one of those that actually makes a difference. After all, I've been in the trenches so long, I could use some good news!

OVERTIME

For those hoping to secure a position with a collegiate athletic department, it is important to understand the basics. Why were these entities formed? What are their purposes and functions? It may sound silly to ask these types of questions, but realize just how far these departments have strayed from some of their intended purposes over the recent decades.

To pick up where Frank Stephens left off, I believe the primary concern for those attempting to work in inter-collegiate athletics should be, among other things, to put the student back in "student-athlete." Contrary to popular belief, this can be accomplished without sacrificing the blue chip high school phenom and/or staggering bowl revenue. In short, this can be done within an appropriately structured program that balances education with revenue generation.

As a prospective employee of, or consultant for, an athletic department, expect to be faced with solving the problems listed below. Accordingly, your academic and professional training should be geared toward the areas that will begin to provide some of the answers to these complex problems.

For starters, one might want to begin by devising a program that helps eliminate the "garbage in, garbage out" problem of high school recruiting. Until a university is able to *really* know the character and aptitude of its recruits, it has little or no chance of stemming this tide of academic fraud. The academic fraud of which I speak begins in high school where the star athlete is unceremoniously passed through his course work without regard to his actual academic skills. Once in college, this athlete regularly continues to be passed through the system as most of the major universities are not properly equipped to help this student-athlete in his greatest areas of need.

Providing and delivering consistent messages about the importance of education and other related matters is yet another deficient area within collegiate athletic departments. Not surprisingly, the creation of a system where student-athletes are sent a clear message, one in which no academic concessions are made, would be met with tremendous appreciation. Specifically, the following issues should be addressed:

- determining whether every institution should accept or reject the Proposition 48 athlete;

- deciding on a national policy regarding freshman eligibility—either all freshman should be able to participate or none should be given the opportunity;

- resolving the graduation rate debate: either commit to educating athletes or resign ourselves to the fact that we prefer to produce winning teams over winning scholars—after all, very few universities have been able to achieve both; and

- informing student-athletes of the reality of just how unlikely it is to have a career in professional athletics.

In short, those individuals with the creativity and patience to diligently study the situation and implement changes to this system would be able to write their own tickets in the world of athletic department management. Reducing the glaring hypocrisy and corruption present in today's intercollegiate athletics is the major challenge facing this industry as we move toward the 21st century. It is possible to begin stemming this tide while still attending college, by conducting directed research and/or interning for the athletic department or sports information department. This work experience can range from simply tutoring student-athletes to assisting them in career guidance matters. Additionally, working with the athletic department to better ensure the overall balance between athletics, academics, and social responsibility is another possibility.

In any event, this hands-on work experience, even if one is only compensated with academic credit rather than income, will provide those hoping for positions with athletic departments the required exposure to warrant future consideration for permanent positions. Moreover, the trend appears to be toward retaining athletic department personnel who possess strong administrative, academic and counseling skills/backgrounds rather than simply promoting the head football coach to an influential position merely because he has won successive conference titles.

Career opportunities also exist for those individuals who are able to enhance the relationship between athletic departments and student-athletes. As previously discussed, a big-brother mentality exists between the two, with athletes becoming increasingly wary of and uncomfortable with the interactions of the two. This growing skepticism is the result of the frequently sent mixed signals previously discussed, as well as the precarious relationship the respective athletic institution has with the NCAA.

In short, the players do not feel comfortable approaching the administrators about the very issues for which athletic departments were founded. They feel guarded about candidly addressing the pressing problems and obstacles that face them as student-athletes. Accordingly, those who are able to break down these barriers will prove extremely valuable to an athletic department, as developing this positive relationship increases the productivity of the student-athletes, both on the field and in the classroom.

In much the same manner as bridging the gap between the student and the athletic department, similar opportunities exist for those who can eliminate the animosity between the athletic department and the university. For example, significantly raising and more equitably distributing "unearned revenue," such as general fundraising and athletic booster donations, may begin to bridge this gap.

This could be particularly effective if and when funds generated by the athletic department are more evenly divided among non-revenue producing programs within the institution, such as libraries. When the university, as a whole, feels as though it is directly sharing in the financial success of the athletic department, it will be more inclined to work *with*, rather than against, the department in accomplishing other athletic and academic goals. These entities, when working together toward a common goal, will be much more successful in containing costs and developing special programs designed to enhance the academic experience of the student-athlete. Again, imagine how well received a program or system would be if it enhances this precarious relationship. Focusing on resolving these current shortcomings allows the analytical professional to build a "better mouse trap" and establish himself as a

valuable asset to an athletic department; and once again position himself
for the long term.

In addition to the opportunities for employment arising from the
delicate relationships between student-athletes and athletic departments,
as well as universities and athletic departments, numerous issues
continue to surface between the collegiate athletic department and its
governing body, the NCAA. The general lack of trust and overall
dishonesty that exists within this relationship is among the most
ridiculous in all of organized athletics.

The NCAA's selective enforcement has been a major cause for
concern for a very long time to the Division 1 athletic departments. In
what appears to be a rather haphazard application of Bylaws 2.1 through
2.13 (see page 35), the NCAA is unwittingly providing those who desire
a career in sports with a tremendous opportunity, not to mention an
awesome responsibility. A review of these bylaws reveals a major
opportunity for interns, consultants, and even staffers who are willing to
roll up their sleeves and begin repairing the rampant problems inherent
in collegiate athletics. In short, select one or more of these and get to
work. Student-athletes, their families, the coaching staffs, and even the
NCAA will be cautiously optimistic, but eternally grateful.

Turning our attention away from the specific inter-relationships, let
us consider other prominent issues likely to be faced by athletic
departments in the near future. First, pay close attention to the activities
of law firms as well as public relations and marketing firms. These types
of organizations will begin playing an even more instrumental role in
collegiate athletics in the years to come. Universities will look to these
organizations in an effort to minimize NCAA sanctions, promote their
athletic department successes, and market their current stars. Not
surprisingly, it will be possible for those employed by these firms to
make the transition from a traditional position to one in inter-collegiate
athletics.

Moreover, marketing and related professionals possessing strong
merchandising experience will be in high demand. Recall the dramatic
increase in merchandise sales associated with a successful football
campaign. This phenomena will only increase as collegiate athletics
continues to enjoy massive domestic and international exposure. This
will likely force athletic departments to place an added emphasis on
marketing and promotion-related activities, essentially creating
additional consulting and employment opportunities.

Next, the notion of athletic departments being sponsored, at least in part, by corporate America may not be far off. In Fact, Spalding Sports Worldwide has already approved a sponsorship agreement with the University of Massachusetts. In this relationship, Spalding will supply athletic gear, underwrite sports camps, and serve as signature sponsor for Head Basketball Coach Jim Calipari's local television talk show. As long as corporate America realizes the opportunity to access this very important target audience and state education budgets continue to be cut, this form of alliance will begin to prosper. Remember, it was only a few years ago that we thought signature sponsors of bowl games were far fetched. The bottom line is that it may be worthwhile to gain work experience with one of these potential sponsors as they may have significant influence when the time comes for selecting candidates for athletic department posts.

Finally, when considering a career in collegiate sports management, one must consider the likelihood of major changes in the structure of competitive collegiate athletics. This is not to say that a major overhaul is imminent, rather that it remains critically important to follow developments in the industry. This may be especially important, for instance, when considering the impact of the minor league baseball system on the financial success of college baseball. As long as a shift from the other major college sports to a more formal minor league system remains a possibility, one must consider the impact this could have on career opportunities.

If this were to occur, athletic department revenue would decline even further, resulting in an even more remote probability of securing a meaningful position. Be mindful of this kind of issue, regardless of how far fetched you believe it to be, as any significant development in a particular industry will have a tremendous impact on the long term success of that industry.

When addressing the necessary educational requirements for prospective athletic department staffers, it is important to recall the breadth of responsibilities handled by these professionals. Accordingly, diverse educational backgrounds and varied work experiences exist in the athletic department. One sees professionals who have degrees in administration; education, including coaching; marketing; finance; accounting; public relations; sports information; and liberal arts. Therefore, combining any of these courses of study, and perhaps others, with the ability to solve the type of problems mentioned above will favorably position a candidate for these elusive positions.

Once this level of education has been achieved and corresponding problem solving ability has been demonstrated, one should expect the first employment opportunity to come from a lower division college or university. Recall that there are only 106 Division 1 institutions combining for approximately 1,500 full-time employment positions. Differentiating oneself as a candidate in this competitive environment at the Division 1 level will be difficult unless other related work experience has been gained, such as serving in an administrative (or volunteer) capacity at a lower (or upper) division school.

Balancing tangible academic progress with the athletic and financial success of the athletic department is, and will continue to be, the major issue facing collegiate athletics. How, as participants in the collegiate sports management industry, can we ensure that both athletics and academics become, and then remain, a right rather than a privilege? Those who contribute to the resolution of this concern will enjoy a long and illustrious career as an athletic department professional.

****

PART III:
Athletic Representation Firms

****

5

AGENTS

*A*gents. Are they star makers or dream breakers? In the competitive field of athlete representation, all too often the nice (legitimate) guy has finished last—But times are changing.

The three most important years in football, if you were or desire to become an agent, have been 1895, 1900 and 1925.

PERSONAL REPRESENTATION

By accepting $10 plus expense money to play for the Latrobe YMCA against the Jeannette Athletic Club, John Brallier became the first football player *to openly turn pro*. The year was 1895. Three years earlier, Yale All-American Guard, Pudge Heffelfinger paved the way for Brallier by accepting $500 to play for the Allegheny Athletic Association in a contest against the Pittsburgh Athletic Club. It was only two years after Brallier's signing that Latrobe became the first team to play an entire season using all professional players.

William C. Temple became the first known individual club owner in 1900 when he took over the team payments for the Duquesne Country and Athletic Club. And finally, 1925 marked the year that University of Illinois All-American halfback, Harold "Red" Grange, signed a contract to play for the Chicago Bears.

What made Grange's signing noteworthy was that he retained an agent to assist him in these discussions. C.C. ("Cash and Carry") Pyle negotiated a deal for Grange that guaranteed him a minimum of $100,000 for eight games over an eleven day period. However, this single event did not begin a flurry of agency activity as evidenced by a now famous quote from the legendary Vince Lombardi, then the active Coach and General Manager of the Green Bay Packers. Lombardi responded to ten-year veteran center Jim Ringo's request to have his agent negotiate with the team, by stating,

> "I wouldn't get discouraged, son. Maybe your new team will talk to him."

Ringo was subsequently traded to Philadelphia, ending his career and relationship with Lombardi's Packers (O'Connor: 2).

Monumental growth did not occur in the personal representation business until the end of the 1960's. In the late sixties and early seventies, a variety of events facilitated this growth including players' enhanced leverage with ownership, stemming from enormous increases in network television contracts; the ability of respective professional athletes' unions to win landmark legal battles, such as free agency in baseball; and, the constant competition generated by newly formed leagues like the USFL, which bid for players services. These events provided the agent with endless opportunities to maximize his negotiating power by representing the largely unsophisticated athlete market.

Simply stated, the sports representation process is comprised of athletes, agents (and their firms), and team negotiators. The athletes, having been consumed by training and a desire to succeed in professional athletics, do not customarily possess the business savvy and/or communicative skills required for securing an equitable contract.

The agent, having witnessed the opportunity to exploit this unsophisticated market, has fully developed what was once a cottage industry. As this representation discipline evolved, unscrupulous and incompetent agents have received an inordinate amount of dubious publicity. This is unfortunate, as most agents are hard-working, honest professionals earning a comfortable living in a very competitive business. As usual, the consumers—the athletes and the general public—only hear the horror stories, not realizing that most agents are performing a very valuable and much needed service for their respective clientele.

Nonetheless, as previously noted, not all agents are "alter boys." Mention the word 'agent' and watch the women clutch their children, the men their wallets. The perception that all (or at very least, most) agents are "bad news" is really unfortunate. As discussed, agents perform an invaluable service for their clientele and usually position the athletes favorably for post career opportunities. This scar on the agency business has been created by the actions of a few agents who are involved in the majority of the controversial and illegal practices. It is these unprincipled characters who are the focus of the scathing articles and endless litigation that continue to plague the industry.

Prejudicial, preconceived notions, and stereotyping have also played a major role in the formation of this negative perception. Many believe that a typical agent is one who wears fur coats and snake skin boots while standing just out of view. Decorated in gold jewelry and holding a cellular phone, as this stereotype continues, the agent approaches the athlete, with promises of instant stardom.

The agent is revered as both persistent and creative when it comes to recruiting prospective clients. Many use "runners" to do their leg work. This "running" is comprised of ferreting out the players and theoretically making informal introductions on behalf of the agency. Since he is not registered as an agent (this process will be discussed later in this chapter), the runner's loose affiliation to an agent(s) can be very hard to trace, as runners are transient by nature, generally associating with whichever agent will give them the best deal for their informal business development.

Runners, serving as "middle men," are known for catering to the needs and whims of athletes. They commonly do so with total disregard for established rules and regulations. Arranging cars, securing personal loans, and/or other financial relations without generating a paper trail are typical responsibilities of runners associating with dishonest agents. Techniques for tracking down prospects range from the obvious (relentless mail and phone calls) to the outrageous (moving in with or next door to a top prospect). The key, whatever the method, is to create goodwill with the prospect while simultaneously doing one's best to keep the other sharks at bay.

Credible, established agents more commonly rely on a referral for developing new clientele and do not associate with runners. Referrals from associates, teammates at both the collegiate and professional level, players' families and occasionally even professional teams, all contribute to offset the practice of and need for "running." This is not to say that these agents sit idly by waiting for clients to appear on their doorstep, but merely that their strategy for initiating introductions is a bit more polished than their less credible counterparts. While every agent solicits business directly, some are more creative in placing a different spin on the process.

When deciding which players to recruit, agents rely upon a wide variety of scouting reports published across the nation. Other not-so-public information also exists, offering details about the athletes on and off the field. For less than $1,000, an agent can have most of the necessary information including home addresses, unlisted phone numbers, and other personal data, at his disposal. He combines this written and verbal information with the personal network he has in place to determine whom he will pursue. Once the market has been segmented and the introductions to athletes have been made, the agent is in a position to "pitch" the player.

This brief look at the recruiting process is only a thumbnail sketch of how agents position themselves to solicit new business. Realize that there are nearly as many techniques for solicitation as there are registered agents. And, as in all industries, some participants play by the rules while others disregard established guidelines.

The legitimate agents, many of whom represent only a handful of players, despise many of the aforementioned business practices used by this overzealous minority. Most agents operate in a very professional office environment. However, the environment that is most often portrayed by society is of the agent working out of the trunk of his flashy car and beginning conversations with the phrase, "Psst—hey buddy, over here."

With the representation business continuing to become more professional and possibly more regulated, the back-alley brand of agent is destined to become a dinosaur. The checks and balances built into the comprehensive management team, to be addressed later in this chapter, will further ensure the athletes' welfare.

THE AGENT'S ROLE

As the sports representation business began its rapid growth in the seventies, agents were successful in informing and convincing players of the numerous benefits associated with retaining professional assistance.

The majority of the reasons for retaining an agent are legitimate. Unsophisticated college-aged, but not necessarily college educated, young men are in an unenviable and extremely vulnerable position when it comes to negotiating. Savvy team negotiators and owners are significantly advantaged because they have been involved in hundreds of these negotiations, are skilled in the art of persuasion/negotiation, and have the necessary salary and financial information available.

In short, those athletes without representation stand little chance of receiving a fair compensation package as dictated by supply and demand in the sports world.

As a result of this lack of relative preparedness and sophistication, athletes now turn to those whom they believe possess the requisite negotiation tools: communicative skills, business acumen, and a knowledge of sports finance. Additionally, an agent is better poised to sell a player's skills since it is universally recognized that a third party provides the required professionalism and tact. A representing party can also be more objective, direct, and understanding in this negotiation process. These financial and legal issues provide the basis for agent/athlete representation and require further discussion.

Collective bargaining is the process through which players and owners (labor v. management) negotiate over disputed economic issues such as free agency, the draft, minimum salaries, pensions, and other rights issues. These negotiations are very intense and extremely important, as they dictate the financial structure and success of the organizations. Accordingly, these disputes often lead to each of the respective entities fighting for benefits, at the expense of the other.

In football, the 1982 and 1987 seasons were interrupted by strikes resulting from the renegotiating of collective bargaining agreements. Ultimate success or failure in collective bargaining is a function of the leverage and the ability, but not the willingness, to pay which each side possesses (Staudohar and Mangan: 3). The results of these agreements significantly alter employment opportunities and salary structure.

Agents provide athletes with the business philosophy of these involved transactions and communicate the impact of such agreements to their clientele. While keeping clients informed on collective bargaining developments and their impact, an agent also continues to educate his clientele about other current events in the sports community that might affect the athletes' well-being. These current events may deal with changes in drug abuse policies or other personal matters such as a player's safety on the field. Agents must also be well-versed in other economic impact matters like expansion and its subsequent dilution of playing talent as well as the creation of new and competing leagues which increase demand for talent, resulting in higher salaries for the more talented players.

It is in these situations that the agent can serve not only as a calming influence, but also as a source of information, educating his client about pertinent events that directly impact his ability to play professional sports for a living.

Sports has become big business, very big business. As the dollars became increasingly significant over a relatively short period of time, the need to have a professional assist the athlete gained momentum. As network and cable television rights escalated throughout the eighties, the players needed a vehicle to help ensure that they benefitted from this increased revenue.

The National Football League Players Association (NFLPA), for instance, addresses such union-wide issues as pension plans and health insurance. It operates for the benefit of the group of athletes as a whole. On the other hand, the NFLPA's member contract advisers, or agents, are responsible for turning this larger success into personal financial security for their clients. The higher these broadcasting contracts became, the better informed and more sophisticated the athlete had to become. It was these types of needs that further demanded the existence of individual representation.

Naturally, as sports steadily grew into an annual multi-billion dollar industry, financial services began to play an important role in athlete representation. What were once regarded as ancillary issues like money management, accounting, and budgeting became primary reasons for the existence of individual representation.

An agent's ability to educate players about financial responsibility quickly escalated and became a serious point of delineation among agents. As we will later discuss, agents can either handle the athlete's money directly or simply refer him to financial managers for assistance. The latter method, where an athlete retains a team of financial professionals, is clearly preferred.

In the event that the agent does not directly manage an athlete's finances, his ability to provide the athlete with the highest quality individual(s)/groups is extremely important since the athlete is unlikely to have established these relationships independently. If this financial team is successful in managing the athlete's risk/return preferences, the agent will no doubt be in a position to develop excellent referrals from satisfied clients.

As salaries surpass the $10,000,000 per year range, this service provided by the agent will continue to grow in importance and remain a major reason why athletes seek reputable representation.

The ability to access marketing opportunities can be a very important service provided by the agent. The need for this form of representation arose from the onslaught of media attention given athletes. Massive television exposure, especially cable television, national radio broadcasts and, to a lesser degree, the print media have enabled certain athletes to become household names. The American consumer, inundated by and drawn to these media outlets, often views these athletes as role models.

The issue of fairness attributed to the "creation" of role models (icons) could be the subject of an entire book. Nonetheless, these icons/media darlings *project* certain images that consumers can relate to. As a result, consumer product and service companies, charities, and other philanthropic organizations use athletes in their advertising and promotional campaigns. Sex sells; so do fear and safety. Convenience, along with craftsmanship, also sells. And, of course, star athletes can sell. Combine a star athlete with one of the previously mentioned categories, and perhaps the formula exists for financial success for the group retaining the athlete.

However, regardless of how marketable an athlete appears, it is still very difficult for him to aggressively and effectively market himself. After all, the primary objective is to maximize his potential as an athlete for as long as possible. Without success on the field, there will be no success in subsequent marketing endeavors. Occasionally, retired athletes and current career journeymen secure deals, but these are few and far between and becoming more so every day. Years ago it was possible for many athletes to secure at least some marketing opportunities. But, as this industry has continued to evolve, the marketing opportunities have drastically changed. Previously, numerous athletes shared in the sports marketing pie, each one making a little bit of money with a select few actually commanding sizeable sums. Now, the number of athletes able to secure marketing deals is shrinking, with only the superstars realizing any substantial income. The pie may be getting larger, but it is being shared by fewer athletes.

It is then up to the agent to access these remaining, elusive deals. Additionally, he can assist a client who is in jeopardy of losing potential revenue due to either a poor work ethic or negative publicity. Ben Johnson, Pete Rose, Jose Canseco, and Mike Tyson have all experienced this in the last few years.

Ben Johnson, for example, had approximately 30 endorsement deals before testing positive for steroid use after his gold medal-winning performance at the 1988 Seoul Olympics. Most industry analysts believe Johnson's indiscretion cost him between $8,000,000 and $10,000,000 in foregone endorsements. Only one of the 30 endorsement contracts remained in place after the disclosure and there is no telling how many new opportunities would have surfaced.

With the help of his agent, Johnson has begun the struggle to repair his damaged reputation by associating himself with charities and other public service oriented activities (Quinn).

In fact, companies which ordinarily would consider Johnson as a spokesman have acted to protect their interests. "Image insurance," as it is called, is offered by at least one major insurance carrier in an effort to protect the company's large investment in a star athlete. The policy pays if the athlete is involved in the "commission of a criminal act, offense against public taste or decency, an occurrence tending to degrade, scorn or ridicule a large section of the community" (Hiestand). This subject is mentioned because it might be possible for an agent, knowing this type of insurance exists, to consider it when marketing his athletes. A firm that is ordinarily skeptical about using athletes may be inclined to give a campaign a try, knowing they have hedged their position.

The specific types of marketing services an athlete may pursue will be discussed below. To summarize, there are several reasons for the existence of personal representation: agents typically have better communication and business skills, often including legal expertise; are in a position to inform their clients about changes and developments in the industry; can be instrumental in building the financial management team; and, have the ability to access and capitalize on marketing opportunities.

THE WORK OF AGENTS

Once the player has realized the need for an agent based on the preceding factors, it is necessary for him to evaluate the functions he would like his agent to perform. Most agents play a combined role of business manager, personal/guidance counselor, and confidant. Operating in this capacity has led agents to offer a multitude of services for the athlete—some needed, others not. As each athlete is different, so too are his needs on and off the field.

Many agents and agencies offer the following comprehensive services: contract negotiation, marketing, financial management, legal advice, and post-career counseling/planning.

The negotiation of a player's contract is, without doubt, an agent's primary responsibility. This role can be very involved and encompass a wide variety of issues. For example, when negotiating a rookie's contract, the agent must determine the financial range in which he is negotiating. This is based purely on the athlete's position in the draft. This range, often referred to as a "slot," dictates the salary range in which the agent can maneuver. Simply stated, the tenth pick in the first round will be compensated more than the eleventh but less than the ninth selection.

It will be the agent's responsibility to determine this range by reviewing historical salary information, current contract signings, collective bargaining agreements, and the financial history of the team in the negotiation. The leverage his client can demonstrate and trends in the sports finance community (for example, is there a new network television contract on the table?) are also contributing factors.

Renegotiating during an existing contract period or signing subsequent contracts require the same thought process, save the slotting. In these veteran contracts, more attention must be paid to the leverage and individual desires of the client. Fortunately, when negotiating a second contract for the player, the agent knows the athlete both professionally and privately, thus enabling him to better serve his client's needs.

The final type of contract negotiated for a professional athlete is the free-agent contract. The free agent, a player who is either not drafted or has been released unconditionally, has special needs. He may need an agent that has the time and ability to market his playing skills to the professional franchises. Distributing videotapes, placing numerous, and sometimes tedious phone calls, scheduling additional workouts, and evaluating the alternatives—such as playing in another league—are all included in this marketing effort.

The more traditional marketing of athletes is comprised of securing endorsements and managing publicity and media relations. The number of quality product endorsements has been declining over time. Unless the athlete is a proven superstar with a squeaky clean reputation, the chances of securing a major endorsement contract are greatly reduced.

Certainly, however, there have been those role-playing bad guys whose personalities have enabled them to capitalize on these opportunities, but this is increasingly rare. For the agent who represents the superstar in a marketing capacity, his role is more as order-taker than marketer. After all, he is not making any cold calls attempting to line up marketing deals; he is awaiting phone calls and screening opportunities for his client.

Other endorsement contracts involve payment for services rendered. The best example of this is the star running back who wears a certain manufacturer's gloves or cleats over a specified time frame and for a specific price. Additional activities, such as autograph signings and personal appearances, also generate additional marketing income for the athlete.

Positive publicity, such as charity involvement and other philanthropic activities, provide the athlete with increased exposure. Serving as a spokesman for a local cause or contributing money or time to community programs can certainly endear the athlete to the team and its fans.

The agent can also assist his client with media relations. Having a positive relationship with the media can make or break the athlete. Preparing the client for the media circus, working on his communication skills, and presenting him professionally will always reflect favorably on the agent and his client.

All of these marketing activities can contribute to better terms in an upcoming contract. The better the athlete's reputation, the more leverage he has as renegotiating nears.

Agents have also handled the financial affairs of their clients. This has proven to be a major mistake over the years, as many agents, lacking the essential expertise, have been sued for mismanagement. Athletes, in dire need of comprehensive financial planning and conservative financial management, including budgeting advice, have relied on their agents for support and guidance.

Unlike marketing, financial mismanagement can be devastating. Instead of concentrating on the preservation of capital and medium to long term growth, agents are tempted by investment advisors who push the get rich quick schemes and exotic limited partnerships. Many agents also receive direct compensation, in the form of kick-backs, from financial advisors for placing their athlete clients in these speculative investment vehicles.

It is highly recommended that an athlete retain an outside group, or financial team, to work with him and his agent on all financial matters. This team, including the agent, would typically be comprised of an accountant, banker, investment advisor(s), insurance specialist, and lawyer. The team will act as a "check and balance" system for the athlete, ensuring prudent financial management.

In this scenario, the accountant assists in tax planning and compliance, as well as budgeting. Other duties may involve bookkeeping, bill paying services, determining the worthiness of investments, and assisting the investment advisors/brokers in asset allocation.

The primary role of the banker is to offer retail banking services. Checking and savings accounts, home mortgages and preferred banking relationships will be critical to the athlete and his agent. It is also possible for the bank to provide certain low risk investments for the athlete's investment portfolio. The banker would interact frequently with the other members of the financial management team.

Investment advisers, or brokers, work closely with both the agent and the accountant as previously mentioned. The advisor takes input from the rest of the team before devising an investment strategy for the athlete. This strategy is a function of where the athlete is in his playing career, his tax situation, spending habits, and risk tolerance.

The insurance specialist, providing disability, health and life insurance for the athlete can be associated directly with the financial team or can perform as an outside party. The important issue is to make sure the agent appreciates the need for adequate insurance and relays this message to the investment advisor, accountant and athlete.

In the event that the agent is not an attorney, one must be retained to resolve issues ranging from wills and trusts to prenuptial agreements and other personal legal advice.

Finally, the agent often provides post-career assistance. Helping the athlete make a smooth transition from the playing field to the business world is essential. If managed properly over his career, the athlete will be in a position to pursue the career of his choice—broadcasting, coaching, or returning to school, if necessary. The point is that he should be able to do so without worrying about his financial security, as his agent should have made this a top priority after signing the initial contract.

Whichever of the preceding services an agent is retained to provide, he must do so within established industry guidelines. These guidelines, which vary from discipline to discipline, often create problems for the agent. That is why it is a current trend in representation for the agent to work with a team of professionals, as mentioned above. This eliminates potential conflicts of interest, establishes a team where checks and balances are prevalent, allows qualified professionals to serve in their primary areas of expertise, and enables the agent to do what he does best—recruit new clients and negotiate contracts.

HOW AGENTS ARE COMPENSATED

The basic premise of this book is to add value by either increasing revenue or minimizing cost. This also applies to the agent when negotiating a professional sports contract. Ideally, the agent adds value in a very quantifiable manner by increasing the compensation paid his client. The value he adds to the contract is represented by the dollar amount he negotiates over and above some pre-determined or anticipated minimum.

Consequently, fees should be charged on the amount negotiated over these levels. Other sums, for which an agent cannot derive a fee, are "honor bonuses." These bonuses apply when players make the Pro-Bowl or All-Rookie teams, for example. All other forms of compensation, such as signing bonuses and other performance related monies, can be counted in the total compensation amount on which the agent charges a negotiating fee.

There are three commonly used methods for compensating an agent: a percentage of total dollar value negotiated, an hourly rate, and a flat fee. Naturally, there are pros and cons of each.

The percentage method is the one most commonly used in football. As stated previously, any dollar amount negotiated (theoretically over and above the league minimum), excluding "honor bonuses," is subject to a fee. Typically, agents using the percentage method charge between three and five percent, depending on services performed. The major drawback to this method is that an unethical agent may sacrifice the athlete's best interests in favor of his own short-term financial gain. Specifically, agents have been known to seek contracts that are longer than appropriate for their clients in an effort to maximize their income.

Despite this potentially dangerous vantage point, players tend to prefer this method because it forces the agent to continue to service the client. The NFLPA, for example, urges its players to pay the agent as the income is earned, thus forcing the agent to remain in an active role, and represent the best interest of his player(s). Another reason players prefer this method is that they are very apprehensive about calling an agent whose "meter is running."

The hourly rate method is also very popular, but has several limitations—including the fact that the agents hate it! The average NFL contract, at most, requires about 40 hours to negotiate. It is the drawn out nature of these 40 hours that creates the appearance that the negotiation process is time-consuming.

Nonetheless, assume an athlete is prepared to sign a contract which pays $1,000,000 over the minimum, not including honor bonuses. Based on the percentage method and using an average of 4 percent, the agent would earn $40,000 over the life of this contract. Utilizing an hourly rate of $250, and assuming the contract takes 40 billable hours to negotiate, the cost would fall substantially to $10,000. The hourly rate, as agents are quick to suggest, does not adequately reflect the recruiting costs and overhead of signing the player. Most agree the true value added is somewhere between these ten and forty thousand dollar figures.

Players typically do not like this method because it does not reward an agent for attaining top dollar. They prefer a built-in incentive. Players are also concerned about whether the meter is running and what additional expenses they are incurring throughout the process. Even in the event that the lawyer or firm charges for every single expense and phone call, it remains unlikely that the fee would ever reach the $40,000 figure. But the athlete is forced to decide which approach provides peace of mind—historically, the percentage method has provided this sense of "value added."

The final method used for compensating an agent is the flat fee. It is the cleanest and most manageable of the options. In these cases, a pre-determined sum—which has been mutually agreed upon—is charged for negotiating the contract. By and large, this method is used with lower round selections where there is little range in potential compensation and where the percentage method would yield little compensation to the agent, as these contracts are likely to be barely over the required minimums. The flat fee, usually a few thousand dollars, may be the most equitable for both parties. Any combination of these alternatives can be implemented, but they become increasingly difficult to administer.

QUALITATIVE REPRESENTATION

The agent also adds value in other, more qualified ways. His industry expertise, including a knowledge of collective bargaining agreements, trends in sports finance, and individual team structure assists the athlete in the representation process. These experiences may not be explicitly noted, but are critical when negotiating on behalf of the athlete.

Most agents conduct their business in a very professional manner. Their educational training and work experience add further positive benefits to the athlete, as he is viewed as having surrounded himself with a qualified team. Over time, this results in a sense of security where the athlete can trust his agent and advisory team to explain any complexities and turn to him/them for professional advice. The agent is seldom paid for advice and peace of mind. It simply comes with the territory when representing athletes.

Lasting friendships, other quality relationships, and player referrals are generated from these activities. It is not unusual for an agent to serve as a mentor, of sorts, to his clients. Assisting the athlete in finishing his college degree, helping him with personal problems, and teaching him various aspects of business often result from this unique friendship/mentor relationship.

The agent also provides another noteworthy value-added service. By acting as the representative of the athlete, the agent is in a position to play the "fall guy" in many situations. Initially, the agent can insulate his client and deflect any negative situation away from him during negotiation. Playing the intermediary allows the agent to protect the delicate ego of the athlete; an ego which would be affected by the negotiating ploys of the team. The agent also prevents the athlete from developing a detrimental relationship with the team during this precarious phase. Petty exchanges, which are not intended to be taken personally but customarily are, can alienate the athlete and the team. These exchanges, coupled with the frank financial discussions regarding a player, can serve to strain this relationship unnecessarily.

While these potentially heated negotiations are taking place, the agent can distance the athlete from the media by fielding all inquiries about the contract. This allows the athlete's reputation to remain relatively untarnished in the process while making the agent look like the "bad guy." This subtlety may actually save the athlete thousands of marketing dollars by not compromising his character with the fans.

The agent is also in a position to protect his client from the numerous "great opportunities" that exist to the young and affluent. It is far easier for an agent to say no to "distant" family members seeking financial assistance than it is for the player. This also applies to risky business investments preported to be "a sure thing" and requests by friends and fellow players. Having the agent serve as the "fall guy" allows the player to maintain these relationships without jeopardizing his personal finances.

THE AGENT/ATHLETE SELECTION PROCESS

Regardless of how the agent is compensated, he performs a much-needed service for the professional athlete. Some of these are easily quantified while others are of a more qualitative nature. Whatever the case, the selection of an appropriate agent is perhaps the most critical business relationship the athlete will ever form.

When forming this relationship, players consider how the agent or agency has structured his representation practice. Many agents concentrate their efforts in a single sport, representing rookies and veterans of all types—high and low round picks, journeymen, and established superstars. The reasons for this are numerous.

The seasonality of team sports and the ever increasing in-season overlap make multiple sport practices difficult for the smaller agencies. Also, the intricacies of each sport's financial structure play a key role as does an agent's personal interest in a particular sport. After all, agents are fans too.

An agent's specialization and breadth of services are also to be considered when examining agencies. As previously discussed, some representation firms prefer to handle all aspects of the athlete's business career. Others focus purely on the contract negotiation. The full-service type of agency tends to have staffs comprised of professionals in such areas as finance/investing and marketing/endorsements.

Some agents attempt to build client lists by approaching players located in specific regions. Developing a strong presence in a particular college town, conference, or region allows the agent to minimize overhead and other expenses while maintaining such specific strategic advantages as a prime office location and referrals.

Other, less common approaches to organize an agency do exist. They include building a clientele based upon the character of a particular type of client. In this scenario, an agent remains extremely selective as to whom he will represent, usually at the expense of representing a larger number of athletes. Yet other agents may differentiate themselves by only representing players occupying a certain position, such as running backs, or those at a certain stage in their career, such as rookies. Still others only represent players who demonstrate some minimal level of financial worth.

Finally, the size of the agency naturally plays a role in the athlete's representation selection process. This section has addressed the smaller, sole proprietor and partnership type agencies; the larger sports management companies offering traditional representation and negotiation services, such as IMG, ProServ and Advantage International, are discussed in Part VI.

AGENT REGULATION (OR LACK THEREOF)

As with most professional occupations, the sports representation business also has governing bodies and professional associations. The most notorious of these is the NCAA, whose primary area of interest is in eligibility-related issues. There is also the NFLPA, which represents the interests of professional football players. Both entities attempt to regulate the activities of agents: the NCAA while the athlete is an amateur, and the NFLPA once the player's eligibility has lapsed.

The NCAA, in particular, has established a very stringent set of rules for agents. These rules were theoretically designed to protect the athlete, as well as the financial interest of the NCAA and its member institutions, while he is competing on the collegiate level.

The NCAA considers any person who intends to market an athlete's skill or reputation to be an agent (*NCAA Manual*: 72). Further, the NCAA has adopted an all-encompassing general rule prohibiting certain dealings with agents:

> An individual shall be ineligible for participation in an intercollegiate sport if he or she ever has agreed (orally or in writing) to be represented by an agent for the purpose of marketing his or her athletics ability or reputation in that sport. Further, an agency contract not specifically limited in writing to a sport or particular sports shall be deemed applicable to all sports, and the individual shall be ineligible to participate in any sport.

Also prohibited by the NCAA are any benefits donated or given by an agent to an athlete, his relatives, or friends. These benefits—consisting of transportation, loans, meals, etc,—if not made available to the general student body, constitute a violation of eligibility.

The rules governing athlete representation fail to achieve the intended purpose for at least two reasons. First, "securing advice from a lawyer concerning a proposed professional sports contract shall not be considered contracting for representation by an agent under this rule (Bylaw 12.3.2), unless the lawyer also represents the student-athlete in the negotiations for such a contract."

How many attorneys, in the event they are asked by a player to provide this authorized legal advice, will turn him down? Probably very few. Also, if the attorney does in fact ultimately negotiate the contract, which occurs most of the time, the student-athlete would have, by definition, already sacrificed his eligibility. Once an athlete relinquishes his eligibility, he is no longer governed by NCAA rules and regulations. The bottom line is that the attorney has no incentive *not* to represent the athlete.

The other reason that the NCAA has failed in its efforts to govern amateurism is that it does not prohibit athletes from meeting with agents. Obviously, it would be impossible to enforce such a rule, so it isn't even on the books. However, agents can (and do) contact and meet with prospective collegiate clients at any time, provided no benefit not available to the general student body is given. In a predominantly cash business, this too, is nearly impossible to enforce.

The only way the NCAA is made aware of a potential eligibility violation is if it is a blatant act witnessed or uncovered by the athletic department or other affiliated organization. Naturally, this is an infrequent occurrence as the athlete is cautious about any undue benefit that either he or his family might receive.

When discussing the potential for an eligibility violation, it is important to consider the recruiting practices of agents as they relate to these amateur status issues. Many agents do not concern themselves with these issues, as they are not generally bound by the same rules and regulations that govern athletes, their respective universities, and/or the NCAA (it must be noted, however, that many individual states have laws which hold agents accountable for illegal practices). Not surprisingly, then, agents have actively and illegally pursued athletes at the collegiate level. After all, the probability of punishment for violating other organizations' rules is remote. To this end, agents have admitted to paying and signing college athletes prior to the expiration of their eligibility.

While they are not specifically concerned about violations, agents still take some rather creative measures to ensure a player's privacy and to protect him from both his school and the NCAA. Agents have secured representation agreements from athletes and placed them in safe deposit boxes. Another common practice is to enter into a relationship where the contract is post-dated, reflecting the date an athlete's eligibility is likely to expire (i.e. January 2nd, after a New Year's Day bowl game).

The NFLPA requests, but does not require, that agents become certified. The certification process is very simple and requires little effort. In fact, all that is required is a completed application, a membership fee and annual attendance at one of three NFLPA sponsored seminars. Not surprisingly, there are currently approximately 735 "Member Contract Advisers" representing just over 1300 professional football players. The old "80/20" rule holds true to form as the top 4 percent ("top" is defined in this case by number, not quality or character, of an agent's clientele) of all registered contract advisors represent more than 40 percent of the current players.

For the sake of comparison, baseball does not require those agents who represent minor league players to be certified. Moreover, there is no maximum percentage that can be charged for negotiating a player's contract as this would allow agents, rather than Union regulation, to determine the market price. Conversely, the NBA has established a maximum allowable percentage of four percent for negotiation of a contract. Additionally, agents wishing to represent basketball talent must be certified by the Players Association. Remaining rules and regulations for the various Player's Associations vary and should be reviewed thoroughly as necessary.

Players' Association applications generally consist of many detailed questions intended to determine one's educational background and work experience, current professional status in chosen field (i.e. whether litigation is pending or if prior convictions exist), and reveal any relevant representation experience. Once the agent has been certified, the Players' Association may require the contract advisor to use its standard contract advisor/athlete representation agreement. This is a very short boiler-plate document which spells out the basic terms of the representation.

Seminars, such as those conducted by the NFLPA, are held three times per year and are offered in different regions of the country. Items discussed at these meetings include "the state of the union" and related legal proceedings, licensing, and other topics such as drug abuse in football and agent regulations. This is as close as it gets to continuing education. However, many of those who represent athletes are in professions that do require some form of continuing education. Lawyers and accountants are prime examples.

Other associations dealing with athlete representation also exist. The Association of Representatives of Professional Athletes, ARPA, was founded in 1978 with the assistance of the NFLPA. Its purpose is to maintain the highest degree of integrity and competence possible when representing the professional athlete. Since representing an athlete does not require that one be a practicing attorney, ARPA is comprised of both lawyers and non-lawyers. Within the Association's code of ethics are the following:

1. The representative can never accept payment from a professional team or its representative. He must always hold the interests of his client primary, and

2. The representative shall not offer, promise, or provide financial support of any kind to the athlete, his family members, his coaches, or any college employee in order to become the agent of the athlete.

One other noteworthy organization associated with athlete representation is the Sports Lawyers Association. As the title indicates, this association's members are exclusively attorneys. Both associations are excellent sources for the attorney who is hoping to learn more about representation and is committed to providing ethical service. Furthermore, these organizations can serve as outstanding networking groups for those looking to expand their contact base.

Numerous state and federal statutes also exist which attempt to regulate and monitor the representation business. These statutes were designed to help athletes in an otherwise loosely regulated environment. Remember that all a person needs to become an agent *is* the athlete himself. The very first state law dealing with agents was enacted by California in 1981 and is known as the "California Athlete Agents Act." Fewer than ten years later, more than fifteen other states had enacted similar legislation. Potential agents, therefore, must be aware of and abide by any state laws that may apply to their representation practice.

Nice guys **used to finish last**. Now, agents that build and manage a team of associated professionals are poised to succeed in the representation business. The growth and evolution of this industry has created numerous financial opportunities for the ethical agent while reducing like opportunities for those who are unethical. The intricacies of the representation process continue to become more involved as the sports economy soars. In the coming years this sky-rocketing economy is poised to create many new employment opportunities in the field of representation and associated service organizations.

CAUSE AND EFFECT

Unlike the obvious effects of Athletic Departments on the sports industry, the contributions of athlete representation firms are a little more difficult to comprehend. However, agent activities do benefit the other four areas discussed throughout this book. A competent agent can have a very positive affect on his client's athletic department. In many cases, the athlete who is involved in community service or becomes a role model through the efforts of his representatives is a positive reflection on the academic institution he attended. Moreover, in the event the athlete has not completed his studies, the agent can be instrumental in persuading his client to finish his degree—thus re-affirming the respective institution's commitment to its student-athletes.

Believe it or not, franchises also stand to gain from an agent's activities. Players whose financial situations and personal lives are running smoothly tend to be more focused on game day. Additionally, the qualified agent performs the much needed function of facilitating equitable transactions between his client and employer. The successful accomplishment of these activities allows a team's players to concentrate on winning.

Sports management companies are in a similar position to reap benefits from athlete representation firms. Those sports agencies that do not directly market their clientele, provide the marketing and management firms with critical player referrals. Prior to this referral taking place, the agent has been responsible for creating a marketing persona. Whether he has done this aggressively or passively does not matter; the point is that the athlete already has some form of marketing identity by the time he is represented by a marketing or management firm.

Finally, the media has been known to enjoy and profit from agents. In a very basic manner, agents are responsible for "getting the product to market." Without this product (athletes), the media would have a more difficult time maximizing its revenue. On a somewhat lighter note, the media enjoys following the trials and tribulations of agents in this country as media personnel commonly view agents with contempt.

6

AN INSIDE LOOK AT THE PERSONAL REPRESENTATION PROCESS

It's All About Service

Stephen P. Freyer, is President and CEO of Freyer Management Associates, a New England based personal representation firm that represents approximately thirty-five professional baseball and hockey players. Steve's storied career in sports management enables him to discuss the various intricacies of the personal representation process. His diverse experiences in sports as an athlete, sports marketer and agent, provide invaluable insight into the day-to-day concerns of a player representative.

A graduate of both Colby College and The University of Colorado School of Bank Marketing, Steve is a certified agent with Major League Baseball, The National Hockey League and the National Football League Players' Associations. He also serves as Chairman of the Board of the Boston Organizing Committee which is dedicated to bringing international sporting events—and eventually the Olympic Games—to Boston.

In retrospect, my long term involvement with sports preordained a career as a player representative. Immediately after graduation from a small New England college, the first three jobs I had were in the sports business.

The first was a short stint with the Denver Broncos as a wide receiver. Albeit brief, and although the Broncos and I seemed to agree that another line of work might be in order, the taste of professional sports was powerful and sweet.

In 1968, agents were virtually unheard of in most circles. In fact, my meager contract was signed somewhat under duress while running through an airport. Having been informed that I would be drafted by the San Francisco 49ers shortly before the draft, I was crestfallen when the day came and passed with no phone call.

However, on the way through the airport to catch a flight back to school, I quite literally ran into the scout who had pursued me. The entire 49er staff, including the scout, had been fired prior to draft day and as he was now working for the Broncos, he had come to Boston to sign me. However, I had to sign that moment or he would pursue someone else. It was a classic "last, final offer" negotiating strategy—and it worked.

We haggled briefly over a signing bonus; I made a call to my parents and my brothers seeking advice. But when pressed by the scout to sign, I crumbled like a saltine cracker and agreed to a very modest contract in the amount of $12,500—with a few dollars thrown in as a signing bonus (remember this was 1968).

I learned some time later that, in that day and age, scouts were rewarded if they were able to keep signees under certain budgeted dollar levels. So it was directly in the scout's interest to pressure and squeeze the last concession possible out of me.

It was a memorable lesson in the effectiveness of power negotiations.

In the intervening 24 years since my experience negotiating without an agent, the use of a representative has become not only accepted practice, but most professional teams prefer to deal with an agent. There have been a number of occasions when management has encouraged a player to retain competent representation rather than negotiate on his own. The two obvious reasons are: 1) Management doesn't want to engage the player in a one-on-one battle. The residual damage of unpleasant confrontation can be severe. 2) The team never wants to be accused of taking advantage of a player's naivete. After all, it is much simpler to note that a player hired an agent who serves as the responsible party.

Shortly after being cut by the Broncos, I returned home to Boston and began work with the American Biltrite Rubber Company which had begun manufacturing a vinyl material to be used for running tracks, field house floors and tennis courts. Practically speaking, I was hired because I knew something about sports and gym applications. Shortly, my responsibility became inducing major indoor tennis tournaments to use our surface, called Uni-Turf, as their playing surface since it was reasonably portable and the price was right (read: free).

Within a year, I received an offer to become Associate Director of an exciting young company in Dallas called World Championship Tennis. Founded by Lamar Hunt, one of the originators of the American Football League, WCT was the first truly organized professional tennis circuit since the introduction of "open" tennis in 1968.

As is today, in the early 1970's a tennis tournament needed marquee names to ensure success at the gate. Lamar's concept was to sign the top pros around the world to personal service contracts wherein the players would commit to playing a certain number of weeks of tournaments in exchange for guarantees of prize money. WCT then could promote events with the knowledge that certain top names like Rod Laver, John Newcombe, Ken Rosewall or Pancho Gonzales would definitely be playing. My specific responsibilities included player relations as well as sales and marketing of WCT tournaments worldwide.

Closing the loop on my training was eight years as a commercial banker. Banking isn't the most scintillating of businesses, but it certainly teaches one how the real world works—which means how money works.

My entry into the business of representing players came about through a chance meeting in 1978 with a fellow named Jack Sands. Jack had a small company offering negotiating and financial management services to a group of successful major league baseball players including Greg Luzinski, Dwight Evans and Jerry Reuss. He wanted to expand that business and do more marketing work for his top clients. We talked for a very brief time and agreed to join forces. It was perhaps the best decision I ever made. Sports Advisors Group became a major force in baseball and hockey primarily because we were one of the first companies to offer a full range of services to professional athletes and their families. Besides the obvious of negotiating contracts, we provided tax planning and preparation, cash management, budgeting, bill paying and investment advice. We could literally take care of every facet of a client's financial life if he wished.

We would even go so far as to locate competent local counsel for him at his home residence, for estate planning and the execution of wills and trusts.

About five years ago, Jack and I agreed to a very amicable split. Freyer Management Associates as formed represents and manages professional baseball and hockey players, as well as a group of radio and television broadcasters. The bulk of our revenue stems from contract negotiations and financial management (although roughly fifteen percent comes from marketing consulting work for companies interested in looking at sports activities for marketing and promotional programs).

One of the more attractive aspects of this industry is that there is virtually no limit to salary potential other than that set by simply calculating how many people one can service effectively. Having noted that, there have been a number of representatives who have become so successful, so quickly, that they have lost the essence of their business—which is service. That in turn, can quickly lead to a loss of clients who feel disaffected.

SERVICE: That is the beginning, middle and end of any primer on how to be successful in this business. The actual act of negotiating a contract is not particularly complex. And, any responsible financial manager can create a plan for a professional athlete that will be sound and secure. In terms of marketing and endorsements, again, this isn't particularly challenging.

The key to success in this business is the ability to offer and to continue to provide a high level of client service. This service is a sincere, constant level of interest and concern for the client and his family.

For example, one of our fundamental policies is to make at least telephone contact with all clients once a week. It doesn't have to be a business call. In fact, it helps if it isn't. A brief conversation inquiring about the client's health and well being is worth a great deal in forging a lasting relationship. It must be remembered that an agent is one of a small group of people that a professional athlete can turn to for support and guidance. This relationship can't be manipulated and/or created in a short time. To be genuine and effective, it is developed over a long period covering a myriad of discussions, some important, most not.

Having noted that a commitment to high quality service is the single most important commodity a representative should offer, there are, naturally other skills (besides the general education behind a collegiate business degree) involved in running a successful company.

One of the less obvious but most important tasks confronting an agent is media relations. My preference has been to try to keep negotiations out of the press since it is seldom helpful and often times disruptive.

Sometimes it's unavoidable and you have to field all kinds of inquiries. How one responds is very important to how the public perceives you and your client.

I have run out of patience with agents who forget they aren't the star—or worse, who carry on nasty, aggressive campaigns against team management. In most cases, the loser is the player's image.

There are two cardinal rules in dealing with the media. First, never, ever, ever lie. The reality is they have long memories and the last word and they will get revenge on you, your character or your client some time down the road. Second, always return phone calls even when there is nothing to report. Certainly the calls can be intrusive and bothersome, but these people have jobs to do and if you can make their lives a little easier and treat them with respect, the close calls will go your way.

A strong financial background is crucial. Needless to say, huge amounts of money are being discussed when many player contracts are negotiated. One needs to have a complete and comprehensive understanding of such financial concepts such as "net present value" and it's affect on deferral and long term contract values.

Further, each client is as unique as each negotiation. A comfort level in dealing with an intimate knowledge of financial options available to you, your client and to the team is critical.

This leads to another issue—possessing an aptitude for negotiating. Naturally, we are negotiating almost everything, almost all the time, from our spousal relationships to buying a new car. We aren't necessarily aware of it, but we are. Like everything else in the world, some people are better at it than others.

From experience, I believe the most important characteristic of an effective negotiator is "open-mindedness." My interpretation of this "open-mindedness" is the ability to sense and be aware of opportunities within discussions that will allow new courses to be charted to solve the differences between sides. Keeping an open mind is often difficult because we tend to focus too tightly on precisely what we need from the negotiations without leaving room for new, creative approaches.

Some within the industry seem to view negotiations as a test of virility with a clear winner and loser in each encounter. Trite and hackneyed though it may be, "win/win" in my view is the best, long term view toward negotiations.

The reality of labor-management relations in sports today is the existence of a palpable sense of mutual and well defined mistrust. An added level of avoidable hostility complete with name calling and public ultimata simply exacerbates the climate of animosity. Therefore, with few notable exceptions, we strive for quiet, mature, high level, non contentious negotiations. The objective is to get what the client deserves while simultaneously having both sides reasonably satisfied at the conclusion.

A list of personal characteristics that an effective negotiator needs might look like this:

1. OPEN-MINDEDNESS. Your primary job is to solve problems, to close gaps, to be creative.

2. FINANCIAL ACUMEN. An ability to deal with numbers and financial instruments and to understand the impact of contract terms on both the client and the team.

3. AN INTUITIVE, DIPLOMATIC INSTINCT. A sincere desire to have both your client and the team satisfied at the conclusion of negotiations.

4. PATIENCE. Things take time—often much more than you expect. Our clients get tired of hearing us say, "Be patient." But time does amazing things to the determination of the other side.

5. DOGGEDNESS. There are times when one is absolutely, 100 percent correct in one's position. Therefore, being determined to gain a fair and reasonable result is a crucial goal. Don't waiver when you know you are right.

6. KNOWLEDGE (sports). Although obvious, it is a matter of concern that there are some practitioners who don't know a foul line from a blue line and that definitely hurts a client. Fakers simply can't get the most for a client!

Our industry is changing with great velocity. Twelve years ago the top agents in hockey could be counted on two hands. Recently, we received a list of 88 certified members of the NHL Players' Association. Competition is on the rise and with that comes unscrupulous recruiting and nefarious marketing techniques. The result of greater competition will likely be not only lower fees but also a lower quality of representation.

The good news is that when quality suffers from excessive, mediocre competition, the opportunity for quality, ethical, experienced representatives increases. Quality shines and stands out. The other nice effect of inferior competition is one tends to pick up experienced veterans who have finally realized better representation is available.

At a recent meeting of baseball agents, a member of the Players' Association referred to those of us with ten years of experience as 'old timers'—and that is a proper perspective. Experience is a factor in having an appropriate view of what is critical in negotiations and what is not. We have been through full career cycles—with clients from their entry into the minor leagues through their rookie seasons and on into their veteran years and retirement. That helps us deal with another reality: the assurance of radical change is absolute in our industry.

In the not too distant future, it is likely that all major team sports will have some sort of salary cap and a wage scale for younger players. There will be increased revenue sharing among franchises in order to support the "small market" teams. Alternative forms of compensation for players will be explored.

The need for an agent will not be as apparent as in the past. However, there will always be a need for representation since all players are not equal and, certainly, not all teams are equal.

The industry sprang from the need of professional athletes to have an advocate promote their individual interests. Since some players will always have more intrinsic value to an organization than others, those players will merit and deserve greater compensation. And to achieve that goal, a representative will be essential.

The reality confronting those trying to enter this business is there are many people chasing few openings. The greatest opportunity is to seek placement with one of the large practitioners who has a staff of specialists handling the details of superstar clients' lives. Entry level positions are available with the large companies and, in reality, "on the job training" is the best practical way to become a representative.

For a medium size practitioner, it is difficult to hire someone at a reasonable wage who is incapable of producing revenue in the near future or who does not fill a very specific niche, providing a valued service to an expanding base of clients. The costs associated with hiring a staffer who will be traveling while marketing and servicing clients are tremendous, and one needs reasonable assurance that revenues will rise as a direct result of the increase in expense.

Perhaps sports will become more homogenized, but the cream will still require special attention and service. And the perspective of the experienced negotiator/observer will be critical in assisting the athlete and his family anticipate and plan for the future.

The gratification in this business is knowing that you did the best possible job for your clients.

The climate in baseball is always changing and the negotiations of the 1991-92 off-season were no exception. We represent a player who was a free agent in the fall of 1991 and we were confident in October that there would be several teams eagerly bidding for his services.

But in early November, we sensed that things were changing; baseball was trying to squeeze the so-called mid career, marginal player out of the game. We immediately changed our strategy and aggressively marketed our client to two teams and then crossed our fingers. Fortunately, one team decided they needed our client and signed him.

When I walked into spring training camp my client rushed up to me, threw his arms around me and said, "I had a feeling you did a good job but I didn't realize just what a great job you did until I started hearing about all the guys who are sitting home right now without jobs." He then handed me a catalogue from one of the top sporting good companies that gives him $2,500 annually in equipment in exchange for wearing their glove. "A special gift to you. Help yourself to all of it. My special thanks for a terrific job," he said. That memory still feels good.

Recently, I played golf with three "retired" clients and someone made the comment that they were surprised to see I was so close to former clients. He obviously missed the point about our business. If you have fulfilled your obligation and done your job well, your client will always be a client since you will always be there to offer help, solace, friendship and advice. Just because they've stopped playing the game, doesn't mean they've stopped needing you.

OVERTIME

Unlike the other four areas discussed in this text, the professional opportunities available in the area of personal representation remain virtually unlimited—unlimited with respect to the varied scope of employment opportunities, earnings potential, and professional flexibility.

Employment opportunities available in the industry range from assisting a sole proprietor in a business development position to actually working for a major agency, possibly in a financial or legal capacity. In any event, these positions are very hard to secure, as a number of extremely qualified individuals are constantly chasing but a handful of opportunities. Alternatively, one can pursue athletes independently with the hopes of securing that first relationship. This method allows for the professional flexibility previously mentioned by enabling a prospective player representative to learn and participate in the business at his or her own pace. Contacting players and building the necessary relationships can occur within the everyday constraints of one's "regular" job.

Whatever the approach, one must be mindful that the only earnings limitation arises from one's ability to service his clientele. If gainfully employed in another line of work, it may be difficult to service more than a couple of athletes at any one time—effectively limiting earnings. However, easing into the representation business may be the most reasonable approach for many working professionals who would like to experience the industry without sacrificing their current employment situation.

When seeking one of these career opportunities, you will continue to hear from and about player representatives who have also participated in collegiate and/or professional athletics. Do not be discouraged in the event your athletic background is limited to participation at either the junior high or high school level. After all, have you ever noticed how many successful corporations are being managed by professionals with liberal arts backgrounds?

While competitive athletic experience may help those agents understand the athletes they hope to represent, today's intrusive media has significantly limited this advantage. For example, today, even the "average" fan has access to the most intimate and personal details of many of the athletes on his or her favorite team. It was this kind of detail that, in the past, enabled agents with playing experience to excel. While this previous "working knowledge" may have been beneficial to the agents of yesteryear, it now assists everyone. However, one major advantage tends to remain for those who have participated in competitive athletics—their contact base is very well defined compared to those outsiders who are attempting to similarly begin a career as a player representative.

In the event that you are either pursuing academic interests or considering a return to Graduate School, there are several issues to note. First and foremost, schedule and complete a balanced curriculum. This may be difficult given the time demands of a Law or Business School, but it is very important to continue to differentiate yourself from "the pack." This balanced curriculum should include course work in marketing, specifically media/public relations; personal finance; strategic planning; journalism, including communications and persuasion/debate; business law; and, sports information/management.

Each of these academic disciplines, many of which are included in most "core" curriculums, will establish the well-rounded base required by most of those in the agency business. The important aspect to remember when considering these courses is to view them from a service perspective. For example, the emphasis within the marketing course work should focus on endorsements and media relations—the elements of marketing that most closely impact a player's (client's) ability to earn additional money "off the field."

Another way to capitalize on your academic training is to interact with the institution's Athletic Department. This interaction can take many avenues, such as skewing your academic course work toward athletic related issues. Additionally, volunteering to assist the Athletic Department at events, fund raisers, and other functions will allow you to interact with and meet many of the people that make collegiate athletics a reality at your institution.

If you are already a working professional, there are still numerous ways to begin to prepare for a career as an agent. For instance, contacting the related professional associations is a great way to begin. Also, many finance and finance-related companies already deal with professional athletes in some capacity. The key here is to determine whether your company does, and if so, which services are offered, in which corporate location these services are housed, and exactly who handles the day-to-day affairs. Similarly, most of the larger law firms have, at some point, represented a professional athlete in some form of litigation. Again, research and confirm the particulars that allowed your firm to represent the client in the first place.

In the event these natural opportunities do not provide you with some form of agent interaction, check the appropriate sources to determine the locations of and services offered by local sports agencies. Begin building your network by taking one of these local representatives out to lunch or inviting him by your office. These early meetings allow you to decide if the agency business is really the profession you would like to pursue.

Whether you are a student or working professional, one point is consistent: make yourself unique. Remembering Freyer's supply and demand comments will encourage (force?) specialization. Once completing the well-rounded curriculum previously mentioned, gaining a keen awareness of a sub-discipline within the representation process will be critical. "Jacks of all trades" are not in a position to offer any unique skills to an agent or agency. Developing your primary area of interest within the discipline increases your marketability and maintains your interest in the representation business.

Who is, or will be, your Biltrite Rubber Company? Since most agents begin their careers in other sports oriented positions, it is critical to consider a position even though it only tangentially relates to sports management in general and personal representation specifically. Notice how quickly Steve Freyer built his contact base throughout the sports industry through a position that many of us would not have even considered. Placing yourself in a position to meet the right people is much more important than the initial function performed at any entry level sports position.

Throughout this learning period—which typically includes the completion of an academic degree and landing that first sports-related job, you must continue to study and research the most important element of the personal representation process: developments in the area of sports finance. A contemporary understanding of the issues associated with free agency and salary caps is most important when networking with those individuals you hope to work with in the agency business. A working knowledge of the financial environment that envelopes sports, along with such related topics as the efficiency of advertising in the sports world, are also very important.

Related to charting these financial developments is the need to be aware of the changes in the representation business. Realize how drastically the representation business has changed over the last fifteen years—what changes do you foresee by the end of the decade? Will this evolving industry play into the strengths you are developing? Referencing Freyer's comment about "radical change," how will you continue to fine tune your skills in order to capitalize on those few employment opportunities?

As previously discussed, there are very few quality employment positions available in the representation business. Many agents will recommend "on-the-job training" at a major agency as the best way to build experience. While this sounds most practical, the fact of the matter (as we will see in the section on sports management companies) is that "large" agencies such as The Big 3 (International Management Group, Advantage International, and ProServ) are still relatively small when compared to corporate America. Nonetheless, the opportunity to work in this type of environment is invaluable and is viewed as excellent work experience. Also recall that, unless your skill or position directly increases revenue or reduces expenses, the chance of earning a respectable living is quite slim.

Over the years, I have witnessed a common thread to breaking into the agency business: luck. This is not the type of luck associated with winning the lottery or "scoring" tickets to the Super Bowl. The kind of luck I am referring to comes from placing yourself in a position to seize an opportunity when it comes your way. Many agents have begun their careers by representing "the kid" next door or college roommate; some have met their first clients through chance meetings. The point is to be prepared to act on the opportunity when it is presented to you. After all, it was once accurately stated that luck is at the intersection of preparation and opportunity.

Regardless of how or when that first representation opportunity arises, if the willingness to provide consistent service is deficient, rest assured there will not be a subsequent opportunity. Perfecting one's ability and capacity to serve is the only way to maintain and build a quality clientele. This point of distinction was well covered by the contributor.

A major part of this service orientation includes focusing on the specific function(s) that you as the agent would like to offer. Will you handle only the negotiation of the player's contract or will you perform other functions such as the solicitation of marketing opportunities and financial services? Recall the discussion about the merits of building a comprehensive financial and marketing team for the athlete. As the agent, it will be up to you to decide how best to form these relationships. Regardless of the number of relationships formed, it will be your duty to service your client (the athlete) by maintaining a professional and working relationship with his entire team of advisors as well as his family, and other parties deemed appropriate.

As a player representative, you will likely be responsible for, or at least apprised of, many of the client's business activities. With this in mind, it is important to realize that there will be situations beyond your control (and professional obligation) in which you may have little or no experience. Do not be afraid to seek counsel from those industry professionals who specialize in the areas in question. Your clients will appreciate your honesty and integrity—two characteristics which inevitably lead to referrals.

Throughout the entire representation process, there are several principles to remember. First, don't sacrifice or compromise your principles or integrity. The area of athlete representation is, by far, the easiest of the five areas discussed in this book where the opportunity for the "quick kill" exists. Most of the established agents and agencies that have survived have done so by operating in a relatively professional fashion; the majority that fail do so because of the lure of easy money and a get-rich-quick mentality.

Next, concentrate and develop your specific role. If other industry professionals cannot differentiate your services, how can you expect an athlete, who has never participated in this process, to tell you apart from the rest of the crowd?

Finally, make the representation process a learning experience for your client. Not involving your client in this process will be tantamount to breaching your primary responsibility—that of service. Educating your clientele about the financial, marketing and management issues related to their participation in professional athletics will enable them to better prepare for life after sports by developing a sense of independence and self worth. Coddling an athlete throughout his career is arguably the most detrimental service any agent can offer.

Once working in the agency business, place great importance on the list of personal characteristics that were presented by Steve Freyer in the previous section. An effective negotiator (agent), stated Freyer, has the following personal traits: 1) Open-mindedness, 2) Financial acumen, 3) An intuitive, diplomatic instinct, 4) Patience, 5) Doggedness and, 6) Knowledge of sports.

****

PART IV:
Professional Franchises

****

7

FRANCHISE MANAGEMENT

*P*ositions in franchise management often involve long hours, low pay, and considerable indifference from above. Furthermore, the unsettling financial structure raises questions about the professional sports franchises and their related organizations.

MANAGEMENT OPPORTUNITIES

It is widely believed that professional sports franchises and, to a lesser degree, league offices and players' unions provide a large number of employment opportunities. These positions are extremely visible, thereby generating a fair amount of publicity due to the inner-workings of the franchise. When a player is traded, a coach is replaced, or the annual player draft is conducted, most of us hear from a team's General Manager, Public Relations Director, and Player Personnel Staff.

Additionally, a fan attending a professional sports contest witnesses staff members serving in a variety of capacities. This staff, which assists in game day operations, serves as front office support during the day, performing duties ranging from marketing to finance and administration. The hosting of a professional sports contest requires *the entire staff* to participate in both the preparation and successful completion of the game. The reason for this franchise-wide personnel involvement is due largely to the size of professional sports franchises.

By and large, most franchises employ between 20 and 35 business professionals. This includes the front office personnel as well as various support and administrative staff. Including the recent expansions, the four major sports leagues currently consist of 112 teams including the NFL with 30, the NBA with 28, Major League Baseball with 28, and the NHL with 26. Simply stated, this translates to approximately 3,100 total employment opportunities nation wide.

It is important to mention that this tally does not include teams in related leagues. These related minor leagues in baseball (AAA/AA/A ball), football (the Canadian Football League and World League of American Football) and basketball (the Continental Basketball Association and United States Basketball League) do offer management positions. Other affiliated leagues, including hockey, also offer similar opportunities for employment. For the basis of this discussion, however, specific focus will be directed toward employment opportunities within the "more traditional" franchises of the four primary sports leagues.

When reviewing these management positions, it is necessary to consider those factors that affect the scope and availability of these positions. For example, how does a team generate enough revenue to pay its employees, including players? Which line items represent the largest portion of franchise expenses? How is a franchise impacted by the rising costs of player development and sky-rocketing salaries? Have recent developments or a lack thereof in the area of minority hiring impacted a franchise's relations with its players and their unions? How financially dependent is a franchise on winning percentage and associated league success or failure? What is the economic impact on the community when a franchise arrives via expansion or relocation? What about the ever-increasing costs to the fans attending games?

These are only a few of the very basic issues affecting professional sports organizations. As these financial and other related issues continue to impact the profitability of professional sports, it is critical to similarly address their impact on employment opportunities. These issues, which are explored in detail later in this section, significantly affect the availability of franchise management positions and employee compensation.

Franchise management and staff positions are usually divided into three rather broad categories. The first includes front office personnel and directors. This category is comprised of the Owner(s), the Board of Directors, and General Management or franchise officers.

These positions are "closed" with respect to employment opportunities. Each professional serving in this capacity is involved in determining the day-to-day policies and procedures of the franchise. Members of this executive staff have long and productive track records in sports management, having served for years in a variety of management roles. Additionally, when a rare opportunity does exist, it is quickly filled by someone who is on a short list of "insiders."

The second category of franchise positions deals with the day-to-day managers who actually operate the team. This managerial staff consists of experts in the fields of marketing, public relations, and finance.

Within the marketing area, specialists are retained to handle general ticket sales, promotional events, corporate sponsorships, team licensing issues, and occasional research. This research may include tracking the effectiveness of advertising and promotional campaigns, as well as analyzing demographics in order to more efficiently market the franchise. Some overlap in duties may exist but, for the most part, the entire marketing function is typically handled by about ten employees.

The area of sales merits additional discussion. Almost every entry level job with a franchise involves primarily sales. This occurs for several reasons. First, since ticket and sponsorships sales are the lifeblood of the franchise, it is important for everyone working for the team to gain experience in a sales-related position. Whether it is the sale of season tickets, luxury boxes, group functions, or advertising time, rest assured that every new employee works in one or more of these departments. At least that is the reason the franchise commonly gives for starting in sales. The real reason, however, is that sales-oriented positions enable franchises to minimize front office expenses. This is accomplished by offering a low base salary plus commission. Designed to compensate employees based on increased sales, franchises only incur additional payroll expenses when revenue increases. This no doubt benefits their bottom line.

The Public Relations staff is similarly divided into subsets consisting of media and community relations, player appearances, and general publicity. Success in media and community relations can be a critical issue for the franchise. For those teams with rich traditions and multiple championship banners, this may require little more than maintenance. But, for average teams and the perennial doormats of the league, these functions can make the difference between profit and loss in any given year. Positive media coverage and established community goodwill can carry a team over short periods of time. However, as a team continues to lose, goodwill is quickly eliminated by the fact or perception that the franchise is mismanaged. Most fans will give *their* team the benefit of the doubt if it is believed the franchise is proactive in its desire to win. This can include pursuing trades or firing coaches. Nonetheless, no amount of goodwill or positive media relations can overcome consistently poor performance on the field or court.

The Director of Public Relations is the individual most involved with the media, handling specific game day requests, arranging interviews and providing statistics, and accommodating the visiting teams' needs in a similar fashion. This is a very time intensive process. It is not unusual for the P.R. Director to work sixteen hours on a game day—arriving early in the morning for an evening game and departing as late as midnight.

Player appearances and general publicity are also managed by the public relations staff. Arranging appearances for athletes at public events and orchestrating community programs are primary responsibilities. Other publicity includes organizing and servicing fan clubs, etc. This portion of the franchise's staff, although consisting of only about five individuals, is most visible to the fan, as they scurry around like mad on game day.

Further behind the scenes are the finance professionals. Within professional sports franchises, a team of about a half dozen perform all necessary finance functions. The Vice President of Finance, Controller, Treasurer, and two or three staff-type accountants handle the traditional duties. On a daily basis they might handle payroll issues, budgeting, and revenue forecasting, as well as assist the owners and front office personnel in studying various financial alternatives available to the team. The biggest challenge faced by these professionals is applying traditional finance and accounting practices in a very uncertain and ever-changing financial arena.

The final category of management opportunities at the franchise level is one of "General Support." Within this extremely important catch-all category, a team employs professionals to handle operations, ticketing, customer service, general administrative functions, and management information systems. Again, these functions are executed by a staff of six to ten professionals.

As previously mentioned, it is likely that most of the staff participates in some type of game day operation. These operations consist of preparing the venue for the contest, securing accommodations for the local and visiting media, preparing for advance ticket sales, and catering to visiting team needs. Other game day functions, such as concessions and parking, are likely to be handled by a venue management firm—this type of sports management company is discussed in a following section.

Unfortunately, most of the positions discussed in this section offer very little in terms of compensation. Once again, the number of people eager to work in this environment drives the wage scale down. The vast majority of a franchise's employees, excluding players of course, earn no more than $50,000 annually, with entry level sales and marketing staffs commanding about half that sum.

Upper management, well aware of this high level of interest in their venture, is often determined to push its staff to the limits. The "request" that the staff work overtime, stuffing envelopes or readying the arena, is a calculated one as General Management knows there are many eager and willing candidates poised to step in at a moment's notice.

This may sound discouraging, but after reviewing a team's sources of revenue and uses of funds, it will appear obvious why the employees are the last to share in the profits and prestige of franchise management.

"CASH IN"—SOURCES OF REVENUE

So, how does a franchise pay for these positions and decide on appropriate levels of compensation? The majority of the answer lies in the financial structure of professional sports organizations. As with most companies, franchises raise revenue through sales of their products or services. In sports, this "product" generates revenue through ticket sales, broadcasting rights, and licensing fees among others. Franchises also incur such expenses as payroll, especially salaries to athletes; research and development costs such as scouting; leases; and insurance. This delicate relationship between rising costs and stable revenues is the primary focus of this chapter.

Until the early 1990's, professional sports franchises were in a position to generate substantial revenue through the sale of tickets and other turnstile-related activities and via network broadcasting contracts. Between the 1988-89 and 1990-91 seasons, the fees for broadcast rights rose more than 110 percent, and have averaged a 20 percent annual rate hike over the last decade (Ozanian and Taub). This massive windfall has led athletes to demand what they consider to be their "fair share" of the pie. Accordingly, teams have begun, begrudgingly, to pay the athletes the multi-million dollar salaries we read about everyday.

But, as it becomes more apparent that these rights fees may be declining by the middle of the decade, teams are scrambling to raise revenue through other, more creative, methods. Realizing that expenses are not likely to fall as revenues decline, franchises seek to offset these skyrocketing salaries by packaging their "product" differently.

Specifically, teams are creating additional revenue in a variety of ways. Skyboxes, once a mere pipe dream, now command as much as $175,000 per season from affluent corporate fans. The ability to wine and dine clientele has lured corporate America to participate in this trendy venture, one that brings franchises as much as $6,000,000 per year in incremental revenue.

Another recent trend in sports marketing at the franchise level is signage. Signage, a process where corporate sponsors advertise inside the arena, has grown by leaps and bounds from its souvenir program advertising roots. It will not be too much longer before ads will be found throughout the field, court or ice. For the corporate sponsor with really big bucks, buying the right to attach your name to the building where the team plays remains a possibility. These stadium title rentals are available for between $500,000 and $1,200,000 annually.

Licensing fees, once an after-thought to the franchises, now provide the leagues with tremendous revenue. The selling of team-related merchandise has witnessed a growth rate of approximately 50 percent per year over the last five years, to the point where each team reaps millions of dollars from these arrangements. Unfortunately, though, even this over all 700 percent six-year growth rate cannot make up for the probable loss of revenue due to stagnating rights fees.

Teams are now turning a portion of their marketing efforts and revenue quest toward the international marketplace. Faced with domestic saturation, professional athletics view Europe as a natural market for expansion. If this potential expansion is successful on a large scale, professional sports may be able to save itself from ever-increasing expenses.

Domestically, teams are hopeful that cable and pay-per-view relationships will help bridge the financial gap created by the leveling off of network contracts. At best, however, these local cable telecasts will only replace a portion of the foregone network revenue. Network contracts are expected to decline by as much as 30 percent over the next few years, with local cable and pay-per-view replacing about 10 percent of the loss through their own programming packages.

"CASH OUT"—MOUNTING EXPENSES

The basic revenue sources are quickly consumed by mounting expenses. Operating expenses such as those related to sales, general and administrative costs, and rent tend to be rising across the board. But, the most obvious and certainly most devastating expense which continues to spiral out of control is that of player salaries. Players' salaries customarily account for 50 percent to 60 percent of team expenses. As reported by *Financial World*, player costs for Major League Baseball were up more than 51 percent during the early 1990's.

As if this were not bad enough, revenue increased by a mere 12 percent during the same period. This statistic alone explains why some franchises are on the verge of financial ruin. Whenever expenses are rising faster than revenues, a firm is in trouble; when expenses increase at a rate of more than four times revenue, most organizations would be running down the path to bankruptcy. A much closer and detailed look at player salaries follows below.

An extremely interesting, but often overlooked expense, is that of player development. Do you ever wonder what it costs a franchise to develop a minor league prospect into a major league player? $100,000? $500,000? Would you believe $1,800,000? That's right, *almost two million dollars*! In 1990, the *Sporting News*, with the assistance of the Chicago White Sox, studied financial data relating to the development of one of the team's 1985 free-agent draft selections, Donn Pall, a right-handed pitcher chosen in the 23rd round.

The findings surprised many, including the Sox front office. What were once considered either hidden costs or negligible expenses began to add up in a hurry. Pall, from the University of Illinois, worked his way through the ranks of the minor leagues over a thirty-six month period; beginning his journey in the Rookie League and progressing steadily through Triple A, before eventually making the White Sox Big League roster on August 1st, 1988.

For the purposes of this discussion, the *Sporting News*/White Sox Organization considered a total of fifteen categories in which they incurred player development expenses. The largest of these, $958,333, was in a category entitled "Minor League Regular Season." This line item noted that the Sox committed $5.75 million to their minor league operation during Pall's three year stay. Since only six of these minor leaguers made it to "the Show," Pall's expense was calculated as just short of $1,000,000.

The "Minor League Spring Training" category also raised a few eyebrows. Using the same method as above, Pall was "charged" with an expense of $382,500 as the organization allocated $2.3 million to this effort during 1986, 1987 and 1988. The White Sox also incurred scouting costs for the 1985 amateur free-agent draft totalling $846,461. Considering Pall was one of only five players selected by the team in that draft that actually made it to the Majors, he represented 20 percent of the overhead associated with that draft. This "Team Scouting System" category incurred $169,292 in expenses on "his" behalf. Not all of the expenses were of a six digit variety. Insurance premiums and medical bills totalled $7,100. He was also "billed" $62,500 for "Roving Minor League Instructors." These specialists worked with the minor leaguers during Pall's three year stay in the minors. Again, since only six minor league players throughout the franchise made it to the top, he was responsible for "his portion" of the $375,000.

The list continued and the expenses mounted—eventually totalling an astronomical $1,812,385. This expense was for a player who never achieved "star status." Of course, it should be noted that this may seem high for Pall, but who's to say that this would not be a bargain for the likes of Barry Bonds or Tony Gwynn?

A far less financial approach can also be applied to the "art" of player development in the NFL. Historically, estimates suggest that the 30 NFL teams (pre-expansion) employed a total of more than 200 full time scouts, at an annual cost exceeding $25 million (Stogel).

Another way to look at this sum is to figure the amount spent per *drafted* player per year during this period. Divide this total by the 336 selections made during these previous college football drafts (excluding supplemental selections), and the average recruiting expense per player is just under $75,000. By the way, since only about half of these drafted players actually make the roster, this expense essentially doubles on a per-player basis.

The high cost of football recruiting is attributed to a massive overlap in scouting and the enormous size of these staffs. For example, in the past, the New York Giants employed 13 full time recruiters, including a career counselor whose responsibility was to evaluate the players "off the field." There is also waste created by duplicate scouting. Each of the 30 teams typically meets with its top prospects on a number of occasions. This repetitive expense could be eliminated if a centralized service existed. Naturally, the NFL teams would not trust a service to determine the abilities of collegiate players. Consequently, each team—rather than just one scouting service—is faced with visiting up to 300 schools and working out and/or meeting as many as 700 players.

While there is little doubt that professional teams must research and develop talent, there are clearly areas within this activity that could use an "overhaul." After all, these high costs are always passed along to the fan and advertiser. A major opportunity is available for the individual or firm that can create a better method for this player development process. One area, intentionally not discussed, is the relative success of these scouting activities. The list of first round "sure things" is equalled by the number of "could-have-beens." The above data does not address the qualitative issues associated with this "research and development".

Once the prospective athlete becomes a contributing member of the professional franchise, a new set of financial concerns envelopes the team—outrageous salaries.

A CLOSER LOOK AT PLAYERS' SALARIES

Player salaries, especially in baseball, have been escalating at an extraordinary pace over the last several years. In fact, the average annual salary heading into the 1992 season surpassed $1,000,000 for the first time despite a major-league batting average of only .256. This salary figure compared most favorably to that of 1982 ($241,500) and 1972 ($34,000) (Bodley).

Individually, Barry Bond's recent contract extension calls for an average annual salary of $7.3 million, dwarfing the leagues first $3 million player, Kirby Puckett. Puckett's 1989 contract shocked many fans and front office personnel with this previously unheard of average. Most recently, the 1993 season provided fans with 264 players earning in excess of $1 million, with nine of those earning more than $5 million annually. Where do you believe player salaries will be in the years to come?

On the franchise level, the Toronto Blue Jays are in a league of their own, with a total player payroll of nearly $52 million, outrageous when considering the San Diego Padres' total is a mere $12.8 million. Many experts believe that the $10 million-plus per year player may not be far ahead, causing numerous franchises to take "financial cover." How, then, is it possible for franchises to agree to these obscene salary demands?

For starters, consider the four factors that determine a player's salary:

the overall quality of player performance; the player's contribution to team performance; the experience of the player; and, the popularity or recognizability of the player, also known as "star" status (Scully: 156). How these factors relate to club profitability must be examined before deciding whether player compensation is unreasonable.

In economic terms, firms are willing to continue production (output) as long as the marginal revenue generated from that activity is greater than its marginal cost. Conversely, firms cease production once the marginal cost of production exceeds the marginal revenue added. This same basic premise can be applied to the salaries demanded and paid in sports. In baseball, this means that the Mets believed, based on the criteria above, that Bobby Bonilla would generate at least $6.1 million in incremental revenue, measured in production, output, and ultimately victories, to the franchise during the 1992 season. The team realizes a "profit" if he generates revenue over this point and suffers a "loss" should he not create at least this added cash flow. This cash flow consists of increased ticket sales, corporate advertising, and to a certain degree, broadcast fees.

Taking this idea a bit further, a study established the fact that a 1-point increase in a baseball team's winning percentage raised its revenue by nearly $31,700 annually. Since there are 162 regular season games, each victory is worth 6.17 points (1000 points—a perfect 162 and 0 record, divided by the total games played, 162). This means that each victory was worth approximately $196,000 (Scully: 155).

So, hypothetically speaking, how many percentage points do you believe the Mets will gain by adding Bobby Bonilla to the line up? And by how much has the value of one of these points increased in the last few years? Welcome to the thought process of Major League Baseball Management.

Consequently, a team already possessing several superstars is theoretically less likely to pay Bonilla the "big bucks," as he will not be in a position to *significantly* raise the winning percentage as he would with a sub-par team. Unfortunately, this model does not take the many intangibles into consideration. Intangibles such as the "star" status and absolute market size affect team revenue beyond winning percentage by increasing, among other things, licensing revenue and community goodwill.

Similar exercises are carried out when a team is considering re-signing one of its own players or trading for an established star. Some teams choose to spend less money on player development and devote more resources to the acquisition of other established talent. Both free agency and arbitration have further contributed to the major rise in players' salaries. Free agency, which amounts to a competitive bidding process, pushes salaries beyond what "the market" would typically bear. In these situations, however, fair market price is seldom paid as extenuating circumstances, such as the owners' egos, often provide the athlete with a financial windfall.

Arbitration has a similar, albeit less severe, short term impact on player salaries. In arbitration, a theoretically unbiased professional determines which party—the athlete or the team, more accurately values an athlete's athletic accomplishments. The arbitrator is forced to choose either the sum advanced by the player's agent or the offer made by the franchise. Historically, the player stands to benefit substantially from either of the aforementioned financial alternatives since he typically increases his salary under either scenario.

The franchise owners, desiring to win, are willing to pursue the top talent available—at almost any cost. Moreover, the owners' egos do not always permit a clear economic analysis based upon available data. Rather, they occasionally make irrational decisions based on personal agendas; agendas that do not always reflect the best interests of "the business side of sports." The major point is that franchises are willing to pay players based upon the team's estimate of a player's marginal contribution to franchise revenue.

As you can see, there exists a reason for rising player salaries. In closing, be skeptical when a team says "they can't afford" a player. The truth is that a team can and will find a way to afford those players who are most likely to increase marginal revenue beyond marginal cost. This very brief analysis demonstrates the degree to which franchises analyze potential "investment" spending on player salaries.

THE DELICATE BALANCE BETWEEN WINNING AND FRANCHISE PROFITABILITY

The NBA has long been regarded as the only major sports league to have a handle on managing the escalation of players' salaries. The often discussed "salary cap" was created in 1983 as part of a collective bargaining agreement and actually took effect during the 1984-85 season. Prior to the cap's inception, sixteen of the then twenty-three NBA franchises were losing money, and as many as four were in danger of folding (D'Alessandro).

For the league to survive, the players and owners had to come up with an idea that would spread the potential wealth more equitably. Accordingly, the two sides agreed that players would share directly in whatever revenue was created by the league. The amount eventually settled on by both sides called for the players to receive 53 percent of the league's gross revenues. In order to determine the actual amount of the cap, divide 53 percent of projected gross revenue by the number of teams in the league, soon to be 28.

Under the extraordinary leadership of the new commissioner, David Stern, the NBA began a massive growth stage. Within a matter of months following the new agreement, Michael Jordan, Hakeem Olajuwon, and Charles Barkley entered the league via the draft. Corporate interest in basketball was at an all-time high and four new teams were about to enter the league. In addition to the $130 million contribution by the four expansion teams in 1988 and 1989, the NBA signed a new network contract with NBC and TNT calling for another $875 million over the following four years.

The financial impact of these events on player salaries was immediate, forcing the salary cap to continue to rise. During the 1984-85 season, the salary cap was $3.6 million with an average player salary of $300,000; going into the 1993-94 season, the cap has risen to $15.2 million, providing NBA players with an average annual salary of over $1.26 million. This translates to a 322 percent increase in player salaries since the 1984-85 season (DuPree)! And the NBA is still prospering and experiencing growth as an entity, unlike the other leagues which have been far less successful addressing skyrocketing player salaries.

The salary cap, however, is not without its problems. Teams are constantly trying to find methods to stretch the rules, resulting in the ability to exceed the established cap. This is accomplished by jockeying the actual payment of reported players' salaries over time, in affect, "freeing" money under the cap. Teams over the cap have used "exceptions" to replace players lost through such activities as player trades, injuries, retirement, and free agency. This has led to as many as 22 teams being over the established cap. Without discussing the specific maneuvers utilized by individual teams, realize that teams have occasionally retained specialists (Capologists?) to help massage their payrolls. This creative financial management is undertaken in an effort to be able to afford the "missing piece" of the team, that final player needed to take the franchise to "the next level."

There is no doubt that the salaries paid to professional basketball players are high. Nor can it be debated that they are reasonable from an economic perspective. After all, the players are compensated according to the revenue they produce, effectively linking pay and performance. Performance, in this case, is defined as the general level of financial success of the league as a whole. Salary caps may not be the ultimate method of controlling player salaries, but they are definitely the most effective system at the present time. And with football recently instituting a cap, the two remaining leagues will be forced to consider a similar revenue sharing mechanism.

Inherent risks are taken whenever franchises are "forced" to pay these astronomical player salaries. Among these risks, is the concern of diminished athletic performance. Teams commonly insure against a star player becoming injured or succumbing to drugs by inserting clauses in contracts which void payment if drug abuse is discovered or by taking out insurance to cover losses associated with a career ending injury. On the contrary, a team is unable to hedge against a lack of effort. This lack of effort, either perceived or actual, can cause a franchise serious financial difficulty.

Question: If you were considered a top salesperson in a Fortune 500-type company where compensation was based on the volume of sales made, how motivated would you be if the firm gave you a long-term, guaranteed compensation package that did not require you to achieve a certain level of sales?

For the most part, guaranteed salaries contribute, at least subconsciously, to a lack of motivation. This is as true in sports as it is in any other occupation.

In baseball, for example, once a star player reaches a certain level of pay, he may no longer be motivated by additional monetary increases. Conversely, players whose salaries increase in smaller increments and more frequently, typically increase their performance more significantly.

For example, in 1988 thirteen Major League pitchers, including Mark Langston and Roger Clemons, *doubled* their salaries. Pitching statistics for this group declined in each of the next two seasons. On the other hand, a "control" group consisting of pitchers who received smaller raises actually outperformed their higher paid colleagues over the same two year period. This seems to indicate that significant salary increases do not serve as a positive reinforcement to athletes (Sector).

General Managers and Owners, therefore, may want to consider their manner of employee compensation, perhaps more closely linking pay to performance. The tendency toward "over payment" of athletes places such hardships on a franchise that they are again forced to hold down the salaries of their own management staff. Front office personnel are effectively subsidizing these large guaranteed contracts by being forced to forego personal income for the "improvement" of the team and financial viability of the franchise.

RACE RELATIONS

Dismal race relations in professional athletics remains a major source of embarrassment and frustration for all involved in the sports community. A lack of front office minority hirings and the well documented "stacking" of athletes has continued to give the sports community a collective black eye. Bowing to civil rights advocates and the media, many franchises have begun employing and promoting minorities in the last twenty years. Unfortunately, however, progress has been slow, painfully slow.

With respect to the lack of front office appointments to minorities, many recent studies and conferences have further highlighted the problem. While minority hirings of Blacks, Hispanics, and Asians within the upper echelons of franchise management has increased dramatically over the last several years, most contend that this figure still remains far too low.

Public pressure of the early 1970's forced Major League Baseball to consider and eventually hire its first black manager. In 1974, the Cleveland Indians retained Frank Robinson to manage the club. Two years later, the Atlanta Braves became the first team to employ a black in senior management, hiring Hank Aaron in 1976. But, as of 1993, only 3 percent of the top front office positions (Chairman, CEO, General Manager, President or Vice President) in baseball were held by minorities (Lapchick). Why is transformation taking so long?

A common excuse is that blacks have not "paid their dues" by serving in management roles in the minor leagues, working their way up to the major league opportunities. As minorities begin to advance to the major league level, they are blocked by an "old boy network." Within this "network," major league opportunities are customarily filled by white, ex-ballplayers who share a common background and philosophy with the relatively conservative, white ownership (Miller).

Another popular theory for the lack of advancement for minorities in sports was summarized by Bill White, the highest ranking black executive in baseball. White, the former National League President, believes that recent increases in player salaries and other financial issues facing franchises have made it increasingly difficult for everyone, especially minorities. As franchises tighten their belts, few opportunities for advancement exist while even fewer new jobs are created (Dorsey).

Even recently, the NBA has been considered the "model" of the major sports leagues when it comes to front office minority hirings. Still, only 14 percent of the front office administrative positions in basketball were held by blacks while 77 percent of the league's players were black. For the sake of comparison, recall that MLB has a dismal record in the area of minority hiring (3 percent) even though roughly one third of the league's players are black or hispanic. So much for equal opportunity!

Perhaps part of this problem can be traced to "stacking." Stacking is the process by which athletes are steered toward playing certain positions in professional sports, based on a racial orientation. This stacking, by and large, is related to traditional stereotypes. For example, black athletes are more commonly found playing football positions requiring "speed" or "quickness" (95 percent of defensive backs and 89 percent of the wide receivers are black). White athletes tend to play positions marked by "intelligence" and "leadership" such as quarterback (92 percent) and center (87 percent) (Myers). Is it possible that this phenomena is reflected, even subconsciously, in the front office?

Al Campanis, Director of Player Personnel for the Los Angeles Dodgers, made a strong case for this point in his infamous April 7th, 1987 "Nightline" interview with Ted Koppel for which he was subsequently fired. When asked why there were so few black executives in baseball—and sports in general, he responded:

> I don't believe it's prejudice. I truly believe that they may not have some of the necessities to be, let's say, a field manager, or perhaps a general manager—I don't say all of them, but how many black quarterbacks do you have? How many pitchers do you have that are black? So it just might be—why are black men—not good swimmers? Because they don't have the buoyancy?

Racism, in and of itself, is not the only reason for this lack of minority opportunities. Closely related to racism is a critical financial distinction not ignored by professional sports franchises. Consider that most of the dollars generated in the basketball business come from the middle or upper-middle classes, which are typically dominated by non-blacks.

As corporate sponsors and NBA franchises cater to this demographic group and market themselves to this more affluent population, certain observations can be made. White fans, especially those spending big bucks attending basketball games, want to see white players. Not all the time, and certainly not at the expense of losing, but they do prefer to see white players on the roster and, more importantly, on the court occasionally. In fact, a fascinating study (Kahn and Sherer) revealed that replacing a black player with a white one who performs equally well, raises home attendance by 8,000 to 13,000 fans per year.

An equally interesting aspect of the study analyzed player salaries based on race. Black and white players earned comparable *average* salaries. But when the study controlled for performance, league seniority and market-related variables, blacks were paid less than whites by about 20 percent, or $80,000 per year. Interestingly enough, this finding paralleled that of society as the pay gap between blacks and whites in the general labor force is very similar when controlling like variables.

Sports is a reflection of society and the preceding examples should accentuate this point rather candidly. All of society's woes cannot be laid at the doors of professional sports franchises, but glass ceilings apply to minorities in every industry, including sports.

All in all, the prognosis for massive minority hirings in the near future is not encouraging. As sports becomes even more of an international business, minority opportunities must increase. This may not translate to major improvements for specific groups such as blacks, but it should begin a trend toward retaining the best qualified individual regardless of race or ethnicity.

Also, as the playing careers of current day minority sports icons come to a close, be prepared for them to play an active role in franchise management. The Michael Jordans of the sports world are prime candidates to consider team ownership. Having run their business careers efficiently and being in financial positions to acquire a team, they will be cognizant of the need for *qualified* minority management. To that end, they will hire the best professionals for the job, not discounting the obvious management skills and contributions of minorities.

Other opportunities will arise for minorities over time. As many of the old guard managers (Al Campanis, for example) are slowly leaving sports management for one reason or another, they are hopefully being replaced by a more reasonable brand of manager. This new manager will understand the importance of having a well-balanced front office staff, realizing its positive contribution to the morale and success of both the players and the staff.

Hopefully, with the on-going development of sports management and executive training programs as well as continuing education alternatives, more minorities will have access to the required tools necessary to compete on a "level playing field" for those management positions available at the franchise level. After all, there is more to preparing for a career in sports than simply participating as a professional athlete.

Expansion, although limited, should provide a small number of positions for minorities as we reach the mid-nineties. We can only hope that these positions are meaningful and visible. If newly created positions or hirings allow minorities the opportunity to assist in the management of a franchise, we will no doubt watch stereotypes disappear as their performance and success is documented. Consequently, when contacting a team to discuss employment opportunities, one must be aware of these dynamics. Understanding a team's general philosophy and track record with respect to employment may provide the applicant with the necessary tools to excel in the initial interview and, eventually, as an employee.

HOW PROFITS ARE AFFECTED BY 'HIDDEN' ECONOMIC FACTORS

The ability of a franchise to turn a profit and offer steady employment opportunities is closely related to more than just the team's winning percentage. It is the franchise's intent to field the most competitive team possible, usually resulting in drastically increased expenses in such areas as "research and development" including scouting, trading and player development; and marketing. It is hoped that these incremental expenses will be more than matched by the added revenue brought about by fielding a successful, winning team. No team, regardless of market size and athletic prowess, will remain successful without outstanding, hands-on management expertise.

Recalling that a team's primary revenue sources are ticket sales and broadcasting revenue, these elements must be examined to determine if they play the deciding role in financial success or failure. Any individual franchise is affected by two basic criteria: the overall success and marketability of the league in general, and its own ability to field a desirable team within this framework, considering local constraints such as market size and local demand (Knoll).

In basketball, for example, the absolute quality of league-wide play, competitive balance, reputation for integrity of play, and sophisticated marketing all impact the success of the league in general. Within any given market, the same variables impact success, only in a microeconomic fashion. If fans believe they are watching the best athletes in the world, competing in fair (with respect to integrity) contests, they will be interested in viewing.

Perhaps subconsciously and certainly economically, these fans require that their team win a majority of the close games over time as blow-outs become old very quickly, thus maintaining a high level of fan interest. Since steady crowds—be they in stadium attendance or home viewership—lead to increased gate revenue and broadcasting fees, an incentive exists to field a club that is *slightly* better than the competition. Slightly better than the competition does not mean a team that simply plays over ".500 ball;" it means a team that consistently outperforms the majority of the competition, allowing for additional revenue through playoff shares, as well as ticket sales and broadcasting revenue.

At the league level, the goal is to keep the competition *relatively* keen while ensuring that over the long run, teams with a larger number of fans and dollars to spend will tend to be the better teams. Not coincidentally, the larger fan bases are located in the major media markets, enabling the league to maximize its revenue.

Parity, as we know it, is not the goal of the league, as absolute parity would transfer financial opportunities from larger markets to smaller ones, reducing the entire league's revenue. Everyone associated with basketball makes more money if the Knicks play the Lakers as opposed to the Denver Nuggets in the NBA Finals. Since league revenue is shared by the teams and players, it is unlikely that too many of them would argue the point. By the way, of the 47 NBA championships from 1947 through 1993, 35 have been won by teams located in "top 10" metropolitan areas.

The bottom line, then, is that a team needs to be "just competitive enough" in order to be financially successful. Certainly the fans from any given city would like to watch a winner, but given the financial dynamics of the league this is neither desired nor possible. To no one's surprise, the most successful teams are located in cities with large populations and consistently competitive teams.

Since many franchises are valuable financial commodities as

previously determined, their ability to create other economic opportunities within the local community and surrounding metropolitan areas are well documented. As franchises are granted to cities via expansion and relocation, a wide ranging economic transformation can take place.

In theory, a team's arrival in a city spurs economic growth by providing jobs related to the franchise. Not only the front office jobs previously discussed, but other positions such as concessions, security, and maintenance are created. Local merchants also benefit from the addition of a franchise. The presence of any tax paying corporation also contributes to the welfare of the surrounding community. All of these remarks seem to make sense, but do they hold true in the "real world?"

Consider that cities cite three major benefits from having a professional sports team in their town. The first two, the satisfaction of civic pride and the creation of a positive image of the host community, are intangible. There is no doubt that winning franchises deliver on both accounts, while perennial losers suffer in some, equally unquantifiable manner.

Whatever the case, the third reason for having a sports team, the ability to provide economic growth, is quantifiable. The likelihood of significant economic growth often encourages municipalities to strongly consider wooing teams to their towns. They do so by building stadiums and providing favorable economic terms to the franchise.

Their reasoning behind this is that they believe that professional sports will have a "ripple effect" on the local economy. In economic terms, this "multiplier effect" is felt when a sports dollar generated by the franchise is continually reinvested in the community. For example, when a salary is paid to an athlete or club employee, he typically purchases goods or services in the community, furthering the economic growth of the region. This original sports dollar is "turned over" somewhere between two and four times (Miller: 297). While all of these factors may actually help the local economy, there are other characteristics which need to be considered; characteristics which may not actually promote economic growth. For example, many believe that the taxes paid by a franchise do not adequately cover the increased costs to the city of additional police, fire, and public transportation. Other problems arise when the affluent members of the franchise, players and management, choose to move to surrounding suburban areas, essentially limiting the inflow of private spending in the immediate area where the franchise is located. Even the hundreds of seasonal employment opportunities stemming from the franchise's presence are limited. Many of these jobs are low paying which limits their impact on the local economy, but others are well paying, such as stadium construction and state-sponsored renovation. Nevertheless, the tax payer ultimately pays for these types of building services.

Conversely, when a team leaves a city, a contraction of the local economy occurs. Simply stated, many of the apparent economic benefits detailed above are eliminated, leaving communities with fewer employment opportunities and reduced civic pride. The degree to which these contractions take place depends upon one's overall belief that the economy was enhanced in the first place by a franchise's founding or relocation (Hiestand, 1992).

Whether the economic impact of franchises is positive, negative or indifferent, really doesn't matter—we love our sports and continue to mandate that our local politicians and lobbyists pursue franchises whenever possible, *almost* regardless of cost. With respect to employment opportunities, do not disregard the ancillary positions surrounding franchises such as venue management.

PASSING THE COST ALONG TO THE FAN

Whenever the demand for a firm's product increases or the cost to the firm of producing its goods and service rises, the consumer tends to pay the price. No where is this more evident than professional basketball. Recently, the cost of attending an NBA contest for a family of four has increased substantially and now stands at $168.68. This sum, comprised of the cost of tickets, parking, concessions, and souvenirs has risen at three times the rate of inflation over the past three years (Hiestand, 1993).

In recent years, it was possible for a major portion of these soaring franchise expenses to be absorbed by the networks which were eager to ante up the necessary millions for broadcast rights. Under this scenario, it was reasonable to assume that the corporate sponsors who purchased advertising time during these sports telecasts were desirous of effectively marketing their wares to this captive demographic market.

Additionally, these firms required that the exposure translate to sales in order for sports advertising to be cost-effective. Ideally, the fan watching the sports telecasts purchased the products or services being advertised, essentially supporting the firms' involvement in sports. Purchasing products or services—which creates successful ad campaigns, pushes up the cost of advertising as the demand for such advertising time increases, resulting in larger sums paid for network contracts. As the prices of these contracts rise, players' salaries rise as total team revenue increases. This is, albeit indirectly, another method for subsidizing the high salaries paid to players.

There are only three ways to curtail this process. The first is to discourage companies from purchasing advertising time in sports. This can be accomplished by not purchasing the products or services advertised. As advertising becomes less effective due to reduced sales, the cost of the spots will fall. Since supply of advertising time will exceed the demand for placing advertising, eventual reductions in the enormous network contracts will be observed; which is explored in detail in Chapter 8. This will force teams to be more fiscally responsible.

Closely related to this advertising concept is the notion of network ratings. Obviously, the more people watching a particular event, the greater the price demanded for advertising during that telecast. Most advertisers justify allocating big bucks to specific events if they believe their product or service will be reaching its intended target market, i.e. males, ages 18-35. This, too, is further explored in Chapter 8.

A final way to reduce this spiraling cost of attending games is to simply reduce the number of contests attended. This will have the same basic effect as those outlined above. Again, all of these will reduce total team revenue, mandating that franchises keep a trained eye on expenses, including player salaries.

Unfortunately, very few avid sports fans will turn away from a particular game based on these principles. But unless and until we do, we should not anticipate sports becoming any more affordable or easy to enjoy.

On the positive side, there lies the potential for employment opportunities. Generally speaking, firms with large and diverse revenue sources coupled with increasing expenses tend to employ more professionals than a small "mom and pop" enterprise. The firm with $100 million in revenue and $90 million in expenses is likely to have a larger employee base than the firm with $1 million in revenue and $900,000 in expenses. This is not to say, however, that the quality and subsequent compensation of the jobs is outstanding, just that, at the margins, the total number of jobs may be greater. As a rule of thumb, as the sports economy grows, the need for qualified employees and professionals also increases.

TURF BATTLES

Internal structure, political bickering, and financial intricacies all contribute to the continual turf battles taking place within professional sports franchises. Inter-office power struggles regarding such issues as when and where to allocate resources and how to deal with outside political forces, including those affecting relocation and facility upgrades, regularly cause friction among upper management. Additional sources of animosity arise over player trades, acquisitions, and coaching changes, often pitting player personnel against ownership. Other areas in which teams battle internally include mid-management's fight for respect. An apparent indifference exists in the front office when it comes to dealing with middle management and staff positions. This lack of respect deflates morale and stifles creativity.

And, if this steady in-fighting is not enough, consider the "labor vs. management" relationship. Players, along with their agents, are regularly battling management for concessions, whether they be over compensation, practice facilities, or chartered flights between contests. At the same time, the players' unions battle management through the league offices over pension plan parameters, drug testing policies, and player safety. Franchise management can never let its collective guard down as it is constantly confronted by a variety of factions.

Even with these skirmishes breaking out all over, teams still have time to follow a set of loosely written rules designed to benefit the predominantly white, conservative ownership. These rules, as previously discussed, include reduced opportunities for minorities, long hours for franchise staffers, and rampant nepotism in the front office.

Believe it or not, however, these dynamics present a fascinating and challenging work environment. The many perceived negatives of franchise management are quickly dispelled as soon as the home team takes the field. Being associated with the hosting of a professional sports contest tends to overshadow most of the day-to-day struggles and frustrations associated with the long hours and low pay. Working for a team can be and usually is a lot of fun, regardless of the politics and financial hardships present.

PLAYER ASSOCIATIONS
AND LEAGUE OFFICES

Although professional sports franchises are the basis for this chapter, it is necessary to also consider players' unions and league offices. The discussion of these organizations is crucial, as they play a major role in shaping franchise management. While each professional sports league has associated organizations, the two serving the NFL are discussed in this section. Players' associations, such as the National Football League Players' Association (NFLPA), were organized in an effort to improve the working conditions of their member athletes.

The NFLPA was formed in 1956 after a group of Green Bay Packers players became dissatisfied with the cleanliness of their uniforms. When management refused to cater to this seemingly minor request, the group of players rallied, calling for a more formal meeting to discuss how best to pursue the matter.

The first player rep meeting was held in November, 1956, at which time the following proposals were made in addition to the request for clean jerseys and dry equipment: a request for a minimum salary of $5,000, uniform per diem pay for players, a rule requiring clubs to pay for players' equipment, and the inclusion of an injury clause in the standard player contract which would provide for continued salary to an injured player.

Nonetheless, the NFL refused to recognize the Association until 1959, at which time NFLPA President Billy Howton threatened to sue the league for violating antitrust laws unless the league would bargain with this newly formed "union." More than thirty years and numerous lawsuits later, this "Professional Association" (union) now boasts an active membership of 1500 and a retired membership approaching 2000 football players.

A necessary point of clarification needs to be noted, however. At the current time the Washington, D.C. based "Players' Association" has re-certified itself as a union and is no longer termed a "Professional Association." The reason for this stems from the outcome of the antitrust lawsuit against the league filed in the U.S. District Court in Minneapolis, more commonly referred to as the McNeil case.

As a "union," the NFLPA has several stated objectives. These are not unique to the NFLPA per se, as similar ones exist throughout the other major sports players' associations. The NFLPA lists among its objectives the desire to enhance, protect, and defend the individual rights of its member athletes. An additional goal of the NFLPA is to prevent, attack, and eliminate any and all limitations or restrictions on a player's ability to market his skills and/or services. The continuance of group licensing efforts, the enhancement of players' incomes "off the field," and post-career preparation are among other primary objectives of the NFLPA.

The Association is comprised of a wide variety of professionals ranging from the members of the Association's Executive Committee to specialty groups. The staff, totaling about 35, is divided into such functions as licensing, legal, membership, public relations, and research. Other departments address accounting, player benefits, and special events. These areas, which are monitored by the executive committee and implemented by the support staff, handle all day-to-day functions of the Association.

Much like the employees at the individual franchises, most of those employed by the PA's are not generously compensated. However, as in the franchises, certain positions at the union level do warrant considerable compensation and provide enormous exposure while commanding a very high level of respect.

As previously mentioned, the relationship between the Players' Association, its members and their representatives, and the League Office and the franchises and their interests, is continually strained. It is precisely these differences which provide some of the employment opportunities mentioned. More numerous, and often times similar positions which attempt to protect the concerns of the individual franchise and its management, exist in the National Football League Office.

By 1920, professional football was in a state of disarray. Highlighted by increasing player salaries, player transiency caused by players "jumping ship" and continually searching out a more lucrative offer, and the ongoing use of collegiate athletes who were still enrolled in school, it was decided that an organization in which all members followed the same rules was quickly becoming a necessity. A final issue that needed to be addressed, which was not publicly stated by this pending organization, was that of gambling and corruption. The potential for fixing an event was, and continues to be, a concern of those managing the business of football.

To this end, an August 20, 1920, meeting of representatives from four professional teams led to the formation of the American Professional Football Conference. Shortly thereafter, Jim Thorpe was named President of the organization. The name was changed to the American Professional Football Association in an effort to lend the cause added credibility. A final name change was made in June of 1922, with the "Association" becoming The National Football League (NFL).

Located in New York since 1960, The NFL Office continues to serve its members' interests. Over time, the functions served by the NFL have developed, becoming more diverse and issue specific. Essentially, the Office exists to help facilitate equitable transactions and regulate the activities of its members. For example, dealing with strikes/lockouts and franchise expansion/relocation, handling disciplinary actions such as suspensions and banishments, and working with the media in securing appropriate network contracts are all functions performed by the office.

In order to best serve these functions, the NFL Office is divided into approximately ten departments, totaling fewer than one hundred employees. Among the largest of these departments is public relations, with a staff of about eight to ten professionals. Other departments, such as "Legal" and "Treasury" employ staffs of only two or three. This number of employees does not include those working for NFL Properties, the licensing and merchandising arm of the League Office. This branch, while run by the Commissioner, is essentially a separate entity, and is experiencing tremendous growth. Accordingly, the size of this staff continues to grow, representing a large percentage of the jobs associated with the NFL, but not accounted for above.

Most recently, two of these groups, the "International" and "Players Programs" Departments have been experiencing the most development. The need for the League to evaluate, monitor, and raise European awareness of the sport is becoming critical, as this market appears to be a major growth opportunity for football. Also, the broadening of the "Players Programs" group, in which players are assisted with the development of post-career activities such as finishing college and/or attaining meaningful employment has become a very important function provided by the League Office.

All things considered, these League employees are moderately compensated. Much like the NFLPA and individual franchises, the League Office offers excellent work experience, exposing the staff member to the fascinating intricacies of professional sports. The quality of this work experience, however, may be partially offset by this average pay scale.

The Commissioner of the League, currently Paul Tagliabue,

primarily serves in an advisory role, regulating the day-to-day activities of the 30 teams. Tagliabue is empowered to protect the integrity of the game through resolving disputes with in the league and imposing disciplinary measures for conduct "detrimental to the League." With respect to specific proposals, however, the owners must vote to approve or decline any measure—23 of 30 owner votes are necessary to approve any new policy.

The relationship between the Commissioner and the Owners can be quite strained as the individual interests of the wealthy owners may not be consistent with those of the League as a whole. Specifically, some owners are concerned with the bottom line while others are more interested in merely being associated with a professional sports franchise. This business vs. hobby concept leads to many differences of opinion, each of which must be considered by the Commissioner.

Realize that an individual owner's personal agenda may not always be short-term profit oriented. Franchises are acquired for three reasons beyond that of "short-term book profit." First, owners seek to earn capital gains through the eventual sale of the team. Historically, tremendous appreciation in franchise values have made "holding" these assets most profitable. Next, franchises can serve to increase the profits of other affiliated businesses held by the owner. An example of this might include a media giant owning a franchise and capitalizing from this relationship. Finally, owners seek to reduce income tax liability by offsetting any book losses due to team ownership against other sources of income (Scully: 129).

These reasons only begin to explain the intricacies of ownership and the potential difficulties experienced by the League when attempting to regulate franchise activities. The above reasons for ownership make comparing the financial status of each team very difficult, further complicating the Commissioner's job.

Delicate player relations issues are also a source of friction between the League and its franchises, as well as with the players, of course. What might be "in the best interest of football" from the league's perspective may seriously hinder the success of an individual franchise such as a prolonged player suspension. These examples provide a flavor for the types of activities and concerns which are "regulated" by the League Office. The NFL Office provides a wide variety of essential functions necessary to the well being of professional football. Without this office, the League would be in the same disarray that it was in 1920.

CAUSE AND EFFECT

Professional sports franchises contribute to the overall welfare of the other four areas in different ways. With respect to collegiate athletic departments, professional sports help build interest in the collegiate game. Granted, there are millions of fans who not only prefer amateur athletics but watch them exclusively. Nonetheless, professional and collegiate athletics serve in a complementary fashion—each benefitting from the success of the other. To a lesser degree, the publicity and recognition given the professional superstar's alma mater draws further attention to the athletic department and its athletic prowess.

The ability for an athlete representation firm to prosper is a direct result of its relationship to franchises. Agents provide the "supply" of talent while the franchises "demand" the top athletes. This basic economic relationship is the basis for agency compensation.

It is the goal of the media to secure television rights to athletic events, broadcast these same events over the airwaves and print the results in local papers and national magazines. Without this ability, the sports media would be in a precarious financial situation. Fortunately, this is not the case as the media is in the position to raise revenue from these activities. As expected, professional sports franchises play an integral role in raising these revenues, allowing media to continue to rely upon a healthy relationship with the major sports leagues.

Sports management firms rely heavily upon the continued success of professional franchises. Without superstar athletes to promote, many sports marketing and public relations firms would be forced to look elsewhere for revenue. Where would sports marketing-driven corporations be without those "franchise" players soaring through the air, graphically displaying the $175 dollar "tennis" shoes? Venue management firms are equally dependent on the success and growth of franchises as they represent the cornerstone of their businesses and the key to their financial success.

8

DON'T STOP THE NOISE—OR I WILL LOSE MY JOB

*B*ryan Deierling is currently in his sixth season with the Golden State Warriors, and second as a media sales representative. Prior to serving in this capacity, Bryan was an account service manager in the marketing department. Deierling is currently responsible for sponsorship sales of Warriors television, radio and in-arena signage. Additionally, he writes an occasional column for **Warriors Playbook**, the team's bimonthly magazine.

Prior to joining the Warriors in 1988, Deierling served in a sales management position at the Oakland Hills Tennis Club as well as Garvin Guy Butler, a Euro-dollar brokerage house located in San Francisco.

The Lutherville, Maryland native is a graduate of the University of California, Santa Barbara and holds a degree in Economics with an emphasis in marketing.

I am constantly asked the question of how, when, and why I decided to get a job in sports. The reality of the situation is that I never planned to work for a franchise like the Golden State Warriors—like most, I planned on playing for one!

My initial dream, like many youngsters, was to one day be a professional athlete. However, I lacked the requisite combination of size, exposure, and of course, talent. The lack of any of these attributes led to an early reality check—I was not going to enjoy a long and illustrious career as a professional basketball player.

Accordingly, I was faced with "getting a real job" upon receiving my diploma from the University of California, Santa Barbara in 1985. The good news was that I had earned a degree in Business Economics, with an emphasis in Marketing. This course work provided me with an excellent theoretical background in business, but lacked any real practical applications of these principles. The bad news was that, like most of my college buddies, I felt relatively unprepared and unsure of exactly what I wanted to pursue in the business world.

I did know, however, that I wanted to take advantage of the interpersonal skills (read: sales!) I had developed over the years. Nonetheless, I was unwilling to go to work for a large corporation where I firmly believed many employees were viewed simply as numbers rather than people. It was not for me.

Surprisingly enough, I was able to locate a job opportunity (in the classified section of the local paper) despite these constraints and personal requirements. I began managing a tennis club in Northern California, a position which combined membership sales with participation in the leisure sports industry. Unfortunately, it was not long before I realized that severe salary limitations existed due to the relatively limited revenue generated by the club; I quickly sacrificed some of my earlier 'requirements' in an effort to make a better living.

After an abbreviated and relatively uneventful three month stint working for a Euro-dollar brokerage house in San Francisco, I knew I was headed in the wrong direction—away from what I truly enjoyed: sports.

That's when serendipity took over! Although I had not initiated an active job search, I scanned the classifieds one evening, looking for that perfect job. Given my cynical state of mind, I never believed that the perfect job could ever be found. Suddenly, a two-sentence opportunity screamed out to me from the endless columns of run-of-the-mill jobs.

"Motivated sales people wanted for professional sports team. If interested, please send resume to—."

I was stunned. I read and re-read the passage several times and immediately called an associate who was working for a local sports team to inquire as to whom this mystery franchise might be. I was particularly surprised to read this passage because my contact consistently reminded me of the lack of career opportunities at the franchise level. He told me that he was certain that the ad was placed by the Vice President of Marketing for the Golden State Warriors. So much for being cynical!

I hand delivered my resume the following afternoon and asked to speak with the person to whom I was to direct my resume. He came out for a quick precursory handshake, thanked me for coming and informed me that I would be receiving a call to set up an interview for the position of season ticket sales, a summer-long employment opportunity.

I was elated to learn that, upon completing the interview process, I was one of six candidates chosen for the available positions. I was also told one more very interesting bit of information: One of these temporary representatives (the one with the best sales performance at the end of the summer), would be offered a permanent position with the club.

As it turned out, our sales results were so strong that the Warriors chose to hire four of the original "temps." This was deemed necessary because of the recent resurgence of the team and the relative lack of "permanent" sales staff employed by the Warriors. Although the six of us tried to take full credit for this sales success, it is possible that the beginning of the Don Nelson Era and the addition of eventual Rookie of the Year Mitch Richmond may have played a small part in this new found success!

In retrospect, this does not seem like the typical career path leading to a position with a professional sports franchise. But, you too will find that many great opportunities are merely stumbled upon at opportune moments or through chance occurrences such as mine.

Needless to say, I had numerous preconceived notions of what life would be like working for a professional sports team. Some of my expectations were confirmed while many others were dramatically contradicted. I envisioned a relatively glamorous, high profile lifestyle with the pro athletes that I had read so much about.

My first dose of reality, as it pertained to life in the NBA, came within my first week of the pre-season (my "rookie" year—if you will). I showed up at the office wearing a crisp, freshly pressed white button down shirt, silk tie, dress slacks and loafers—fully prepared for the privileged life of an NBA'er.

I was eager to witness the first game of my new "home" team. Instead of being able to acknowledge the roar of the sell-out crowd, I was assigned the task of unloading a truck load of boxes containing that evening's promotional give-away: magnetic Warriors season schedules (perfect for the tacky refrigerator door, I might add). Within seconds of receiving this first assignment, I realized I was over dressed for the evening as my shirt was sweaty and soiled, my tie already badly wrinkled and my ego firmly in check. Welcome to life in the NBA!

I also anticipated both a friendly personal and professional relationship with the players. After all, I reasoned, if we were selling the product, we would have to get to know the stars in order to more efficiently sell them to the community. While I was never one to be star-struck, I regularly held professional athletes in very high regard for both their physical ability and the discipline required to reach such a level of athletic competence. As a result, I looked forward to sitting down with the players, getting to know them and talking 'hoops'.

As I spent my first summer as a "temporary" employee, I just figured all the players were out of town for the off season and I would get an opportunity to rap with them when they returned to training camp. Well, as training camp came and went, I realized the only real opportunity to interact with them would be a quick greeting in the catacombs of the arena as they headed to the locker room after practice. However, as time went on, I eventually reached a first name basis with only a few of the more gregarious players.

However, not long thereafter, the first couple of players that knew me (or at least my name), were summarily traded or waived; I was forced to question the coincidence of these transactions. Finally, I reached a first name basis with a number of players that retained a spot on the roster for a longer period of time. At least I was reassured that their friendship with the front office staff was not the reason for the previous players' dismissal from the team.

In addition to the glamorous lifestyle I was convinced I would lead, my expectations for compensation were equally, and unreasonably, lofty. I theorized that I would make a salary comparable to any other sales-related industry at an entry-level position. I mistakenly assumed that professional sports was such a lucrative business that I would be a beneficiary of this greater financial success. As it turns out, the limited beneficiaries of these high level dollars are the marquis figures in the professional sports experience—the players.

Related to this point is the belief that professional sports is a big money maker for the owners. This may not be an accurate statement if you are evaluating profitability based on year-to-year franchise operations. As discussed earlier by the author in the section entitled "Cash Out," there are numerous, significant expenses involved in the operation of a franchise. The yearly balance sheet of a franchise commonly shows, at best, a break-even level of financial success. This is because the books typically reflect the necessary debt service required to repay the initial loan used to purchase the franchise. The primary economic profit that exists in franchise ownership is based on the eventual sale of the team, where a return on the initial purchase price can be several hundred percent—a tidy profit. Because of this lack of profitability in the day-to-day operations, a pro sports franchise attempts to keep personnel costs at a minimum. Due to the collective bargaining agreement between the players' association and the league (in addition to the pressure to field a winning team by acquiring as many top athletes as possible), players' salaries remain the largest expense item to the team.

As a result, a team's personnel cost containment must come at the front office level. In spite of all this seemingly discouraging news, you need to know that, although you won't be in a comparable tax bracket with the players, you can earn a living that will allow you to live comfortably. The entry level salaries for NBA front office personnel is generally in the low twenty thousand dollar per year range, although it obviously depends on the position available and the cost of living in the team's market. I have known individuals with other teams that have started with salaries that were both higher and lower than this range.

Perhaps the most important thing to bear in mind is, if you are searching for a job that will result in a lucrative salary, the front office of a professional team is not for you. If, however, you are looking for a job in sports because of the emotional reward and exhilaration of associating with the team, the opportunity to work in an industry that is not only interesting but simultaneously allows you the luxury of actually having fun most of the time, then a job in sports is worth the required sacrifice and effort.

Having been with a franchise for over five years and moving from an entry level ticket sales position to an account executive in the media sales department, I have become quite familiar with just how difficult it is to secure a position within the sports industry. Lest you become discouraged by the bleak picture I am presenting, let me suggest that there is hope. I am pleased to tell you that the Warriors have hired four new full-time employees in the past two years and four new part-time employees during the past two seasons.

With my background as an "insider" of sorts, allow me to share some of my personal observations. Due to the high demand for positions in professional sports, competition among prospective employees is extremely fierce and involves a large number of highly qualified (and often over-qualified) candidates. The qualifications required to garner consideration for a franchise position include: a college degree, extensive sales experience and prior internships or experience with other sports entities. Sports franchises view all of these as pre-requisites for handling entry level responsibilities (which vary depending upon the position involved).

In addition to the high demand for jobs, the number of actual available positions within the industry is extremely limited. As I will explain in more detail later, a pro sports team employs a surprisingly small front office staff and, more often than not, will increase the responsibilities of the current staff when the team enjoys success (on the court and/or at the till) rather than add an additional staffer. Understandably, this combination of high demand for employment and low supply of positions available makes it incredibly difficult to land that first job.

After observing the success (or lack thereof), of applicants to secure that elusive job in pro sports, I have made note of several approaches that appear to yield relatively successful results. Experience, at any level, in the sports industry will look great on a resume. You immediately appear that much more qualified for a position. As a result, look for an opportunity to work at *any level* of sports; don't limit your job search to your favorite sport or team. Many potential participants in the sports industry have been unsuccessful in their job searches, and subsequently (and reluctantly) returned to a standard 9 to 5 job because they were discouraged by their initial lack of success. Very likely, the problem, in addition to a basic lack of credentials, was a series of misguided efforts; setting their sights solely on the franchises in their immediate area. Any time you limit your employment universe, either team-wise or geographically, you substantially reduce the likelihood of successfully gaining that first job.

The best approach to finding employment is to discover a way to just get your foot in the door. That is, make every effort to gain entry into any area of a pro sports team, regardless of whether it is in your particular area of (long term) interest. This initial involvement will most likely involve only game night operations in a volunteer capac-ity—promotional staff or stat keeper, for instance. Game day operations involve many highly laborious tasks and, as a result, most teams are in need of a number of competent and responsible individuals to assist in these duties. To gain access to these positions, make an effort to contact game operations managers and promotional and media relations managers and volunteer your services. Through diligence and perseverance, you can prove your worth to the organization and increase your chances of gaining full time employment with the organization.

Another essential component to your job search in professional sports management is the all important art of networking—making yourself known and available to those individuals involved in the hiring process. It is extremely difficult to land a job without having personal contacts within the industry to help distinguish you from all other applicants.

Bear in mind that teams receive an average of 20-25 resumes per week and if, through your personal contacts, you can differentiate yourself from the other applicants, you will gain a decided advantage. Be advised that 99 percent of these resumes come from unsolicited applicants. Of these, about half are addressed to the specific person responsible for hiring, which at least required a little extra effort. Unfortunately, an alarmingly large number of these applicants have misspelled the name of the hiring manager.

There are a number of different approaches to make yourself visible to the appropriate people. Depending on your level of creativity (and bank roll), you have several alternatives regarding entree into the world of sports management.

A typical environment for making sports industry contacts would include industry-specific symposiums and seminars which feature guest speakers from various segments of the sports industry. You can obtain information about when and where these take place through the different sports industry publications. These situations will afford you the opportunity to make some personal contacts with sports executives in a professional atmosphere. These conversations could mean the difference between your resume (or phone call) being lumped with all the other applicants or being considered for future opportunities because of a qualified prior contact.

Another approach (one that will potentially yield even higher employment opportunity dividends), is making an effort to volunteer for any sports related event that is held in your area. Even if this event has no apparent relation to your desired field, it helps to expand your recognition amongst the people in the sports industry. When I say "everything," I mean events ranging from 3-on-3 basketball tournaments to charity 10 kilometer races. Even if you don't initially make contact with the individuals directly involved with hiring in your field of interest, the people you work with will often times serve as strong personal and professional references, essentially adding one more credential to your growing list of qualifications.

Finally, a more aggressive (yet not necessarily more effective) means of getting yourself recognized involves posting some major frequent flyer mileage. All it takes is a little research to determine where the major sports gatherings will be held throughout the country. For example, the NBA, NFL and Major League Baseball all conduct annual meetings, most of which are open to the public in some capacity. Attending these functions and making yourself visible may pay off if you are able to make a good and lasting impression on those individuals responsible for hiring at the franchise level.

Obviously, opportunities exist, but you must use your own personal agenda as a barometer to ascertain which approach best suits your needs and time-line. Nonetheless, all the hard work you do to market yourself could be for naught in the event that you are viewed as a nuisance instead of a potential resource for the organization. This requires a very delicate balancing act.

As I mentioned earlier, there are few similarities between working for a franchise and holding a more traditional 9 to 5 job. To further demonstrate this, I will describe the typical work load of a season ticket sales representative, my first position.

The day I was hired, one thing was made crystal clear to me by my superior: sell season seats, or else! Ticket sales are generally the life blood of a sports franchise and, as such, season ticket sales are extremely important to the over all financial health of the organization. To this end, my focus that first summer (as well as the next three) was to work the phones in search of that elusive group we knew as potential Golden State Warriors season ticket holders. So, contrary to both public perception and my own ridiculous beliefs, I quickly learned that the front office, unlike the players, does not have the summer off. In fact, our seven person marketing staff came to the office day after day to make both solicited and unsolicited calls to prospective Warriors season ticket holders.

These calls made for some very long days but, at least, the conversations revolved around the Warriors past successes and forecasting their future performances (topics of general interest to most Bay Area sports fans). This brief description does not even begin to discuss the difficulties encountered in most of these calls. Earlier, I referred to solicited and unsolicited calls—the distinction between the two being that solicited calls refer to individuals who had indicated some basic level of interest in a season package. These are in stark contrast to the unsolicited call, or cold calls, which were basically shots in the dark.

The seven of us quickly tried to maximize our sales results by devising different means of lead generation—everything from referrals to targeting athletically related industry lists, such as athletic club membership rosters. This work is very labor intensive and, more often than not, horror stories are exchanged about how one of us called a "hot" prospect, only to be told that the person in question had either died or moved away years ago. Back to the drawing board!

I cannot believe how times have changed. With a little help from a competitive team on the court, the season ticket solicitation process now revolves around contacting a limited number of our "Warriors Reserve Team." This "team" refers to members that have submitted a deposit to become part of the season ticket waiting list.

Even with this success, we still don't get the summers off. Since we have sold out for five consecutive seasons, someone is required to service each of these accounts, ensuring that payments are made and seat locations are improved whenever possible.

Once the season begins, our duties take on a dramatically different role. As previously stated, game day tasks comprise a large portion of the marketing staff's responsibilities. For instance, these can range from placing a "Beat the Bulls" placard on every seat in the arena prior to the Chicago contest to placating the large numbers of disgruntled fans who inevitably show up at the Will Call booth on game nights either in need of replacement tickets or complaining that tickets which were supposed to be left for them are nowhere to be found. Often times, many of the staff are only able to catch a small portion of each home game due to these types of responsibilities. This makes these assignments especially tough because one of the main reasons we are willing to work so hard is the opportunity to see our product (the Warriors) compete. These game days (and nights) regularly consist of a 15 hour work day; long hours which can be rewarded by watching the Warriors post a big home victory.

The morning after one of these grueling days is always a little bit tough. After all, the morning comes a little too quickly and, depending on the success of the team the previous evening, can be very depressing. All in all, the mood ranges from somewhat energetic to downright lethargic. These are some of the rare moments when life in professional sports feels like a "real job."

On days when the team does not play, the season ticket representatives are responsible for servicing between 450-750 season ticket accounts. These service calls can be someone voicing a complaint ("the pizza man doesn't come to my section"), making a recommendation (some of which are actually implemented), or a season ticket holder simply interested in discussing the teams performance. It is this attention to service that allows a team to build and maintain a satisfied season ticket base even when the team encounters a rough season or two.

In addition to the aforementioned duties, there are other, lesser known responsibilities that make the inner workings of professional sports organizations even more unique. For example, I remember how surprised I was to learn of the relatively small size of the front office. As I stated earlier, management prefers to increase the duties of current employees, rather than increase staffing.

This "lean machine" approach necessitates that *everyone* be involved in the day-to-day tasks of the organization. As a result, performing the important tasks to the most menial chores are completed by whomever is available at the time, usually regardless of status or position in the organization. Since there is no strict adherence to job responsibilities as they relate to a traditional corporate hierarchy, task flexibility is extremely important—do not allow your ego to get in the way of "pulling your own weight." During the season, since more time is spent with your co-workers than your own family, it is important to maintain a magnanimous nature; as nothing will ostracize you from your colleagues more quickly than a blatant disregard and/or unwillingness to pitch in when needed. The major benefit of this team approach is that it builds much closer personal relationships among your co-workers than in more structured corporate environments.

Of course, due to the involvement and time constraints of this business, it is very important that your family and friends support you in your efforts and are willing to make certain concessions in your personal life. While franchise employees do indeed have lives outside the office (er, arena), the combination of work related responsibilities requires a complete commitment. But on the up-side of things, this is the only business I know where sometimes being a couch potato and watching sports on the tube is "just doing my job!"

Not unlike many other small businesses, the Warriors' front office management is readily accessible to everyone within the organization. An informal "open door policy" is the rule, rather than the exception. Interaction, on both a formal and informal basis, with the team president and vice presidents is encouraged—it's not unusual to carry on a discussion with the team president while preparing lunch in the snack bar area. This accessibility allows a large amount of freedom and willingness among the employees to offer suggestions and exchange ideas with their superiors. For a firm that grosses tens of millions of dollars a year, it's a refreshing and productive way to run a business.

Additionally, because of the athletic nature of the business, there is a somewhat casual and health-conscious atmosphere around the office. Most often, a dress shirt and tie is only worn to the office when appointments have been scheduled. The majority of the day-to-day fashion involves more casual active wear which serves a dual purpose: it allows an employee to be more comfortable and, more importantly, makes it easier for the employees to pitch in and help with the necessary manual labor at a moment's notice—without having to concern themselves with ruining their dress clothes.

Through much hard work and ethical work habits, I have enjoyed some success and, as a result, have enjoyed a measure of upward mobility within the organization. I have been very impressed with the opportunity the Warriors afford an individual to progress within the organization through promotions when a position does become available. The "small business" aspect of a sports franchise allows an employee to regularly demonstrate his worth to the franchise. Through these promotions, the team sends a message to its employees that hard work is rewarded, leading to a much more productive and satisfied work force.

In my efforts to grow within the business, I have set some long term goals in terms of advancement, most of which revolve around continued growth within the Warriors organization. In this regard, please realize that patience is a definite virtue in this industry. While your job title may not change very quickly (due to the 'lean' nature of franchises), your responsibilities will certainly begin to mount. The way a staffer manages these increasing responsibilities determines his or her value to the team. Again, if patience is demonstrated in this process, the promotion will follow, paying much larger dividends in the long run.

Like most industries, the competition stiffens as one moves up the company ladder, as both exemplary qualifications and extensive personal contacts begin to play an even larger role in the process. When the available position is at a higher level, the organization is more interested in opening up the competition to include candidates from outside the office. They typically do this in order to have a more comprehensive, and possibly more qualified, group of candidates from which to choose. They deem this necessary because a higher level position very likely requires a more specialized area of knowledge and, as such, may limit the internal applicants and dictate bringing in prospects from outside the franchise.

Obviously, this reduces the "promotion from within" factor which is a decided disadvantage for me. Already a member of the organization, however, I do possess greater insight into the team's philosophy and management style; attributes that could prove very beneficial to the organization.

Having already moved from marketing (ticket sales and servicing) to media sales (television, radio and signage sales), I am in the process of becoming proficient in two of the major areas of revenue generation in sports. As I have stated, I strongly believe that it is extremely important, with regard to future advancement, to familiarize yourself with as many different areas of sports management as possible.

Should I decide to leave franchise management at some point, there are many opportunities that I now feel qualified to pursue. Through the numerous contacts I have made in my years of working with the Warriors, I could effectively move into any of the other sports careers mentioned in this book, as well as various other sports related industries, such as athletic equipment or merchandise sales. It is difficult to predict if these contacts would lead directly to a position within one of these areas, but the use of networking that I highlighted earlier would definitely help me secure a job in whatever field I chose to pursue.

After considering my future in the sports industry in general, my remarks would not be complete without briefly discussing what the future of the NBA appears to hold in store. I've already mentioned the unbelievable growth in popularity of basketball internationally. This immense interest in hoops has not gone unnoticed by the league and NBA Commissioner David Stern. For the past several seasons, the NBA has scheduled a two game series between NBA teams at the start of the regular season in Japan and plans to continue the tradition in other foreign cities in the future. Additionally, for the last several years, an NBA team has travelled abroad during the pre-season to participate in the McDonald's Open against several of the top international club teams, and there is continued talk of expanding this tournament to include many other top club teams from additional countries.

It appears unfeasible to actually locate NBA teams in foreign countries, but there is talk of having the European club champion face the NBA champs following the season. The NBA has already placed offices in Melbourne, Hong Kong, and Barcelona to promote the league. This certainly reinforces the notion that widespread international interest in basketball is long term.

As the NBA's international presence increases, some unique job opportunities may become available which have never previously existed. The ability of an applicant to fluently speak other languages and/or be familiar with the cultures of other countries will provide that individual with the qualifications necessary to land a job in the NBA overseas.

Upon writing this contribution, a process which required a tremendous amount of soul-searching and self-evaluation, I can now begin to answer the questions posed at the beginning of this piece regarding the how's, when's and why's of getting a job in professional sports.

First, as I've stated, the "how" involves a little luck and a lot of perseverance—and that's just to get your foot in the door of the organization. After that, it is entirely up to you to get in the door before it slams shut!

Second, the "when" depends on your personal agenda. The sooner you want it, the sooner you have to make the effort to get it, because most often acquiring a *full-time* job with a pro sports team takes time. I should mention one thing regarding timing—one of the biggest mistakes applicants make is assuming that the easiest time to get hired is when a team is enjoying success in the standings and/or at the box office. This is not normally the case. The reality is that most teams need creative, hard-working professionals when the team's performance is suffering and some new ideas are necessary to re-create success off the court.

Finally, the most enlightening aspect of writing this piece from my vantage point is the "why" of having a job in sports. I realize now, even more than before, that I endured the manual labor, long hours and relatively low pay (if you were to figure my salary as an hourly wage) because I love my job! There isn't a day that goes by without at least one person commenting on how lucky I am to work for the Warriors—and they are absolutely right.

There is only one remaining part missing from this fantasy world I call "work;" my team, the Warriors, have not yet brought an NBA World Championship home to the Bay Area. And, when they do, it won't take me very long to measure my world championship ring size!

OVERTIME

Bryan Deierling accurately and thoroughly describes the duties performed and qualifications required by participants in the franchise management business. Accordingly, I will spend very little time reviewing these topics. However, I will remind the reader that if one is not interested in sales, and entry-level sales at that, a paying position with a professional team will be virtually impossible to attain.

Additionally, one must be prepared to contribute in the form of game day operations; moving boxes, setting up sales booths, appeasing disgruntled season ticket holders and/or passing out promotional materials. It is not until these unpleasantries are completed is it even possible to *think* about watching the game (which, by the way, is seldom earlier than half time and not uncommonly as late as the fourth quarter!).

Many other potential employment opportunities in the "Cash In" category are also important to re-visit as they represent significant sources of franchise income and, consequently, provide employment. The first of these, the procurement of luxury box sales and signage sponsorship, will be considered as one entity for the purposes of this discussion. One's ability, in the absence of a formal job opening, to help a franchise secure one of these major revenue sources would be a tremendous display of salesmanship and hard work.

I am personally aware of "consultants" who cultivate their own sponsorship leads, shape this potential corporate relationship into a tentative deal, and then present it in to the franchise. At this point, since the team did not have to spend any time or resources cultivating the lead, they are generally quite pleased with this "found" revenue. One must be careful, however, not to be placed in the precarious situation where the franchise and corporate lead can secure the deal without your assistance, as this would tend to reduce any potential revenue to you, the consultant. This is why it is particularly useful to have a working knowledge of the franchise's staff and have developed a trusting relationship; a relationship that may have been formed through one's volunteering for game day operations, for example. The formation of this informal or volunteer relationship will also make it far easier for the franchise to consider your efforts. After all, teams do not want just anybody serving as a de-facto business development officer.

It is this type of creative approach that clearly demonstrates a potential employee's worth to the franchise. This worth would not only be reflected on the candidate's resume but, in all likelihood, would enable him to make a franchise's "short list" of final candidates.

Another similar example of this may exist for the current working professional in the field of law or business. As previously mentioned, franchises may actually begin negotiating directly with networks and other media sources regarding the issuance of broadcast rights. But, for the most part, professional franchises have not yet employed a professional staffer who is both a media expert and conversant in the legal issues of structuring this type of deal. Again, outside consultants have begun to fill this void, proving to the franchise that they are able to bring a much needed area of expertise to the table.

It should be noted that in each of these examples, the independent consultant has quantifiably raised marginal revenue or reduced marginal costs—adding significant value to the operation of the franchise.

With my previous references to sports merchandise, I would be remiss if I did not address the importance of merchandise sales to a pro sports franchise's bottom line. Both team and player identified merchandise is a major and rapidly growing source of revenue in which teams are placing an increasing priority as a means to partially offset the spiralling cost of operations. As these operating costs, including players' salaries, continue to rise, teams need to be creative and find alternative sources of revenue; and merchandise appears to be the best opportunity for future, steady growth. Moreover, merchandise has become such big business that teams are capitalizing on this popularity by implementing changes in team logos and colors in an effort to capture a larger share of the market.

Another substantial appeal of merchandising which has enormous potential, is that of international merchandising opportunities. Basketball has become the new international sport of the 90's, as evidenced by the success of the USA "Dream Team" in the 1992 Summer Olympics; and this popularity is clearly illustrated by the dramatic increase of team merchandise sold overseas. As a result, the opportunity to tap into this relatively new audience should produce a significant increase in a team's revenue generated through this type of sales, not to mention making a valuable addition to the team's publicity efforts. These licensing efforts, both domestically and internationally, will continue to provide tangible career opportunities within the existing franchise structure.

Minimizing a team's "Cash Out" category can also provide employment opportunities at the franchise level. Remember, minimizing costs to the team can, theoretically, contain the cost to the family of four who typically attends one of these professional sports contests. While it is understood that most franchises do not pass a cost reduction along to the fan (in fact, they usually view this increasing gap between revenue and reduced expenses as additional, or "found income"), it is still an important perspective to take because a franchise's ability to profit is solely based on this mythical family of four's desire and ability to watch and/or attend games.

For the purposes of this discussion, it is assumed that the 50-60 percent of a team's expenditures that are devoted to player salaries cannot be reduced. Accordingly, when one seeks a position with a franchise, there exists a limited percentage (sometimes as low as 40 percent) of expenses that can be reduced. But, nonetheless, issues do exist at both the franchise and league level for cost reductions.

For example, internally it may be possible to devise a more efficient scouting system that reduces duplication in recruiting efforts and streamlines the actual player development costs detailed earlier. Computer programs which more accurately and quickly summarize a player's personal data and athletic performances or a new accounting system or internal audit which reduces some of the numerous and burdensome layers (trimming the fat) present in an organization would be well received. After all, a single percent reduction in expenses to a team on an annual basis will more than pay for that added employee or consulting fee.

Moreover, the appropriate application of fundamental economic principles can be a major assistance to leagues and franchises looking to quantify growth and/or evaluate the merits of league expansion or relocation. Granted, the resolution of many of these high level front office issues are not employment opportunities available to the entry level staffer. But, for the professional with significant and related professional experience in other industries, these are the issues that will experience growth in importance in the years to come; especially the expense related issues involved in international franchise management and player development.

A far less quantifiable measure of cost reduction exists in the area of player relations. Many professional sports franchises do not enjoy cohesive relationships with their players, a scenario which often translates to a lower level of performance on the field or court. It has always been this author's opinion that a player who has his personal life in order and is content off the court, will be a much more focused and productive player during the game. Moreover, it is not unusual for the players' agents to be neither qualified nor particularly interested in assisting their clientele with non-contract issues.

For instance, professional athletes occasionally have well documented financial and other difficulties that eventually find their way to the local, if not national media. Additionally, it is unfortunate that many athletes do not feel comfortable confiding in management when they experience these difficulties. To no one's surprise, the problem remains hidden, eventually festers, and at some point, becomes a major distraction to the team; and, *possibly*, in the case of a star, may cost that team a victory. As we well know, victories translate to incremental revenue, etc. Therefore, I believe franchises should consider building relationship with parties who are capable of working with these potentially troubled athletes *before* they experience this situation.

The major obstacle to the team seeking to form these professional relationships is the general air of uneasiness felt between the players and management. As discussed in the section on athletic departments, a 'big brother' feeling commonly exists with the athletes, which does not enable them to feel as though they can freely discuss their personal situations with management. Nonetheless, a major opportunity is presented to those individuals willing and able to structure this relationship in a mutually beneficial fashion.

With respect to gaining the proper academic background and professional work experience, it should be noted that an undergraduate degree in almost any related field would suffice for the entry level sales-related positions. Also, credible work experience in sales with a consumer products or services firm would be equally desirable. In most cases, those individuals making the final entry level 'cut' have both a degree from a major university and a proven sales record. The area of entry level franchise management, unlike the other four areas discussed in this book, allows for a wide variety of professional backgrounds and personal experiences. Unfortunately, due to the limited number of these opportunities, the competition is quite fierce as indicated by Deierling's comments about the short supply of (and heavy demand for) these sales positions.

Much has been made the last few years about the lack of employment opportunities, and eventual advancement, for minorities at the franchise level. In the future, this hypocrisy will continue to wane as qualified applicants of all backgrounds will be recognized for their ability to add value to the bottom line of the organization. Perhaps NBA front offices will never proportionally reflect the same percentages in the front office as are seen on the court but, one thing will remain constant: franchises will always discriminate. They will discriminate against those employees who are not willing to work the long hours, check the ego at the door and make the necessary sacrifices in their personal lives, as described by the contributor.

This is not intended to disregard the blatant inconsistencies in franchises' hiring practices. They do exist. However, with respect to many professional sports franchises, the staff is often comprised of predominantly white males for one very apparent, albeit unacceptable, reason: league and franchise research continues to indicate that this is the same demographic group consuming the majority of the product. Therefore, they believe it is important to display this sense of belonging to the fan. Cynical? Absolutely. Far fetched? No way.

Finally, employment opportunities with franchises may begin with gaining corporate experience. As we move toward the end of the decade, franchises are being purchased more frequently by those that can truly afford them—huge domestic corporate concerns and multi-national business conglomerates. Paramount Communications (owners of the New York Rangers and Knicks) and the Walt Disney Company (granted a National Hockey League expansion team in Anaheim, California) represent the type of organizations that not only have the deep pockets required to pay increasing player salaries, but also have the ability to cross-promote their products and services to captive target markets. Accordingly, many of the employment openings at the franchise level may very well be filled by those currently employed by the parent company. Maybe the best way to work for the Atlanta Braves is to first work in Ted Turner's WTBS mail room!

The ability to analyze and think through these different types of employment scenarios will provide you with a much better chance of finding or creating that first job in franchise management. After all, doesn't it beat sending a resume blindly, and often without specific purpose, to the local professional sports team? Serendipity may have worked for Deierling, but you must place yourself in a position to capitalize on it when it presents itself.

****

PART V:
The Media

****

9

THE MEDIA:
The Tail Wags The Dog

*E*mployment opportunities on the media side of sports are associated with either radio, television, or print. And, historically, the individual role of these media has been evolving over time—creating opportunities for some and professional difficulties for others. "All sports radio," for example, is now available in most major metropolitan areas. Only a few years ago, this concept would have been neither financially feasible for the radio networks nor heavily demanded by its general listener-ship. Today, however, "sports junkies" are flocking toward this inexpensive means of entertainment with audience participation programs experiencing steady growth.

HISTORICAL INFLUENCES

In the last forty years, television has witnessed an even more fascinating development. Television viewing, once considered a fad, has now evolved into a multi-billion dollar industry. And by the mid-nineties, pay-per-view is likely to be a formidable competitor to the traditional networks. After all, "standard" cable television has already eaten into the profits of major networks over the last ten years. Cable television has been able to accomplish this by offering attractive sporting events, as well as motion pictures, during prime time to a very captive, predominantly male audience. Collectively, American sports fans are relishing this added sports coverage.

With the massive growth of televised athletics and the increased emphasis of sports on the radio airwaves, print media has perhaps suffered the most. The ever-changing broadcast communications previously mentioned have changed the role of the written media drastically and forever. Initially, the primary source for sports information was the print media, but it has since been surpassed by the immediacy and tangibility of the other forms of sports communication media.

Each of these media is examined in detail throughout this chapter. A special focus is placed on the relationships of these media to one another and their impact on the sports economy, especially players' salaries and industry trends. This includes the influence each has on the scope and quality of employment opportunities in the media.

America began its love affair with radio more than seventy years ago during the inaugural broadcast of President Warren Harding. Harding, taking the oath as the 29th President of the United States in November of 1920, unknowingly paved the road for the electronic media (Klatell and Marcus: 25). The demand for additional broadcasts of all types rose dramatically as America became hooked on radio.

All that remained for radio to become a major source of entertainment in America was financing. At the time, few realized the potential of electronic media as an effective source of advertising. However, within fifteen years of the inaugural broadcast, radio had surpassed newspapers as the nation's primary news source. The creativity and spontaneity of radio allowed it to grow as advertisers quickly sponsored programs with the hope of generating publicity and sales for their products and services.

Live radio, especially sports telecasts, cast a luminous shadow over the print media. That is, with radio, loyal fans were no longer relegated to waiting for the morning paper to determine how their favorite team had fared. Instead, these fans were able to almost participate in games by listening to the broadcasts and creating their own images of the action. This was preferable for many fans, as it served as a means of entertainment; after all, reading a day-old account of a ball game in the local paper was far less entertaining than enjoying the game live on radio. Hearing the crack of the bat and the roar of the crowd quickly made print the second choice of most fans.

A similar and equally important transition took place in the early 1950's, as television replaced radio as the media of choice. Also, bear in mind that television would have been a more powerful media even sooner had World War II not depleted critical materials and the necessary labor. Fortunately for television, corporations were quick to believe that, relative to the radio experience, advertising during television programming would be an excellent avenue for marketing their products. Within a few decades, these advertising dollars would become critically important to the growth of collegiate and professional athletics. Currently, teams receive more than half of their revenues from television.

This transition from print to radio, and subsequently from radio to television, launched sports into what was then considered "big business." Nonetheless, the evolution of the media also caused economic difficulties for some in the sports community.

For example, some felt the relative success of baseball was significantly diminished by the presence of television broadcasts. It was believed that the opportunity to see a major league contest in the comfort of one's home reduced the attendance at minor league ballparks. As this demand declined, so did the number of minor league operations. (Miller: 6). Branch Rickey, the legendary front office manager of the early fifties, noted that radio *created* the desire to see baseball while television *fulfilled* this desire. What might Rickey say today about the relationship between television and baseball? To date, his fears have hardly been realized.

What, then, is the prognosis for radio in the 21st century? If one believes that radio has indeed become a step-son to television, it stands to reason that radio will eventually share a similar position with print media: a distant second place to television. Regardless of the fact that radio forever changed the print medium, newspapers are still an invaluable resource to the fan. The reason for reading the sports page today may be different than it was seventy-five years ago. Yesteryear, we read the paper for final results and game summaries; today we read for such details as statistics (for rotisserie leagues) and general interest.

Radio is likely to undergo a similar change in purpose. As a continuing source of inexpensive entertainment, radio will not become a dinosaur any time soon. It may, however, become an increasingly specialized market playing a different and more supportive role in the broadcasting of collegiate and professional athletics. Also, as the international marketplace for sports competition develops, radio will enjoy added exposure and growth, capitalizing on previously untapped markets and listeners. The general trend toward international competition will surely present this media with the enormous challenge and opportunity to remain a viable source of information.

SPORTS AND TELEVISION

As previously discussed, the advent of television changed the way Americans live their lives. Television and American culture were to be forever inter-twined. The immediacy of this media, coupled with the visual stimulus generated by the telecasts, was responsible for the rapid growth of television.

Historically, television was a media used for the reporting of newsworthy events and previously recorded entertainment. However, by the late eighties and early nineties, television allowed us to watch the news as *it was being made*. This live theater has brought America infamous telecasts including the Space Shuttle Challenger disaster and wire to wire coverage of the Gulf War. It has also served as the perfect stage for athletic competition.

The first known sports telecast took place on May 17th, 1939 as Bill Stern "broadcast" the play-by-play of the Columbia-Princeton contest in Manhattan. Approximately 1,000 households tuned in to watch this initial telecast. The game was telecast on an experimental station, W2XBS. This isolated incident was the origin of sports programming as we know it today. More than a half a century later, sports and television have almost become synonymous. The attractiveness of sports on television was accurately stated by David Klatell and Norman Marcus in their work, *Sports for Sale*. These authors noted that:

At its best, television sports is the finest programming television can offer. In many respects, sports may be the quintessential television program format, taking fullest advantage of the role television plays in our daily lives. Sports on television have visually attractive elements—splashy colors, attractive locations, motion and movement galore. They have expansive vistas, exquisite details, and larger-than-life images. Compared with the austere hush and 'studio' sound of most programs, sports are alternately loud and brassy, and painfully hushed: you can tell the moment you hear the sound of the crowd what's going on. There is drama, tension, suspense, raw emotion, real anger, unvarnished joy, and a host of other responses. Most of all, you are watching real people compete for real, as unsure of the outcome as the viewer. The script, being written in front of you, is subject to few constraints common to the formulas of standard entertainment fare.

In sports television, the 'bad guy' of the script often wins, unexpected things happen, virtue doesn't necessarily triumph, and goodness is not always rewarded.

Perhaps this could have been best summarized by the old Wide World of Sports adage, "the thrill of victory and the agony of defeat." But this would be too simplistic, as sports is more than that, and sports on television is truly big business. Sports on television works. It works for the fans, the media, and the sponsors.

This is validated when one considers the evolution of the corporate sports sponsorship. These corporate sponsored sporting events provided fans with the programming they so heavily craved. In exchange for these telecasts, the consumer was constantly reminded of the product line and/or service offered by the sponsoring company, usually through commercials. The television network, then made its money by taking in more revenue through advertising sales and corporate sponsorships than was required to produce the event.

The first such corporate sponsorship belonged to the Gillette company in 1935. Gillette began this sponsorship process by sponsoring entire broadcasts of sporting events, primarily boxing matches. This was accomplished through the company's purchasing of the broadcasting rights to the event and then selling this package to a station (Klatell and Marcus: 116). Gillette continued, in the following years, to become more aggressive and proactive in the arena of sports sponsorships. Their bold leadership and corporate philosophy served them well as they became the corporation most associated with professional athletics throughout the 1940's. Needless to say, Gillette was very successful selling razors to its predominantly male audience during that decade.

The entire sports industry began to change as these sponsorships continued to make economic sense for the sponsoring firms. The ability of a firm to indirectly and, at times, directly "manage an event's timing" became commonplace. For example, major team sports in this country have added "TV time-outs," 24-second clocks, 2 minute warnings, and the like—mostly to appease the sponsors. These changes in the events' formats are directly related to a sponsor's desire to capitalize on the contest at hand. Individual sports such as tennis and golf have also changed their formats, adding tie-breakers in tennis and 72 hole total tournament scoring in golf. Don't be fooled, even for a minute, that these changes were made exclusively to enhance the event itself. As these changes have made the contests more exciting, ratings have risen, enabling networks to charge more money for the available advertising time.

While the concept of managing an event's timing became more prolific, other changes also followed. Baseball moved many of its games to the evening in order to accommodate television. Realize, however, that there is no strategic advantage—athletically speaking—from having the dreaded "twilight" start. In fact, players often voice their dismay at these starting times, noting that the shadows on the field affect their judgement and timing. This is truly ironic since these are the very same athletes seeking the multi-million dollar contracts—contracts that are financed by the corporate sponsorships and related network contracts.

As the major networks and athletics industry continued to witness this corporate interest, they began evaluating the concept of network contracts. Believing that it may be more reasonable to sell the broadcasting rights to the networks, professional sports stumbled onto a goose which was poised to lay the proverbial "golden egg."

The three major networks (ABC, NBC and CBS), realizing that corporations were eager to purchase their advertising time during sporting events, possessed significant leverage during negotiations. Negotiations over the cost of sports advertising led to a rapid escalation in the price of the commercials since the demand for advertising spots during sporting events exceeded the supply of commercial time available. The major networks could afford to pay exorbitant prices for the rights to these sporting events as they were confident that the corporations would bail them out financially. This bail out would come in the form of paying premium prices for the ability to market their products and services to this captive audience.

Naturally, increased costs of advertising are passed on to the consumer, costs which further escalated as the three networks competitively bid against one another for the exclusive broadcast rights to certain sports or sporting events. This vicious cycle continues and is addressed again shortly during the discussion of cable television.

Today's advertisers believe that the captive sports audience that the Gillette company discovered and subsequently capitalized on in the 1930's still exists. This captive audience, typically males ranging in age from 18 to 54, was and continues to be a critical demographic group for advertisers. They are attentive, have decision-making capacity, and possess discretionary income. Given these demographics, it is no surprise that beer and automobile manufacturers, insurance and financial services firms, and other office product manufacturers including those selling copiers and computers, spend millions of dollars annually in order to gain access to these consumers.

Even with the attractive viewer demographics and relatively captive audiences, corporations must continue to study the financial feasibility of advertising in sports. Additionally, the networks must decide exactly what is a reasonable expenditure for broadcast rights—and, more importantly, how much is too much?

Before bidding on a contract, the networks must consider various external economic issues as well as their own financial ability and corporate agenda. Specifically, the state of the national economy, forecasts of inflation, and the financial stability of the sports industry in general all contribute to the firm's bid on a network contract. Internal issues, including a company's profitability, corporate strategies, and existing commitments also play a role in determining the value of the bid.

Once this preliminary research has been completed, the network must consider the feasibility of acquiring the actual broadcast rights (Klatell and Marcus: 114). What is the optimal length of the proposed contract? How unique is the contest or sport? Is the event or sport gaining or losing popularity? What are the fixed and variable costs of producing the event? What kind of ratings can the network expect from such events? And, the critical question: will the advertisers buy it?

These types of questions and issues must be resolved before a network tenders a bid. In fact, it is likely that the major networks will come up with slightly different figures; and often times, these differences in forecasts will decide which network ultimately acquires the broadcast rights.

The critical question, previously proposed, was whether the advertisers will be willing to buy advertising time during the events covered by the network contract. These potential advertisers must be able to quantify the success of participating in a sponsorship capacity. This success can be measured as a function of sales, either absolute or incremental, exposure/publicity, goodwill, or perhaps a sense of belonging/association. Whatever the reason, the advertiser must feel confident that the sporting event will deliver a certain and often specified number of viewers within their specific target market.

By and large, corporations must have believed that, over time, these sponsorships and advertisements have been successful since the cost of network advertising has grown significantly over the last twenty years. Again, as the demand for advertising time has basically exceeded the supply of commercial time, the cost of network contracts has been allowed to grow steadily over time.

The reason for this monumental growth has been that the professional athletics industry, having witnessed the increase, continued to raise the price of network contracts. They realized that their product, the broadcast of a sporting event, was in very high demand—so they "hiked up" the price to the networks, which in turn, charged more to advertisers. The advertisers, feeling the pinch from these higher rates, passed a portion of this increased cost on to the consumer. The most critical issue, whether this trend will continue, is discussed below.

THE IMPACT OF VOLATILE RIGHTS FEES

The total cost of televising sporting events has soared over the last decade. After growing steadily throughout the middle of the century, television rights fees have increased dramatically since the beginning of the 1980's. Major League Baseball (MLB), for example, witnessed a doubling in its rights fees within the last ten years from $183 to $365 million. This windfall for MLB had been reflected, in part, in the enormous salaries given to the players during this period. Shortly after the previous network pact was signed, fans were bombarded by accounts of the "newest multi-million dollar player." And, as previously mentioned, it was not unreasonable to assume that the first $10-15 million a year superstar was not far off.

But recall that CBS, the owner of the major network's baseball rights, purchased them for the astronomical sum of $1.06 billion over four years in 1990. At the same time, ESPN acquired the cable rights package for $400 million over the same period. At the conclusion of these contracts, each carrier had lost a small fortune. CBS was forced to accept losses in excess of $500 million over the life of its contract while ESPN absorbed an approximate loss of as much as $200 million on its package.

The miscalculation of the rights fee was likely to be felt by both the franchise owners and their players—since revenues had been increasing at the moderate rate of 12 percent while expenses mounted much more quickly—about 35 percent per year. Former Baseball Commissioner Fay Vincent warned the major league clubs that the revenue per team derived from the network contracts would likely fall by as much as $5 million per team per season under any new contract. To no one's surprise, other less conservative estimates placed this decrease closer to $8 million.

What could have possibly led the right's holders to believe that their billion dollar deal was a good investment? Three possible reasons may now explain why the carriers took such a bath. By most accounts, baseball's audience was down by about 20 percent since the major network contract had been negotiated. The alternatives for television outlets had increased, providing advertisers with other, seemingly more attractive, options. And finally, advertisers were not willing to pay the traditional inflationary increases during a major recession.

While hindsight is no doubt 20-20, CBS should have been able to analyze the industry-wide variables that led to their massive losses more accurately. After all, the emergence and popularity of cable had steadily syphoned ratings away from the major networks. As for ESPN, the sheer number of baseball telecasts makes the sport less appealing to many fans. Who wants to watch the ESPN game of the evening when it is possible for the fan to watch his own local team on regular television? Perhaps Curt Smith, author of *The Voice of the Game*, summed up CBS's contract best by calling it "the Exxon Valdez of sports contracts."

As the prognosis for future increases stalled, the networks and MLB searched for appealing alternatives. Given these massive losses, new network contracts were sure to command heavily discounted prices or, alternatively, take on a different look. Since industry experts forecasted a decline in the rights fees by as much as 50 percent, the parties involved created "The Venture."

In this arrangement, MLB pioneered a partnership with NBC and ABC for its next TV contract that will run for six years, beginning in 1994. Rather than receive a typical rights fee from the network, baseball will take a percentage of the revenue from the sale of advertising and corporate sponsorships and essentially share the risk with the networks. If successful, The Venture may very well help the networks, MLB, and corporate advertisers as well as the players, provided the advertising rates charged are reasonable.

The industry-wide variables mentioned above have had a pronounced effect on the networks. Consider, for example, that only about a decade ago, local/regional cable operators and national superstations were in their infancy. Competition with network sports programming was relatively non-existent, allowing the networks to focus on the competitive advantages enjoyed by only two or three other major industry participants.

Now, these local and regional cable operators and superstations are providing formidable competition to networks, forcing them to pay

closer attention to this ever changing marketplace. For instance, the
Madison Square Garden Network currently provides the New York
Yankees with more cable revenue than several teams derive from all of
their revenue generating activities combined. This enormous presence in
the sports communications business has sent the networks running for
financial cover as they continue to witness their domination of televised
sports slip away.

Enormous regional cable television packages present yet another issue
that warrants discussion. If a franchise is in a position to command as
much as $50 million per year from a cable operator over an extended
period of time, does this affect the team's incentive to win? If large sums
of money are guaranteed to the franchise, why spend all that money on
players' salaries? Hopefully, this cynicism will be overshadowed by an
owner's competitive, rather than financial, desire.

Is football faring any better? First, consider that CBS, NBC, ABC,
ESPN and TNT were locked into a four-year NFL deal running from
1990-1993; the cost of these comprehensive rights was $3.65 billion.
This average per year of $912 million reflected a 96 percent increase
over the previous contract; a contract which ran from 1987-1989 and
averaged $466 million per year. Final projections suggested a $315
million combined loss for the CBS and NBC over this latest four-year
period. Appropriately, the experts believed the next national TV contract
would be reduced by approximately $352 million, or 39 percent from its
previous rate. They had good reason to believe that the NFL, much like
MLB, would come to terms with either a reduced rights fee package or,
alternatively, develop their own version of "The Venture."

CBS, for its part, figured to continue its broadcast of the National
Football Conference under any new arrangement, but were out-Foxed by
Rupert Murdoch. Seizing the moment, Murdoch's Fox Network
postponed (at least until 1997) the "Dooms Day" that many NFL owners
stated was "just around the corner." Thanks to Fox, who will pay the
league an unbelievable $395 million per year for four years, the owners
have more money in their coffers. Moreover, the deal raises the new NFL
salary cap from an estimated $32 million per team, per year, to a hefty
$34 million, translating to more money for star athletes (and sport
agents). Furthermore, the franchise owners will certainly keep a portion
of the increase in television revenue, which approaches $6 million per
team, for themselves.

But it appears that not everyone will benefit from this deal *financially*,
as Fox is already predicting losses of $600 million over the course of the

$1.58 billion deal. It is widely held that Fox did not acquire the rights, for which they shelled out 49 percent more than CBS did on its expiring contract, to broadcast the NFC as strictly a sports deal. Rather, they purchased legitimacy and credibility, essentially becoming the fourth major national network much like ABC did in 1970 when they joined NBC and CBS as one of the "players" in televised sports by beginning their broadcast of "Monday Night Football." Apparently Fox paid at least $600 million for this "Prestige Factor."

Now Fox must sell advertising to sports sponsors in an effort to offset as much of this $1.58 billion as possible. How will they do this given a weaker affiliate lineup that forces them to charge, at least initially, 10-15 percent less for advertising due to the lower ratings?

They begin by attracting (new) sports-oriented advertisers who then might be persuaded to buy time on other Fox programming. This allows the network to be creative when striking these advertising agreements as they face the enormous task of filling this new advertising time. Also, the lead-ins to the prime time lineup aired during the football games will hopefully build viewership during prime time, eventually driving up the cost of advertising during non-sports programming. Relatively speaking, smaller sports sponsors, especially those who could not afford the advertising rates on the other networks, may be wooed by Fox who will be searching for avenues to mitigate these huge forecasted losses. The new network presence provides new opportunities for sponsors of all sizes as creative sports advertisers now have a new vehicle for reaching the younger viewer—the one typically watching Fox. In short, look for Corporate America to wheel-and-deal with the Fox Network, ultimately spending significant amounts of their advertising budget chasing their target markets around the television dial.

College football is similarly feeling the pressure. In April of 1992, NBC agreed to televise the next three Cotton Bowls for a total of $8.1 million. This average of $2.7 million per year is $1.4 million less than CBS had previously paid for the event. This 34 percent decrease appears to be yet another twist in this decade of fluctuating rights fees. In the years to come, college football will likely continue to experience this "Cotton Bowl" phenomena—until CBS fully reestablishes itself in the football marketplace.

This abbreviated look at rights fees applies to all major sports, including the Olympics. However, the focus here was on the two sports that generally receive the most media attention and closest financial scrutiny. The obvious short term solution, as we have seen, is to renew these major contracts at either reduced rates or under very different circumstances. Furthermore, long term adjustments in the structure of rights fees will be required in order to maintain (and increase) the financial viability of professional and collegiate athletics.

Some of these adjustments appear inevitable, other probable, and yet a few down-right creative. As most "traditional" rights fees face a decline through the remainder of the decade, players' salaries will ultimately reflect this potential deflation. Of course, there will still be a number of multi-million dollar superstars per team. However, the number of roster players making less money will increase substantially. Essentially, a polarization of salaries will occur. For example, in baseball, three or four stars will continue earning the big bucks as they are the primary gate draw. The middle tier player—the average starter and many of the pitchers—will experience a decline in absolute salary. Additionally, utility players and back-ups will earn salaries hovering closer to the league minimum. The bottom line is that the middle class in baseball will be squeezed. Ultimately, there will be four or five multi-millionaires, four or five extremely well-paid players and approximately fifteen athletes earning salaries in the several-hundred-thousand dollar per year range. Teams will be forced to control their players' salaries in particular, and expenses in general.

Another inevitable adjustment will be derived from increasing the number of events carried on a "pay-per-view" basis. Many sports finance professionals do not seem too concerned with this, *yet*. They believe, due to the number of games still carried on free TV, that pay-per-view will only work with selected events. These events, many of which occur only once, will generate a substantial pay-per-view audience. The jury is still out on this, however, as NBC absorbed losses approaching $100 million on the 1992 Summer Olympics. "Everyday" sports such as baseball and basketball are safe, *for now*.

It is interesting to note that these industry experts do not consider ESPN, TNT, or the USA network as pay-per-view channels. The last time I checked, I was still paying a basic cable bill. Cable television, even the standard packages, have built in a fee for these sports and sports-related channels. The real argument at hand is not whether pay-per-view will succeed, but rather how much the consumer/fan is willing to pay for it. Stay tuned.

Among the recent developments in baseball, for instance, are inter-league play, an expanded play-off format, and divisional realignment. The purpose behind these moves was two-fold. On the surface, the teams and networks will suggest that these changes will increase fan interest. In reality, the reason for these changes is clear: these activities add revenue to the bottom line of the teams, the players, and the networks. Skeptics, on the other hand, respond quite differently. They believe that inter-league play will lower the interest in championship match-ups and maintain that the season is long enough already—additional games, even play-off games, would only lengthen the season unnecessarily. Moreover, realignment, it is believed, can cause numerous financial hardships to both the leagues and the networks.

Just ask the Chicago Cubs—a team which was nearly embroiled in a legal battle with Major League Baseball over its unwillingness to move from the National League's Eastern Division to the Western Division. In short, the franchise was primarily concerned with playing a greater percentage of its contests at 7:30 p.m. Pacific Standard Time. This later starting time for those in the Midwest (9:30 p.m. local time) would have been reflected in lower television and radio ratings, essentially reducing the cost advertisers were willing to pay to promote their products and services during Cubs games. Since fewer viewers would have been watching or listening to these later broadcasts, the value attached to advertising during this period would have diminished. As advertising and sponsorship revenue declined, the team would have been forced to consider reducing expenses such as higher players' salaries. And, the inability to attract top athletic talent would not have allowed the Cubs to be competitive in the baseball business—either on or off the field.

The future holds many technological and creative changes within the media and among the sports franchises. It is possible that the leagues may decide not to sell their television rights to anyone. Rather, they will maintain control of their own product, selling it as they see fit. In this scenario, the leagues would merely use the networks as distributors. At some point, it may even become feasible for the leagues to produce their own contests, thus enabling themselves to generate additional revenue and maintain creative control.

In addition to these financial changes, the technological advances are certain to alter the way sports are viewed in America. As fiber optics becomes more commonplace and satellite transmissions become an even more ordinary occurrence, the traditional media industry will have to evolve in order to remain competitive. The 21st century promises to be an extraordinary one as the relationships between the media and athletics is certain to undergo massive growing, and perhaps shrinking, pains.

THE EVOLUTION OF CABLE TELEVISION

Cable television's impact on the networks over the last ten to fifteen years has forced the networks to rethink the marketing and production of their product. But this has not always been the case. The first sporting event to appear on cable television was the 1953 University of Southern California—Notre Dame football game in which the Irish beat USC 48-14. Even though only about 200 subscribers watched this game from the Palm Springs, California area, the consensus was that this fledgling cable concept had merit. Unfortunately, the general viewing audience was not as enthused. Consequently, the cable firm offering these early telecasts, Telemeter, was unable to remain in business.

Not until the early 1960's was a professional sports contest viewed on cable. This event, the second heavyweight title fight between Floyd Paterson and Ingemar Johansson, was made available to the 25,000 viewers willing to pay $2 over and above their standard monthly cable fee (Klatell and Marcus: 53). These first two telecasts, while not wildly successful, set the stage for the enormous cable industry we have today.

One telecast, in particular, appears to have been responsible for the marriage of cable television and athletics. In September of 1979, ESPN began operation. Televising athletic events which were not perceived as "main-stream" by most fans, ESPN offered the die-hard sports enthusiast a 24 hour sports alternative (Klatell and Marcus: 54). These early telecasts regularly showed softball, wrestling, and news-format programming. Within a few years, ESPN was able to secure the America's Cup, the NCAA College World Series, the Davis Cup, and other respected athletic events. The response to this was soaring ratings and wide-spread viewer appeal. Continued evolution and respect eventually delivered college and professional football, as well as NCAA basketball. Today, ESPN is the networks' primary competition. The cable station's personality, quality of programming and delivery, has created millions of "sports widows" in this country.

As the previous section indicated, ESPN is now sharing in the broadcast rights of the major sports leagues. This competition from ESPN and the cable industry in general has proved detrimental to the major networks. Before the emergence and success of cable sports, including the so-called "Superstations," advertisers were at the mercy of the networks. The networks, fully aware that they had "the only shows in town," were in a position to increase advertising rates by as much as

15 percent per year. The advertisers had two choices: either pay these escalating rates or not advertise.

Then along came cable. Cable's presence in the 1980's significantly increased the number of venues where rights-holders could sell their products—sporting events. This sizeable increase served to fragment the sports audience, effectively lowering ratings. As is usually the case, lower program ratings lead to reduced network advertising rates (Klatell and Marcus: 34). As ratings fell and advertisers took their business elsewhere—to cable—revenues of the major networks declined noticeably.

This fierce competition for sports viewers has been dramatically beneficial to the fan viewing the telecasts. Years ago, most sports fans were limited to the three or four sporting events televised in their local market on weekends. Today, it is not unusual to have three or four games on *simultaneously*. As if this is not enough, the VCR generation has been quick to videotape any important sporting events which may have to be missed due to "extenuating circumstances," i.e., work or social commitments. The bottom line, to date, is that America's sports fans now enjoy the opportunity to watch whatever sporting event they wish—and do so whenever they feel so inclined.

What does the future hold in store for cable television? The immediate future looks pretty bright, but growing pains are sure to be felt. The continued growth of the cable industry will be assisted by increasing international opportunities. The globalization of the sports marketplace will provide cable with an expanding market hungry for sports telecasts. This international—and domestic—demand for programming will result in a relentless menu of programming alternatives.

It appears likely that the proliferation of sports on television will expand to meet the demand of the viewership. This will enable the fan to watch what he wants, when he wants, while forcing advertisers to pay close attention to the expanding marketplace. And, while all of this is taking place, pay-per-view will be carving out its piece of the sports broadcasting pie, further complicating the financial viability of sports on television.

How much sports will the 'average' fan want to watch? Is it possible that fans will experience "burn-out" due to the mind-boggling number of sporting events on TV? Will the fan be willing to pay an additional $10 to see his alma-mater play on a Saturday afternoon? These questions and many more will have to be addressed by the cable industry in order to ensure an ongoing economic profit.

FORECASTING MEDIA'S IMPACT ON SPORTS

Sports in the 21st century will be distinguished by its international flavor and enhanced by its global appeal. This globalization of sports will create opportunities for the networks, advertisers, and athletes. The anticipated international growth is likely to generate an increase in the supply and demand for sports around the world. These new opportunities will be beneficial to all—including the foreign markets which have not previously enjoyed extensive athletic coverage. Additionally, the cultural diversity and political ideologies of the international participants should add to both the interest and excitement of the competitions.

Given this evolving marketplace, how will the networks, corporate sponsors, and athletes profit from this expansion? The networks and advertisers will be facing intricacies not previously applied to the sports industry. To date, the networks have primarily been concerned with catering to the needs of corporate sponsors and advertisers attempting to market their products in North America. The networks, as well as the prominent cable stations, have based the price of advertising on this fairly defined market which is comprised of the United States and Canada. But with continued international expansion, advertisers will have to evaluate, in greater detail, whether they are still getting the same "bang" for their advertising buck.

While the absolute number of viewers exposed to the sponsors' advertisements may increase, there is no guarantee that this increase will translate to greater sales or publicity. The reason for this lies in the demographics of the audience viewing the event. Target marketing a product in the United States is much more of a "rifle shot" than the "shotgun blast" associated with international marketing. The added expense of researching and dividing these consumers into the appropriate target markets around the world will prove cost prohibitive for many corporate sponsors. The variables involved in marketing a product or service in North America can be quite different than those in Europe. Consequently, this international opportunity will require the advertisers to closely scrutinize their sponsorships when choosing to participate in international athletics.

As this advertising and corporate sponsorship environment becomes more involved, the network possessing the rights to the events will have to be cognizant of these issues—or face the potential for stagnating rights fees. The networks will similarly have to be concerned that any price paid for the rights of a particular sport or sporting event is reasonable given the potential demand for advertising. As sports becomes more international, the supply of athletics on television will surely increase. It will be up to the media to create an ongoing demand for advertising time by broadcasting contests that an international audience will want to watch. Again, as the interest level of these audiences increases, viewership will increase, spurring a rise in ratings. And it is this rise in ratings, provided it is within an advertiser's target market, that will lead to an increased demand for commercial time, effectively driving up the cost of advertising. As this cost of advertising rises over time, the networks will be in a position to turn an economic profit.

As athletes witness the financial success of the networks, including cable and corporate sponsors, they will demand their piece of the international pie. To a very small degree, this is already occurring in professional basketball. Several top NBA prospects have fled the States in search of European riches—that is, large contracts which were the result of a player's leverage. As world class athletes are presented with alternatives, the cost to a team of acquiring these "assets" will increase. This phenomena has been observed in the sport of international soccer, but has not yet spread to America's 'main-stream' sports.

BROADCASTING

Decades ago, most sports broadcasts were delivered by at most two commentators, who concentrated their efforts on the action at hand. With generally only one camera angle providing the coverage, the broadcasters of yesteryear were truly "calling" the game. Often providing their own angle and insight, these personalities commonly made the difference in the quality of the telecast.

Today, however, a broadcast staff of at least three is customary when announcing an event. This staff, rather than focusing all its energy on the action on the field, is often consumed with other duties. Networks, realizing the opportunity to market themselves during these telecasts, utilize these announcers ("sports personalities" as they are sometimes called) by having them promote additional network programming such as their prime-time line-ups and provide running commentary designed to maintain the interest of the non-sports fan. This is made possible during the telecast as the numerous camera angles and replays have reduced the need for focused commentary. The more technologically advanced the broadcasts have become, the more the announcers serve as "information managers" rather than broadcasters. A case in point is the statistical data provided during the telecast. These computerized graphics have become such a vital part of the broadcast to the fan that most commentators welcome this ability to cheat.

As the production of sporting events continues to become more involved, the sophistication of the support staff must also be maintained. The intricacies involved in coordinating a three or four hour live sports telecast are at times unbelievable. The different feeds, potential delays, break-aways, and an overall ability to "make or break" a broadcast all require the staff's undivided attention and preparation. Without them and their concentration, many of the multi-million dollar announcers we so often hail as legendary would simply be scrambling to save the telecast.

The support staff also helps with pre- and post-game shows as well as the halftime pieces. Often times, the commentators and analysts featured in these programs are not the same on-air personalities who deliver the game. This may require the support staff to work with as many as five broadcasters during any one contest. As if it has not been made clear already, these behind-the-scenes professionals are at least as responsible for a successful production as the on-air personalities.

As the broadcasting industry has grown to accommodate the fans' demand for information and entertainment, so too has the dollar amount commanded by the top industry broadcasters. These elite broadcasters can be roughly divided into two categories, essentially serving either local or national markets. While there is certainly some degree of overlap, the local personalities are those whose primary duty is to announce one team's games, while the national network level professionals may broadcast several events, or a series of events, carried on any one network.

At the so-called local level, "the voice" of a major metropolitan franchise can earn more than $1 million annually. In contrast, the top broadcasters at the national network level commonly earn twice as much. However, much like the rights fees for sporting events are expected to fall, the salaries of the broadcast personalities are certain to follow suit. Consider that when networks are forced to reduce expenses as revenue declines, one of the first and most obvious places they will turn to is the broadcast booth.

The future salaries of commentators will no doubt parallel the polarization of players' salaries discussed earlier. The elite broadcasters and animated analysts will still earn seven figure salaries, but many of the other commentators may experience a leveling-off and possibly even a decline in compensation.

Two other major variables, both of which have been explored in this text, still remain when discussing the future of broadcasting compensation. They are the increase in the supply of sporting events through the emergence of cable television and pay-per-view, and the globalization of athletic competition. Each of these will significantly impact the number of broadcasting positions available internationally, as well as the levels of compensation associated with these newly created jobs.

THE "FINE" PRINT

While the print media was essentially the first to devote significant resources to athletics, it is discussed last. The reason for reviewing print last is that it has been most affected by the evolution of both radio and television. An understanding of the impact of these two media on print is critical when discussing the history and future of the written media.

Due to the effects of radio and television described above, the print media has changed its role in sports communication. Print's relative immediacy has been supplanted by the absolute immediacy of the other media transmissions. Accordingly, print has altered its focus when covering athletics. Newspapers and magazines still cover athletic events very thoroughly, adequately, and professionally, but due to the nature of the publishing business, print is not able to compete as effectively as in years past.

In order to remain a viable media for sports information, print has pursued the coverage of athletics from a different angle. Rather than primarily reporting the outcome of athletic contests as was the case a half century ago, the various print media are now interested in sporting event related topics. For example, there is no better place to find the most accurate and frequently updated statistics than in the newspaper. Additionally, specialty sports publications such as *Baseball America* have joined the more traditional sports newspapers (*The Sporting News*, etc.) in reporting extensively on collegiate and professional athletics. These publications provide an exhaustive statistical look at the world of athletics as well as fulfilling other critical fan needs.

These other fan "needs" include biographical data, investigative reporting including the police blotter, salary/financial information, and the political issues involved in sports. Radio and television broadcasts can seldom devote the time or necessary resources to provide a comprehensive report about these "behind-the-scenes" sports issues. Nonetheless, as fans continue to spend significant portions of their disposable income attending sporting events and purchasing licensed products, they all but demand this increased coverage.

It is with these types of issues that the print media can continue to compete with radio and television. Unfortunately, many of the truly outstanding resources for written sports information have had a difficult time surviving financially. *The National*, which lasted fewer than eighteen months, attempted to become the nation's first daily publication devoted entirely to sports (Rosentiel). *The National*, which had retained many of the top sports writers in the country, posted an estimated $100 million loss during its brief publication. Inadequate channels of distribution limited the paper's ability to provide for its timely delivery to the newsstand. The lack of a detailed business plan also contributed to the paper's demise, as did inadequate production equipment.

Additionally, certain distribution contracts made it impossible to post the "late scores," providing their chief competitor, *The USA Today*, with a tremendous strategic advantage. This advantage could not be adequately offset by the feature articles and outstanding investigative reporting provided by *The National's* top columnists. At the same time the quality of the product was being called into question, the paper was forced to raise its cover price in order to cover mounting expenses. These increases—of as much as 100 percent—signaled the beginning of the end and, on June 12th, 1991, the paper ceased operation.

It was evident at the time that the demand for a quality sports daily existed; however, the ability to deliver this product appeared to be cost prohibitive. If anything was learned from *The National's* brief printing, it was that money and influence cannot overcome managerial shortcomings and poor strategic planning. The creators of *The National* correctly understood print's changing role in sports communication, but were ultimately incapable of capitalizing on the opportunity. One final and perhaps random observation on the written media. Ever notice that in many daily newspapers, such as *The Los Angeles Times*, the sports section comes before the business section? The subtle implications of this are quite interesting. Clearly the Editors have a reason for placing the various sections in the order delivered. What does this say about America's love affair with sports?

MEDIA'S FUTURE

Media's employment picture has evolved in accordance with the industry's growth over the last seventy-five years. The number and breadth of the positions has encouraged universities to offer such majors as "Sports Information" and "Radio/TV." Each of these broadcast and media related majors usually falls under the umbrella of "Communications" at most colleges. The demand for these academic disciplines has grown, at least in part, due to the need for more personalities and specialties in the industry.

In the years to come, however, many issues will have to be addressed in order for the media to maintain an overall level of success and continued growth. For example, which industries will remain as the primary advertisers in sports? These industries, struggling for profitability, will continue advertising in only those markets where the return on their marketing dollar is greatest. This may sound obvious but, in years past, firms have advertised in sports without regard to financial feasibility. When determining the financial feasibility of an advertising campaign or sponsorship, firms will have to examine such issues as the saturation level of sports and the degree of exposure brought forth from their involvement in athletics. To some degree, the media will be responsible for delivering quality events—events that will interest the sponsors and excite the fans.

As the viewing public is inundated with sports through the various media channels, advertisers must be aware of this potential saturation. This type of market, if indeed fragmented and saturated with sports coverage, will lead to an overall reduction in the effectiveness of the campaign. With respect to exposure, changing technologies may make it possible for certain types of companies to maximize their returns by advertising in or avoiding sports. These returns, enhanced by the media's ability to capitalize on a captive market, will rise as the intended target market is personally and aggressively pursued. Local cable television companies have already begun this process by selling advertising time to the local community vendors and focusing on community awareness issues.

An additional issue that will affect the media in the next few years is that of new forms of media. These new forms of media may simply consist of enhanced variations of today's alternatives. Or, a new type of media may be developed entirely. In either case, as the media becomes more state-of-the-art, corporate advertisers must be prepared to change direction and/or philosophies as the media continues to evolve.

The focus here has been on the corporations sponsoring athletic events or purchasing advertising time in collegiate and professional sports. This has been the focus, quite simply, because these are the areas that provide the revenue for the employment opportunities in the media—a topic addressed in the overtime portion of this section.

The three media discussed in this chapter will each experience change which will impact their stability and viability. Radio, by and large, is not viewed as the same entertainment vehicle today as it was by previous generations. Our "MTV Generation" is more interested in visual forms of entertainment, de-emphasizing radio as a primary source of non-music related entertainment. Recall that when sports was being heard on the radio back in the thirties and forties, few alternatives existed for those who wanted to participate in an athletic event; one could attend the game or read about it in detail the following day.

Today, however, a myriad of choices awaits the fan who does not wish to attend the event or read a day-old account of a ball game. He can watch television, especially the cable sports channels, for an extensive report, phone a sports service, or even tap into his computer for the latest scores and statistics. These media outlets and services continue to force sports radio to provide a superior product in order to retain listeners. Accordingly, and in order to captivate a generation less enamored by radio, all-sports networks will be presented with the challenge of attracting these elusive listeners. Over time, one would expect that a single all-sports station could compete nationally for this audience. Presently, local and regional markets offer similar all-sports programming; however, these stations may not be in a financial position to compete with the large networks over long periods of time. Radio will continue to provide its listeners with an inexpensive form of information and entertainment while simultaneously playing an even more specialized role in the athletics industry.

Television in the 21st century will be faced with the challenge of creating new sources of revenue. This must be accomplished while facing declining or at least stabilizing rights fees and fierce competition for the televised sports dollar. By decade's end, revenue sharing between sports and the networks will be the norm. No longer will it be possible for the networks to bid unrealistically for sporting events, as to do so would be financially irresponsible and lead to massive losses. Consequently, an athlete's compensation will be more closely tied to the success of his sport. In short, players will be paid in accordance with the supply and demand of media alternatives.

Cable television in general, and pay-per-view specifically, will provide formidable and on-going competition to the traditional networks, continuing to syphon ratings and profits from "The Big Three" (ABC, NBC and CBS). The development of pay-per-view (PPV) might eventually allow American consumers to order sports as though it were food at a Chinese restaurant—a little of this, a little of that, and a large helping of something else—and charge it to their account. This continued development of PPV may begin a trend in de-emphasizing corporate involvement in athletics since PPV telecasts are commercial free and generate revenue through viewer subscription. Additionally, PPV might have the same impact on cable television that cable had on regular television in the eighties.

The future success of television of all varieties lies in its ability to sell itself as the premier media. It must also demonstrate that it remains cost effective to sponsors—network and cable advertisers—and to subscribers—the PPV customers. This is critically important to anyone seeking employment in the media side of sports because any expansion or contraction in the sports economy will significantly influence the number of positions available. While reduced rights fees would typically hinder the growth of the sports economy, it is possible that the pending globalization of sports and increased competition from cable stations will counteract any such decline.

Sports within the traditional print media—newspapers, will remain competitive in the sports information market as it is only one of several sections in the daily publication. Its ability to piggy-back on local and national news and business partially insulates it from the constraints faced by all-sports factions such as cable sports. However, as a survivor, print must continue to develop those primary areas where competitive advantages exist. These advantages will be in the areas of sports which are not necessarily game specific. For instance, an added emphasis will be given to human interest stories.

Political developments, drug testing, and the like will comprise more of the print media's product as the immediacy of television reduces the need for detailed game summaries. This is not to say that stories and game summaries will be eliminated in the daily press, but merely that the focus of the stories may take a different tack. More emphasis will be devoted to the broader issues in sports that have piqued fans interest over the last few years, namely money and influence. Print will be in the enviable position of providing this investigative reporting, educating the reader about the numerous off-the-field issues that impact players' performance and the success of the sports industry in general.

All three of the media are facing rapidly changing industry dynamics. One must wonder just how much the sports economy can continue to grow. The increase in the supply of commercial time arising from the globalization of sports is likely to influence the price of sports-related sponsorships and advertising. This will occur unless this increased supply is met with an equal or greater demand for the product we call sports. The media must provide the fan with events that are engaging and offer wide international appeal. Also, the increased number of standard and cable television stations broadcasting sporting events could similarly reduce the cost of sports related spending.

With the combination of the evolving industry dynamics and the current squeeze in middle management in the broader U.S. economy, perhaps the employment picture in the media side of sports does not appear especially bright. Corporate America's reduction in the number of mid-level managers is most disconcerting and this is certain to affect the media conglomerates as well. Hopefully, however, the pending international opportunities will at least partially offset this.

Unfortunately, the technological advances described earlier may hurt the prospects for employment. Much like robotics has changed the assembly line, it remains a possibility that the media industry will employ fewer support staff in the future. Adding this to the mid-management squeeze could very likely reduce the compensation paid for these remaining jobs.

It may be that a new media, or a hybrid form of an existing media, will emerge in the next few years, providing both economic growth and new jobs. In the meantime, a keen eye should be trained on the sports economy and its expansion into Europe. Radio, television, and print will all benefit from this market growth and will need this financial "shot in the arm" in order to remain profitable when providing sports telecasts and information.

CAUSE AND EFFECT

Media's enormous influence and pending international expansion presents opportunities for each of the other four areas described in this volume. Universities will prosper from the international exposure derived from having their athletes participate abroad. This may positively impact international enrollment in the institution and increase goodwill. Domestically, the ability to market the university during a sporting event also contributes to the welfare of the academic institution. In some cases, in fact, the media is providing the institution the time to air an "infomercial." This will continue to be evidenced at the larger schools which boast a tremendous following, as they will be able to form lucrative relationships with the media.

The agents directly benefit from the media as they are positioned to use their clients' increased visibility, including international exposure, to their own financial benefit. Agents have also been known to use the media as a negotiating tool, allowing the general public to determine which side is acting unreasonably during prolonged contract squabbles.

Professional franchises profit from the media in a number of ways, not the least of which are soaring licensing revenues and an increased fan base. At every turn, the attention given to sports through the various media channels further reinforces America's love affair with sports, especially the professional sports leagues in this country.

Sports management companies such as IMG, Advantage International, and ProServ will be eager to market their superstars in these growing markets—markets which were more fully developed by the media. Organizations driven by sports-marketing, such as Nike, and corporate divisions like Gatorade, will greet media's international expansion with open arms.

In short, every area within the sports community is in a position to capitalize on the media's influence and expansion. The exact success of these groups will ultimately rest in their ability to plan strategically and produce quality products at a fair price.

10

STAY TUNED, THE MEDIA MAY BE CHANGING

Lonnie White attended Asbury Park High School in New Jersey where he earned All-American honors in both football and track. He then went on to complete a successful football career at the University of Southern California where he holds the single-season record for kickoff return yardage.

*Upon graduating from Southern Cal in 1987 with a degree in broadcast journalism, he joined the staff of the **Los Angeles Times**. He served as both the **Times'** prep editor and as a beat reporter prior to his current position as staff writer. As a staff writer, Lonnie's primary responsibilities include covering the Los Angeles Raiders and the USC's Men's basketball team.*

Sports has always been a major part of my life. As soon as I was able to walk, my father, who played professional football with the New York Giants for a season, had a ball in my hands. I knew the difference between a touchdown and a home run practically before I learned my A-B-C's.

I was fortunate that I became a talented, multi-sport athlete as a youth. My immediate role model, my older brother Timmy, was also an excellent athlete and enjoyed a career as a professional football player.

I tried my best to follow in his footsteps and, eventually, attained star status at the pop warner, high school and collegiate level.

However, the difference between my brother and me was that it was increasingly difficult for me to duplicate his outstanding athletic accomplishments. Timmy was the absolute best in whatever he did. And, while I was a pretty good athlete myself, I was *no* Timmy White. This led me to consider a career outside of professional football—but not too far from the sport I loved. When it came time for me to be recruited out of high school by colleges and universities, the recruiters frequently asked, "What do you want to study in college?" I gave this basic question a lot of thought, maybe too much consideration. I would sit down and list all the things that I enjoyed. Every time I did this exercise, one thing became evident: I wanted to work in the sports business.

Like many young African-American athletes, I was caught up in sports and fascinated by the television media. It seemed that blacks were given a fair chance to prosper as commentators provided their playing careers were a success. I was not convinced, however, that those same opportunities existed for play-by-play. At any rate, I was convinced, upon graduation from high school, that I wanted to pursue a career in sports broadcasting.

I desperately wanted to be in a position where I could educate people from a black athlete's perspective. Too often, people are influenced by the media's inaccurate portrayal of black athletes—and I wanted to change that. My goal was to have the viewer see the whole story.

However, once I enrolled at the University of Southern California (USC), I decided that I did not want to be in television broadcasting but that I preferred writing instead. I simply enjoyed writing more than being in front of a camera. I also felt that I would have a greater opportunity to be creative when working with the written word as opposed to describing a particular event as it occurred.

It immediately became clear to me that many of the writers I was meeting looked as thought they had never played any competitive athletics. I though to myself, "—these guys have the power to influence the public with whatever they write?" This frightening thought helped me determine that sports journalism—not just 'any' journalism, but *sports journalism*—was my calling. It was my goal to provide the public with a former athlete's view to complement to traditional sportswriter's angle. Basically, I wanted to give sports fans the balanced reporting I felt they really needed.

As a football player at USC, studying journalism was difficult. I had to schedule most of my classes in the evening, after practice, rather than during the day. This forced me to miss many of the extra-curricular activities associated with the major as well as forfeit numerous educational and networking opportunities.

The only major benefit of being a football player/journalism student, was that I was able to concentrate on being a sportswriter. Not surprisingly, I was able to combine my playing experiences with my early professional writings and course work. However, at a school like USC, where the journalism program is highly regarded in the industry, I missed out on all the year-round paid internships being offered. But, I knew that hands-on work experience was important, so I tried to seize all possible opportunities, squeezing them into my already hectic schedule.

In my last two years at school, I wrote part-time for the school paper, *The Daily Trojan*. The job was excellent experience for me because I gained my first by-lines. However, the staff, which consisted mostly of journalism students, was very large, so my opportunities to write were limited. To make matters worse, I made it a point *not* to write about sports. This turned out to be a great move as it forced me to deal with hard-news and features.

While writing for a school newspaper is highly recommended, it is also important to obtain work experience outside of school. For me, this experience came from a small local Los Angeles area paper called *The Wave*. This was my first experience as a "sportswriter" and I truly enjoyed it. Although I was not paid (because of the NCAA rule restricting athletes from getting paid for working while in school), I immediately knew that this was the profession I wanted to get into full time. In an effort to gain meaningful experience, I began covering local high school and college sports for *The Wave*.

Even though I was still playing football, it felt reassuring to know what I wanted to do for a living—after football. I was fortunate as an athlete to participate in four bowl games for the Trojans and also spend a season with the New Orleans Saints. After my release from the Saints due to a shoulder injury, I eagerly pursued my career as a writer.

The first lesson I learned upon my return to Los Angeles was that the journalism field was tough to break into—almost impossible. Years ago, it was easier to become a writer because of the number of newspapers and magazines, however, with the recent economic turmoil in the media business, many publications have folded, eliminating a great number of journalism jobs. In fact, I was turned down by 34 newspapers and magazines before I was given my first opportunity. Thirty-four! Believe it or not, this first offer came from *The Los Angeles Times*, a prominent, well respected paper with a reputation for excellent sports coverage.

I was lucky in landing that first job. *The Times*, with a sports staff of about sixty, has several zone sections along with its main sports department. A zone section is basically a subset of the larger metropolitan circulation such as the Valley, South Bay or Westside Editions. Originally, I thought that I had a better chance to get a job working for one of the zones because it provided more coverage of prep sports as it focused more on a specific city's sports news coverage. But, after I was turned down by four zone sections, I decided to call the main department to find out where to send my resume. It was this move that eventually led to a couple of extensive interviews and, ultimately, the position.

The ironic thing was that when I was hired by *The Times* for roughly twenty thousand dollars per year, I had also received a solid offer to return to the NFL and earn $75,000 per season. The timing couldn't have been worse but, although it was a very tough decision, I opted to become a writer.

The major obstacle in choosing *The Times* was that, as a journalist, your salary is far below that of an NFL player. However, because it was *The Times*—a major daily in a huge metropolitan market—it was worth the challenge. After all, there are no guarantees in the NFL.

Even though USC had an excellent journalism department, classes are not the same as the real world. The course work taught me how to organize stories and line up sources, but it did not prepare me to deal with "real" interviews. So, when I started at *The Times*, I realized that I really did not have much practical work experience in the industry. Everything was new to me.

Essentially, I was hired as a desk assistant where my duties primarily included answering phone calls and typing schedules. I was told that I would get a chance to write but I was scared to death, thinking to myself that my stories would be published along side those of Pulitzer Prize winner Jim Murray!

Learning the duties of the desk assistant were not particularly challenging—certainly not as challenging as my first story assignment: golf. I didn't know the first thing about some aspects of the game; I was lost. Here I was, an ex-football player, interviewing the groundskeeper about his horticultural techniques for an off-season golf story. I thought I was supposed to write about sports. Somehow I survived that first assignment and, before long, I had my first beat, "Arena Football." It turned out to be the most difficult beat to cover because the games had so much scoring and ended so close to deadline. However, because I didn't know any better, I always made deadline (which, by the way, is 10:30 p.m.), a skill that has helped me ever since because it taught me to deal with the everyday pressures of the newspaper business.

As a sportswriter, there are times when I have to pinch myself because I genuinely enjoy what I'm doing. It was a job that I knew I would enjoy; an opportunity that allows me to get paid for doing something I would consider doing for free (if I had the time). Not unlike any other profession, though, dues must be paid before one advances. Sure there are long hours, busy weekends and a general lack of respect but, in the end, it is worth the struggle. Being a former athlete gave me a solid background in dealing with many of the adverse conditions found in this high pressure form of employment. For example, working your way up the pecking order is much like climbing up a team's depth chart. Also, being able to perform under less than ideal circumstances is a big plus—just like it is in the world of competitive athletics.

Sportswriters commonly perform a thankless job. You have to cater to your sources and, the more of these you have, the more time you have to spend developing them. For example, when a game is over, fans can go home, change the channel or begin the weekend chores. However, for us, the job is just beginning. The writer has to locate players and coaches for post game quotes and interviews, all the while thinking about a unique angle to present to the reader.

The best advice I can offer someone who wants to be a sportswriter is to write. The more you write, the better you become. Practice, practice, practice. Also, do not limit yourself to any one subject area. You have to be able to write about all sports, and possibly even non-sports topics.

A great entree into sports journalism is becoming a "stringer" for a local paper. A stringer is someone who works part time and only gets paid by the contributing stories. Acting as a stringer allows you to cover games and events and be paid on a part-time basis. With every assignment, you gain a new story clipping; this is important as you move on in your writing career, as it allows you to build a portfolio of sorts, enabling you to present this track record to a prospective employer.

As you grow as a journalist, you will learn that there are some things that you may not like to cover. For instance, I do not like to deal with court room stories. However, in today's world, sports has moved, at least in part, from the field to the court room. Attorneys, for example, can either be your friend or a pain. Regardless of the quality of this relationship, writers must make a concerted effort to remain objective. I firmly believe that objectivity, in its purest form, is almost impossible to achieve in all cases.

I have always felt that you have an opinion or feeling before you begin any story or feature. For whatever reason, it is there—whether you choose to admit it or not. You may change your opinion during the story but, rest assured, one will always exist. The only objectivity one has is how you deal with the story once you begin your coverage.

Yet another difficult area to deal with as a writer is that of privacy. Specifically, what should you, as a writer, do when someone's personal life is exposed—and you are forced to draw a line. Should I or shouldn't I cover the story? How will the press coverage affect the person's ability to deal with the personal issue at hand? Should I even be concerned about this ethical dilemma?

For example, I had to cover a story following the tragic death of a high school football player, a player who collapsed and died on the field due to heart failure. His family was aware that they had a history of heart problems. Nonetheless, they allowed him to play, despite the well documented risk. They felt that their decision was the right one for their family at that particular time. My feeling was that the family, who listened to the athlete's desperate plea to play high school football, had a particularly difficult time making this decision. Accordingly, I felt uncomfortable writing this story because I knew that the family would be criticized by the general public as "heartless," even though this could not have been further from the truth. In short, it is easy for me to have a personal opinion about a story, but it is far more difficult to keep this personal bias out of the final story.

Personally, I feel that every person has a right to privacy and that the media should be respectful of this privacy. However, that is never the case because the competitive nature of the industry requires us to cover the story—or risk losing our readership. Readership or principles? Unfortunately, the ability to make a profit from these stories often out-weighs an individual writer's personal beliefs—and every year it seems to be getting worse.

Moreover, with television and the other forms of media always looking for the ultimate, sensationalized story, the sportswriter is often faced with covering the story he would rather forget. Additionally, it is tough to follow your heart when your competitor doesn't share the same personal philosophy—and eventually beats you on a story that you were already aware of, but were too principled to break. These are issues that every writer faces at some point in his or her career and must be dealt with carefully. My suggestion would be to check with the editor, asking his professional opinion; unfortunately, though, the editor typically suggests that you cover the story in question. After all, he is being paid to cover stories, not pass judgement on them.

Despite this, there are relatively few disadvantages in being a newspaper reporter. Nonetheless, one area that I feel compelled to discuss, is the hypocrisy associated with the hiring practices in the media. Collectively, the media is very quick to point out any of these unfair practices throughout the sports industry, while simultaneously neglecting its own situation.

As we know, many of today's superstar athletes are black and a great percentage of the dominate teams are led by black players. Over all, a majority of the basketball and football teams have more black players than white. Moreover, for every five stories seen in a sports section, three of them describe blacks in a starring role. But, in the sports newsroom, less than 5 percent of the reporters are black—as are fewer than 1 percent of the editors.

Consequently, blacks as a whole are not represented in the media with the same percentages that are seen on the field. And I don't see this practice improving any time soon. Consider the hypocrisy with respect to major league baseball. The media assaults the sport for not having minorities in administrative positions but, upon even an abbreviated review, it is evident that their own hiring practices are lacking. Moreover, I believe this is the case whether one considers the major metropolitan dailies or the small local papers.

Another concern of mine is the changing influence the print media has on sports. The audience print enjoyed (and took for granted, to a certain degree) is literally dying. The generation who grew up with newspapers as the primary source for information is being replaced with the television generation. People who have news in front of them 24 hours a day, do not need to read as much as their parents once did. Ten years from now, the impact of the print media will be reduced even further, forcing it to present an even higher quality publication. While I agree that print will never be totally replaced, I am certain that it will serve merely as a secondary form of sports information.

This will be the case because of standard television, and the continued growth of the cable television market. Think about it. Why read about today's game tomorrow when you can receive an abundance of coverage tonight? This may force the print media to compete for those individuals unable to gain employment in one of the more "mainstream" media. My immediate interests will be heavily influenced by these trends and I must continue to keep them in mind when planning the rest of my career.

In reviewing my journalism career, I moved from the Arena Football beat to high school sports and, several years later, am now a staff writer. Throughout all of this, I have grown to realize that 'good' jobs are few and far between *today*, and I can only imagine how scarce they will be in the future.

In fact, I am fortunate to be with *The Times* at this early stage in my career. Ultimately, it would be great to begin *and* finish my career as a sportswriter with *The Los Angeles Times*. Only time well tell. Stay tuned.

OVERTIME

When considering future employment opportunities and the financial structure of the media heading into the 21st century, I believe it is helpful to analyze a real world example. While the sport of soccer has never really taken off in the United States, it remains the most popular sport in the world. The Super Bowl, World Series, and NBA Finals pale in comparison to the international recognition and magnitude of this soccer event, which is held around the world every four years.

Accordingly, the audience for the World Cup is many times greater than that of our Super Bowl, World Series or NBA Championship Finals. Not only is the absolute number of viewers far greater from an advertising perspective but the total employment opportunities are also equally and dramatically increased. Think for a moment about what a production the Super Bowl is on a domestic level: advertisers willing to pay as much as $1,000,000 for a single television commercial during the telecast; the host city's economy is significantly and positively affected by the exposure, including tourism; and international media members work feverishly to deliver the telecast back to an often times less-than-enthusiastic home market. While this it is a major international media event requiring significant manpower to present, it is nothing compared to the World Cup.

Support staffs, technical experts, translators, and skilled administrators in the media industry are increased many-fold for an event of this size. And this is true not only domestically, for the World Cup is seen around the world, thus providing thousands of media opportunities worldwide.

To most Americans, soccer stars such as Pele and Diego Maradona were and are merely viewed as extremely talented international athletes, but not necessarily icons as Wayne Gretzky or Shaquille O'Neal are viewed domestically. We as a society, and particularly those of us affiliated with sports, have missed the boat. We are forgetting, or even more inappropriately, disregarding, the potential in this expanded sports market, a market sure to grow by leaps and bounds in the years to come.

With growth comes opportunities, including employment. Lonnie White highlighted the diminished role he anticipates the print media playing in the next ten years. Thus, in the event that one is still interested in a career as a writer, perhaps it would be beneficial to develop proficiency in one or more of the major international languages: French, German, or even Japanese. How about writing a sports piece for a local foreign language paper in your area? Maybe your *Wave* should be a Spanish speaking weekly. Whatever the experience, use the creativity inherent in being a successful writer or, in a broader sense, a successful member of the media, to your advantage by contacting and utilizing what will surely be an expanding employment base.

As previously discussed, the media pays everyone's bills. Accordingly, as international competition continues to blossom, Corporate America will begin selling its products and services abroad. Corporate America will apply many of the marketing techniques, such as target marketing and demographic research, that it has used for years—on a much larger scale. As companies consider and ultimately participate in these international events, the media will be poised to share in this added influence and cash flow.

And, not only will American companies enjoy this added exposure, but foreign interests will similarly participate in the process. As the size of the total sports market expands, those corporations hoping to enjoy increased publicity will also increase dramatically. Naturally, the combination of foreign and domestic advertising and promotion dollars will lead to fierce competition among the advertisers vying for a captive audience. Moreover, as this competition grows, so too will the competition in the media. While you are attempting to gain experience and exposure to international markets and with foreign publications, the foreign media will be attempting the same thing; theoretically resulting in well-covered and professional events from a media perspective.

Whatever the scenario, the media stands to profit from additional programming rights fees, increased total advertising dollars, and from the position of maintaining tremendous power and influence through the staging of international athletic events. The Super Bowl is a micro concept; the World Cup is a macro one. It's been said many times before: think "big picture" and apply your personal media skills to this changing marketplace.

What will the new media look like? Many of us in the financial area of sports believe that it may very well take on a more technical appearance. In fact, career opportunities may be more readily found in areas dealing with the intricacies of delivering and producing an international event. Remember, radio replaced print and, over time, television replaced both of them. It remains likely that high-tech will provide, or at the very least contribute to, the next form of media. For example, using fiber-optic technology, it will soon be common place for the major phone companies to offer cable television over the phone lines. As White said, "Stay Tuned!"

Perhaps the continued development of pay-per-view will signal the beginning of the end to what we once regarded as "free" television. And, as a member of the media, it will be critically important for you to gain exposure to this new technology, whatever it eventually becomes. Remember that many of the wealthiest participants in the sports community are those who had a vision in the media industry. Does the name Ted Turner ring a bell? How about the always colorful Don King? Each of these businessmen quickly capitalized on the emergence of cable and pay-per-view—granted each accomplished his fame in a slightly different manner!

The immediate and timely delivery of sports information will continue to be the driving force in the industry, separating those who are simply in the business from those who are wildly successful in their endeavors. Rest assured that the computer will steer media's employment picture over the next decade, creating new jobs while simultaneously eliminating others. As White suggested, it is important to keep your eye on the ball at all times or face the consequences of being made an obsolete member of the media. Creating a new communications system whereby sports news is more efficiently and instantaneously delivered to the consumer will be met with great demand. After all, consider the concept of desk top publishing; it has redefined certain aspects of the industry and has been well received universally. Once again, product differentiation with an emphasis on immediacy, efficient target marketing, and low overhead will signal the next industry leader with respect to the new media.

When pursuing a position in a new or even hybrid form of media previously discussed, several issues will become critical to keep in mind. First, the cultural diversities and political ideologies will be much more dynamic as the media takes on an even greater international scope. These concerns will not only make covering athletic events more complicated due to the implications of competing international interests, but will also provide the individual members of the media with a more challenging arena from which the actual events will be covered. The press area will resemble the United Nations rather than the local donut shop.

The actual press area is the second issue requiring comment. It has been my experience, as a member of the media, that the press box and related working areas are an excellent venue for meeting and networking with others. This is the case as sporting events are an ideal place for the different types of media to converge and share ideas. The radio personalities interact with those from the written press, the beat writers mingle with the television people, etc. However, and it is a big however, those individuals attending the game on a press credential are there to work, either producing a telecast, analyzing the contest, or writing a story for a paper or magazine. Therefore, it is very important to "pick your shots" when networking in the press box, as disturbing someone who is in the process of earning a living can be quite detrimental. Remember, there is a very fine line between acting as a proactive professional and being an outright bother.

Finally, and related to the previous point, be prepared to play the political game. Building a professional network consisting of all types of media participants will be invaluable in the long run. This bridge-building needs to be accomplished without the proverbial "kissing up" that we frequently hear about. To the contrary, this base building is the result of working a little harder and smarter than others, as well as consistently demonstrating an unequalled level of professional competence.

The absolute number of jobs in the media may increase or decrease in the years to come. Some theorize that with the growth of the international sports markets, the number of employment opportunities may actually increase, even if the scope of these positions is limited. Opponents of this line of thinking believe that as high-tech takes over, actual sports reporting-type jobs may decrease as journalists and others are replaced by a more efficient form of transmission. Consider, say these proponents of a shrinking media, the large number of media covering a particular NBA or NFL ball game. Isn't there a tremendous amount of overlap, or saturation, in coverage? Maybe, they suggest, the volume of media that covers each event can be trimmed.

And what about the networks which have badly over-valued the worth of broadcast rights fees? If rights fees fall over the next few years, what might this do to the total number of domestic media jobs available in sports? At best, a decline or leveling off in revenue to the networks will have no impact on the employment situation in the broadcast media.

However, when large corporations lose money consistently, the work force is usually the first to feel this belt tightening. When hearing or reading about these types of sports finance issues, make a concerted effort to apply the impact of the news to your personal sports career. After all, a fluctuation in rights fees affects everyone in the business, especially those professions mentioned throughout this book.

In any case, rest assured that sports communication will always be a people-intensive business and this will prevent the best members of the media fraternity from ever being displaced.

Given the possibility that there may actually be more jobs available in the media in the years to come, what academic disciplines might one want to pursue in order to access these new opportunities? The contributor mentioned receiving formal training in journalism and/or a related major such as communications or sports information. I feel it is important to add marketing, and specifically, personal selling, to this suggested list. In a business dominated by outgoing personalities and unusual characters, it will always be beneficial to present oneself (personal selling) in the most positive light possible, subtly reminding others of your industry strengths while minimizing the exposure to your weaknesses, shortcomings that are in the process of being overcome.

With respect to earning potential in the media, White indirectly suggested that those who are primarily motivated by money may have a difficult time breaking in as a journalist, broadcaster, or other associated member of the media. The money may eventually come, as it has for the media's elite; however, most of those in the media were more passionate about what they did for a living than how much they received for doing it.

Consequently, those who have succeeded in the business spent less time worrying about how much money they *weren't* making and focused more attention on a particular piece of White's advice: write, write, write; and then, just when you are getting tired of it, write some more. Practicing one's writing skills or broadcasting technique requires a tremendous amount of time and personal sacrifice, a sort of sweat equity that will not be reflected in one's paycheck for a very long time. But, until or unless a particular skill is mastered, the ability to write for *The Los Angeles Times* or broadcast for NBC Sports will be non-existent.

****

PART VI:
Sports Management
Companies

****

11

KEY INDUSTRY PLAYERS

When we envision sports management companies, we often think of elitist organizations representing and/or marketing the nation's superstars. The clientele of these firms is comprised of individual and team sport athletes who receive tremendous attention due to the high profile nature of their specialties.

While this may be somewhat accurate, these firms also provide a wide variety of very important complimentary services to both athletes *and* consumers. These services include: event management, sponsorship procurement, financial services, and consulting. These services, more uncommonly associated with these entities, are reviewed throughout this chapter. Furthermore, the type of sports management firm generically referred to in the previous paragraph is not fully representative of the types of firms which comprise the broader sports management industry.

THE SPORTS MANAGEMENT BUSINESS

For purposes of this discussion, the sports management industry will be divided into four categories. Each of these industry participants provides a series of critical client services designed to enhance the careers of their clientele, while simultaneously providing fans and other businesses the opportunity to participate in the collegiate and professional athletics business. While the four categories described in this chapter may not comprise an exhaustive listing of sports management specialties, it is my belief that most activities fall into one of the following disciplines: Sports Marketing/Public Relations Firms, Special Event Marketing Groups and/or Venue Management Companies, Sports Marketing-Driven Corporations and finally, Financial and Consulting Interests.

Employment opportunities in the sports management business are as wide-spread and diverse as the firms themselves. This enables prospective employees to match skills and interests with the expertise of the firm. Additionally, many of these sports management entities retain numerous "traditional" professionals—accountants, financial analysts, marketing experts, and strategic planners, to mention just a few. Throughout this chapter it is important to consider which are the requisite background types and skills required by these respective management firms. You will notice that this aspect of the sports industry closely parallels that of Corporate America.

The first type of sports management entity to be reviewed is the Marketing and Public Relations Firms. It is important to note that these groups do not always perform *exclusively* sports marketing activities, as many management firms handle clients from multiple industries. Before discussing the actual marketing activities undertaken by this type of firm, it is necessary to understand some of the other functions they perform. These functions, which do not produce a tangible financial return for the group, are very important with respect to building and retaining a client base. An assumption has also been made with regard to the athlete's choice of a sports marketing representative; it is assumed that the athlete has "done the right thing" by not retaining his personal representation agency or friend or family member to provide these intricate marketing services.

Much like the personal representation process, sports marketers often serve as insulation for the athlete. This insulation allows the athlete to defer to his staff those uncomfortable situations where the athlete is approached about unworthy ventures. Specifically, the marketing firm can assume the role of the "bad guy." Essentially acting in a managerial role, the group can serve as the "sounding board" through which all marketing inquiries must be made. This will allow the marketers to say no on the client's behalf without portraying him as the "bad guy." These situations commonly arise from overzealous friends, family members and occasional die-hard fans who long to involve their friend or family member in the next "can't-miss" marketing opportunity.

While serving in this capacity for the client, it is not unusual for the firm to be an integral part of the athlete's overall management team: recall that this team usually includes the agent, an attorney, and financial representatives. As a team member, the sports management group customarily works as closely as required with these other members, providing input and details about the various available sports marketing alternatives. This is very important, of course, as each alternative may have very different legal, tax, and financial implications.

In addition to serving as a traditional team member, the sports management firm retained to market the athlete may be performing a very defined role. That is, it is not uncommon for athletes to retain multiple groups, often providing firms with the non-exclusive marketing rights. In this scenario, the athlete allows several groups to develop business for him. As business is created, the management firm is compensated accordingly, usually as a percentage of the gross revenue generated from the project. The specific compensation methods employed by the sports management industry will be discussed in detail later in this chapter.

Another example of where a management firm performs a very defined role is when the athlete chooses different entities to handle his marketing, promotions, publicity, etc. This is somewhat unusual but has occurred. At any rate, the point is that the marketing representative(s) play an active role as a member of an athlete's team, regardless of the disciplines performed.

Other activities that may not produce a tangible financial return include athlete recruitment and general client development activities. For example, a firm may not charge for the creation of the initial portfolio. This portfolio creation, along with other "sweat equity" activities such as those free services designed to "close" the client, is standard within the industry. The question that quickly arises, however, is how much time and/or complimentary services can a management group afford to offer while courting their next prospective client?

One final note on the positioning of the sports management groups within the industry: the discussion below reviews the sports marketer, not the *order-taker*. Order-takers, those individuals, as opposed to organizations, representing "hot properties," usually perform the role of *responding* to inquiries rather than *creating* them. While in a most enviable position, these individuals do not customarily face the same marketing dilemmas and constraints which are placed upon the market as a whole. Additionally, these "hot properties" may actually be only a fad, associated with a particular event or season. Accordingly, the individual or individuals marketing the star capitalize on the short-term opportunities, usually at the expense of developing a long-term marketing plan.

Order-takers may, in fact, be non-marketing professionals positioned to handle these one-time or seasonal opportunities. The reason for making this differentiation is that the focus of this section is on the more traditional sports management firms; those that devise and implement larger, more broad-based marketing strategies. This discussion is not intended to belittle the obvious contributions of order-takers, but merely to point out that the focus of the two types of marketers is quite different, requiring very different resources, time and expertise.

SPORTS MARKETING/PUBLIC RELATIONS FIRMS

Now, back to the first major group comprising the sports management industry, marketing and public relations firms which specialize in athlete marketing. Once the sports management firm has been successful in acquiring sports personalities in need of marketing, there are several services likely to be provided simultaneously. The first, and most obvious marketing activity, is that of securing product or service endorsements. The most common of these include athletic apparel—such as basketball shoes and consumer products—soft drinks, for example.

Lately, the emergence of the trading card business has provided an enormous source of revenue for the star athlete who enjoys a favorable reputation. For instance, the right to place a player's likeness on a "bubble-gum" card can command upwards of $1 million. It should be noted, however, that this trading card market appears to be leveling off after several years of unprecedented growth. Nonetheless, it is an interesting component of sports marketing and merits continual monitoring.

When reviewing the market place and soliciting prospective companies, marketers must be aware of several critical issues over and above their client's anticipated compensation from an endorsement. Is the image of the potential product or service one that is consistent with the athlete and/or the firm's reputation? Does this even matter to the parties involved? What effect might there be on future endorsements due to one's relationship with today's product? Does the acceptance of a specific endorsement essentially eliminate the opportunity to work with a similar company (mutual exclusivity)? For example, an affiliation with Coke would all but eliminate any potential relationship with Pepsi. Is there a conflict of interest present whereby either the marketing firm or the athlete would jeopardize ones credibility?

This list could go on practically forever—but it is clear that securing the *best* endorsement among the many alternatives may involve numerous non-financial variables. Remember, one of the primary objectives of the management group is to build and maintain an athlete's favorable reputation and exposure over a period of years; not simply to seek out the short-term "kill."

The areas of client promotion and publicity are also very important. Often these two activities take place concurrently with personal appearances. Arranging promotional work may not pay the client very well or generate significant revenue for the firm, but, as part of the larger plan, promotions are invaluable as they build client recognition. Promotions, such as attending a store's grand opening or speaking on behalf of a company whose new product or service the athlete may use, often provides added exposure and experience. This activity generates goodwill in addition to exposure, each of which are typical prerequisites for larger, more comprehensive endorsement campaigns.

Other appearances, such as attending special events or scheduling autograph sessions, also help create the marketing persona. This public persona, created from promotional activities, personal appearances, and other types of publicity is also supported by an athlete's involvement with charities. Whether serving as a charity's spokesman or merely allowing a charity to use a celebrity's name or likeness in fundraising events, the association with what society deems "a good cause" is always beneficial. The marketing benefit of devoting time to a charitable group is that it establishes the perception of genuine concern and commitment to the community.

Each of the activities described above, when taken as a whole, comprise the majority of the firm's marketing efforts. Building and maintaining a professional image, while simultaneously maximizing marketing income, is the delicate balance being struck by this type of sports management company.

As with most businesses, marketing and public relations firms acquire new business through referrals and recruiting. Satisfied athletes are easy to spot, especially in the locker room, when teammates comment on the latest commercial or endorsement. Recruiting, on the other hand, is more complicated. While it may be slightly more scrupulous than the recruiting that takes place for personal representation, this corporate environment is still most competitive as there are only a handful of new athletes looking for marketing support in any one year. This places added pressure on the staff attempting "to land" the next David Robinson.

The size of these marketing groups varies as much as the services they provide. Many athletes, searching for a firm's undivided attention and marketing efforts, may in fact choose a relatively small group consisting of no more than two or three professionals. But, retaining a marketing firm, based primarily on size, can be a big mistake. The quality of the group's work and not their size should be the key concern to the athlete. Advantages and shortcomings can be associated with any sports management group—whether it is a smaller group, as previously discussed, or a larger, full service organization, employing hundreds of specialists such as the "Big 3" which are described below.

In general terms, these organizations are compensated for their marketing efforts using one of two basic methods. The percentage method, typically ranging from 10-25 percent, requires the athlete to pay the marketer a pre-determined percentage of the gross receipts from an endorsement or marketing campaign. This percentage can include the expenses incurred on the athlete's behalf by the marketing agency or can be separate from any direct marketing costs.

For example, assume Firm A charges 15 percent for marketing, but also requires the athlete to pay any pre-approved expenses in addition to this percentage. If the firm spends $500 arranging a $10,000 endorsement, then the athlete owes Firm A $2,000 ($1,500 from the percentage method and $500 more for direct costs).

Firm B, on the other hand, charges an all-encompassing 20 percent fee for marketing services. In either case, the cost to the athlete is the same—$2,000. Where a difference may arise, however, is in the accountability required by the athlete. Some sports management firms may attempt to "run up" or pad their expenses in order to make a little extra off the deal. Still others, using the absolute percentage method, may be less enthused about incurring too many expenses without immediate results, as these out-of-pocket expenses will not be recovered. The problem that arises here is that the marketing group may not be marketing its client as aggressively as the client would like.

Charging a monthly or quarterly retainer is the other basic way in which sports marketing groups are compensated. On a stand alone basis, providing a firm with a quarterly retainer (say $2,500), can be very dangerous for an athlete. Occasionally, marketing firms will accept this payment and be in a position to demonstrate to the client that steady marketing progress is being made. Unfortunately, it may take as long as a year for the athlete to realize that none of these programs are going to come to fruition. At this point, the athlete would be out of pocket $10,000.

An alternative method is to arrange a retainer with a pay back scheme tied to it. For example, suppose the firm arranges $30,000 worth of endorsements for the client during the year, and the firm typically charges 20 percent, expenses included. This means that the firm has "earned" $6,000 during the course of the year while charging the athlete $10,000. Under this scenario, a rebate, of sorts, worth $4,000 is due the athlete. This type of arrangement would be entered into with the belief that the firm would be able to generate $50,000 worth of endorsement income for the athlete. This break-point allows the player to pay in installments, while enabling the marketer to receive a series of payments, essentially earning revenue as expenses are incurred.

In the case where endorsement revenue exceeded the $50,000, the athlete would be charged an appropriate rate or the retainer would be increased in the next contract. This method most accurately ties pay to performance and provides the marketing specialists with an ongoing incentive throughout the relationship. As with contract negotiations, a blended method could be used but would serve only to further complicate the situation.

These methods are the ones most commonly used when dealing with athletes and sports organizations. As for consulting arrangements in which a sports management firm might help a corporate sponsor solve an important problem, hourly rates or a pre-determined total fee may be negotiated. These methods also apply to the sports management organizations described throughout this chapter. The bottom line is that sports management firms and their clientele design and implement the most appropriate scheme for both parties.

SPECIAL EVENT MARKETING AND MANAGEMENT GROUPS

Special Event Marketing (Management) Groups comprise the second group of sports management companies that are examined when considering sports management in the nineties. Many of today's marketers believe that the marketing industry as a whole must begin to change the way it views and, more importantly, gains access to consumers. These marketers sight enormous market fragmentation, increasing product parity, declining brand loyalty, advertising clutter, media inflation, and increasingly powerful retailers as a few reasons why there must be alternative means of reaching those increasingly skeptical, message-resistant consumers.

Witnessing this change in the marketing environment, many believe that special event marketing may provide part of the solution. The goal of special event marketing is to build relationships and demonstrate differentiation of the sponsor's product or service. Sponsors participate in these special events because they understand and would like to capitalize on the opportunity at hand—that of large concentrations of consumers possessing decision-making ability.

A prime example of this might be Cadillac's sponsorship of the 1992 America's Cup. After all, the "sailing fraternity" which is comprised of the Cup's Event coupled and a captive yachting audience—both in person and on cable television—is the ideal demographic market in which to promote Cadillacs.

Event Management is not limited to specific athletic series such as the America's Cup. It can also be effectively used at more traditional sporting events, even in conjunction with federations and organizations, as well as at entertainment and cultural events. Other examples of where special event management/marketing takes place include the Olympics, equestrian shows, and racket sports, as well as golf tournaments, collegiate football bowl games, "All-Star" weekends, and other individual sports such as city marathons and 10 kilometer races.

It is at these events that sponsors can personally sell their product or service. This can be accomplished by discussing the merits of the product and overall quality of the company and its employees, while casually sipping champagne in the hospitality tent. Moreover, as a title sponsor, the unique opportunity exists to be the lone company present from any particular industry. This is very important, especially for those sponsors promoting high-end services. This stage, which provides for the most intimate form of personal selling, is set by the event marketing firm.

When a firm is involved as a corporate sponsor at one of these special events, they are establishing tremendous goodwill and invaluable name recognition for their firm. Building awareness, while not translating directly to sales, is critical in the marketing mix. Participation in a special event such as Wimbeldon or the Olympics also has other benefits. It creates the opportunity for a firm to cross promote and/or direct market its wares. These are some of the reasons why sports management firms would like to involve Corporate America in the sports business.

Accordingly, sports management firms specializing in event management offer a variety of services, all revolving around a specific event. In the early stages, detailed strategic planning takes place in which the conception and development of an event takes place. This includes a thorough review of the competition, general financial and marketing issues to be addressed, administrative concerns, as well as an analysis of the pending representation issues.

With respect to representation, a sports management firm focuses on the areas of rights acquisition, and subsequent sales, and corporate packaging. The firm's marketing experts concentrate on promotion and publicity, paying close attention to hospitality, merchandising and licensing, and advertising sales. The financial team is kept busy with budgeting and other financial issues such as expense minimization. All of these functions are fulfilled while the executive and administrative staff oversees the full implementation of the strategic game plan. These professionals must work closely and effectively together to ensure a successful special event for both the firm and the corporate client.

VENUE MANAGEMENT FIRMS

Venue management firms are also a part of this second group of sports management firms. These organizations receive far less attention than the event marketing groups, but perform a set of very important functions. Without these services, many of the sporting events we attend would not be possible. The reason for the lack of attention given to venue management firms is that they perform activities that are buried behind the scenes of the sports world.

Specifically, these companies specialize in the activities involved in managing an arena, stadium, or other venue. Venue management firms negotiate the terms of leases for franchises and other occupants who use a given facility during the year. Other areas where these firms can assist in the hosting of an athletic event include the procurement of the necessary insurance, security, concession, and parking arrangements. They may not be directly responsible for securing these arrangements, but the overall preparedness of the venue is their primary responsibility. In general terms, these groups can be compared to commercial office building management companies. These commercial real estate companies are accountable to the tenants, their own corporate headquarters, and even local government.

Venue management firms make their money in one of three ways. First, they can charge for their services in the form of a management fee. The fee, based on a percentage of gross revenue, is a result of the time and labor required to manage the event. Alternatively, the firm can charge a flat fee for managing the venue. This flat fee is fixed and covers a specified period of time, such as a year or more. Finally, the firm can earn revenue by increasing the number of events at the venue. Since many costs are fixed, adding events throughout the year can have a profound effect on the bottom line. Accordingly, management firms charge a percentage over and above some agreed upon minimum. For example, the firm may charge double its standard management fee as described above for any amount of revenue generated beyond a certain point. This type of incentive may serve the interests of both parties. Regardless of the method of compensation, these firms are continually involved in a number of fascinating sports management issues.

Recently, an interesting development on the viability of luxury boxes has been receiving an extraordinary amount of coverage. This development addresses whether the construction and maintenance of luxury suites is a financially worthwhile venture given the generous amount of valuable space they occupy. Both franchises and management firms must determine if this specific renovation adds to marginal revenue or simply creates another administrative nightmare.

The larger issue, that of stadium renovations, has been a major source of frustration for both the management firms and local governments. In fact, teams in several markets, including the Raiders in Los Angeles, have threatened to relocate unless their renovation demands are met. These demands included a new press box, numerous luxury boxes, a lowering of the field, and a reduction of the total number of seats in the Los Angeles Memorial Coliseum. Had most of these issues not been resolved to the satisfaction of the Raiders, Al Davis would have likely moved his franchise to a more "user-friendly" stadium.

On the one hand, venue management firms are in an unenviable position. They must provide both a safe and comfortable venue for the fans, while simultaneously providing the franchise with the optimal viewing arrangement that will allow the team to maximize revenue. It is not uncommon for these two agendas to conflict as the number of fans in attendance and the quality of the viewing environment are often at odds. For example, the smaller the stadium the greater the likelihood of a sell out. Sell-outs lead to the lifting of blackouts, which serve to enhance the teams' financial and marketing positions.

On the other hand, as managers of the venue, they find themselves in a powerful and advantageous position. It is possible for a well organized and efficiently operated management firm to significantly impact the quality of sports in a particular city by providing the fans with a safe, comfortable and pleasant viewing experience. The major advantage lies in their ability to charge a premium for a well managed event. This will be discussed in greater detail shortly.

Financing for renovations can be obtained through the public or private sector. In either case, the sale of luxury boxes, usually priced in the tens of thousands of dollars per year, is a critical new source of revenue for franchises and has created many new employment opportunities for those with sales experience. The luxury boxes are, as one would expect, a tremendous setting for entertaining—a concept not lost on major corporate sponsors. The acquisition of a luxury box commonly reflects a sponsor's larger commitment to sports marketing. This commitment to sports at various levels often leads to participation in specific events. At this point, an event management firm would be retained—thus completing the sports management cycle.

Venue management firms also oversee the events held at their locations by working with event marketers and local/state governments. In short, these organizations are responsible for most of the detail work associated with the planning and completion of an athletic event.

Venue management firms are usually a subsidiary or affiliate of a larger, entertainment-oriented holding company. This relationship, with its "behind-the-scenes" nature, can make it difficult to learn about the organizations and associated employment opportunities within this type of management group. Contacting the local professional team(s) or municipality may provide sufficient information about the venue management firm in your area. At this point, it would be necessary to research the services offered by the group and determine its areas of expertise and office locations.

The staffs of these firms can vary in size, depending primarily upon the number of events managed. As a rule, the total staff ranges from about 25-50 employees. Of this group, about twenty-five percent are so-called "white collar" positions, while the remaining positions function in the upkeep of the specific venue(s). For example, one of the larger venue management firms has a staff of about forty, with groundskeepers, electricians, and other maintenance staff comprising well in excess of half the total positions.

With respect to the 'white-collar' positions, the staff is fairly lean. In addition to the General and Facilities Managers positions, about a half dozen professional opportunities remain. The finance/accounting functions would be performed by a staff of about three; the Public Relations Manager would handle the marketing/publicity function; and Event Coordinators would oversee the specific teams. These Event Coordinators are responsible for managing all the details associated with any one team. For instance, if a particular "sports complex" houses a football, basketball and hockey team, three Event Coordinators would be retained. As the entry level position, the Event Coordinator is relegated to long hours, ensuring that the team or event for which he is responsible runs smoothly. This requires being the first person at the venue in the morning and the last one to leave in the evening. It also requires a tremendous amount of overtime, as these events are commonly held at night or over the weekend.

As with most entry level positions, the compensation for an Event Coordinator is usually minimal. These very competitive and draining positions begin at an average annual salary of about $35,000. When calculated by the hour, these coordinators are making about as much as the Public Relations Director for the affiliated professional franchise! At the other end of the salary scale, the General Manager positions can command in excess of $100,000 annually if the venue they manage is of substantial size and has a similar propensity for revenue generation.

SPORTS-MARKETING "DRIVEN" CORPORATIONS

Since they comprise a major portion of sports management positions available today, sports-marketing "driven" corporations are the focus of this third group within the sports management industry. When the term "sports-marketing driven" is used, it is not intended to mean that sports-related activities are responsible for the success or failure of the firm. The term is used to describe those firms which have a large stake in the athletics business—either as a sponsor, advertiser, or owner.

Sports-related activities may "drive" a firm but, without other important business cornerstones such as a qualified executive management staff and competent strategic planners, etc., the firm will be doomed to failure. People, not sports-related activities, are responsible for well-rounded, successful firms. However, combining quality personnel with appropriate sports marketing activities will often lead to successful campaigns—at least that's what many of America's largest corporations believe.

In the early 1990's, U.S. corporations spent nearly $25 billion annually on sports advertising, sponsorships, and related events. The three largest companies accounted for $1.25 billion alone: General Motors ($445 million), Philip Morris ($405 million) and Anheuser-Busch ($400 million).

As previously mentioned, these firms participate in sports for a variety of reasons—not the least of which is the ability "to pitch" to a captive target market. The employment opportunities are enhanced as these "Fortune 500" companies continue to devote significant portions of their advertising budget to athletics. Within these larger "sports-marketing driven" firms, it is commonplace to have an in-house sports marketing division comprised of twenty or more management professionals.

Numerous Sports Marketing Managers report to the Director of Sports Marketing. As managers, these staff members are responsible for negotiating deals, working with wholesalers, and devising marketing strategies and other business plans for the event or team they represent. For example, certain managers handle amateur sports while others work the franchise market. Individual sports, such as golf or volleyball, will be the primary concern of other managers, as appropriate. In short, these managers earn in the neighborhood of $50,000 annually to ensure that the event runs smoothly and to the satisfaction of the Director who may be earning up to $100,000 a year.

Assisting these managers are a number of entry level associates. Associates implement the plans and strategies of their superiors. With a starting salary of approximately $25,000 annually, these well educated, hard working professionals make sure the banners are properly hung, the sixty foot inflatable beer cans are free of leaks, and that all associated "grunt" work has been effectively completed.

This cynical undertone is because these functions do not typically call for "skilled labor." Many of the marketing professionals at these larger corporations have been classically trained in marketing. That is, most have received excellent educations and have previous product or sports marketing work experience. Witnessing these incredibly qualified individuals perform relatively menial tasks says quite a lot about our collective desire "to work in sports."

Naturally, these associates are also responsible for more traditional marketing functions. Unfortunately, the majority of their time is spent following up on details and assisting their managers.

In addition to this sports marketing division, many large sports marketing "driven" corporations have an in-house media group. This media group, which may have its own staff of a dozen or more, handles the purchase of advertising time. While they do not necessarily devote their entire time to sports, they are responsible for coordinating sports advertising for the firm. Other duties carried out by the group include the acquisition of advertising time for non-sports campaigns, in addition to serving as a liaison between the advertising and public relations agencies.

Since these "Fortune 500" corporations are so large, they customarily have multiple advertising agencies which handle different product and service lines or market to a specific demographic market. These agency representatives, or account executives as they are sometimes called, work closely with the firm to ensure the most successful campaign possible. An agency may have a number of account executives working on sports related issues but, once again, sports is likely to comprise only a portion of their time.

Public relations firms are also retained by these larger companies. Like the advertising agency, public relations firms play a very specific role in the sports marketing process. Basically, they handle all media related issues including the creation of promotional campaigns, the publicizing of sports related events, and community relations such as product giveaways at events.

Once again, however, these public relations firms spend only a part of their energy on specific sports-related matters for the client. Accordingly, the half dozen or so public relations representatives in each region spend time working in other areas such as general publicity, community relations ("Don't Drink and Drive," for instance), and "damage control."

We have just touched on a number of the reasons why corporations participate in sports on the sponsorship level. To review, these firms are willing to spend big dollars in the sports marketplace in order to advertise and promote their products or services. An organization's specific objectives include increased publicity, the generation of goodwill, and a sense of belonging. Additionally, devoting large portions of the advertising/marketing budget to sports is a terrific idea when those consumers attending the event, or watching it on television, are within the established target market for the product or service. The ability to cross-promote, direct market, or build product awareness is also an important element of sports marketing.

Those corporations which do not have a distinct sports marketing orientation but do participate as sponsors have relatively small staffs devoted to the sports marketing function. It is not unusual, for example, for a financial services firm, such as a bank, to employ fewer than six mid-level managers to fulfill these duties. This is not uncommon for regional or local firms where limited resources are devoted to sports and sports marketing activities. Even in the event that a half dozen corporate professionals are involved, it is not likely that sports marketing activities require more than 25-30 percent of their time. In many cases a full-time staff of one or two can effectively handle everything.

A primary reason for this is that an outside advertising agency typically is responsible for the media related activities. This leaves the corporate marketing staff in a position to "trouble shoot"—that is, make sure the program advertisements are correct and that appropriate signage is visible at the venue. Essentially, then, the sports marketing staff of a sponsoring company confirms that the agency is effectively implementing any established marketing strategy.

Much of the sports marketing staff's time is spent managing the personal relationships that have evolved from their participation in athletics. This would include the institution's strategy for allocating the "merchandise" received from the sponsorship—like season tickets and vouchers for pre-game cocktail mixers.

Some of this merchandise is distributed to valued customers and business acquaintances, while the remainder may be given to an internal unit based on performance. For example, the division which increased sales the most over a given period of time may be given the "Company's Seats" for the night. The ability to attend a sporting event with a colleague or prospective client is a great way to build a relationship; allowing the firm's top producers to attend a big game is a terrific way to build morale and recognize a job well done.

Other duties of the sports marketing staff include incorporating the sports marketing activities into the firm's master marketing plan. Since sports comprises only a part of the total marketing budget, it is critical to have the message presented to the consumer in these sports related ads carry a similar message as the one created for the overall marketing strategy.

These limited sports marketing opportunities are usually salaried positions with an occasional bonus. Nonetheless, the professionals are compensated based on their position in the firm as a whole. Since sports marketing may represent only 25 percent of the staffer's duties, compensation is based on the sum of the functions performed. In the case of the financial service firm described above, the base pay ranges from $30,000 for an entry level staffer to about $100,000 annually for upper management. It is important to note that sports marketing experience at the regional or local level may serve as an excellent "springboard" to an opportunity with a firm for which sports marketing is a significant focus and priority.

Sports marketing positions similar to those addressed in this chapter are available throughout Corporate America. While these jobs may appear difficult to find, and even tougher to land, one must only use a little imagination and a lot of ingenuity. For instance, have you ever checked a game day program to find local sponsors or firms who participate in sports? Upon your next visit to a sporting event, purchase a program and scan it for event sponsors. You will find financial institutions, airlines, automobile manufacturers, consumer products companies, publishing interests, breweries, and manufacturers of consumer durables. You will be astounded by the number and size of the corporations, both locally and nationally, which participate in sports marketing.

The idea of thumbing through a game day program may seem a little far-fetched. If so, why not pay attention to a few television commercials run during your favorite team's time-out? You could also listen to the names of the firms sponsoring the local sports news on radio and television for ideas. Whatever the approach, you will quickly notice a number of organizations attempting to capitalize on the popularity of sports—why shouldn't you be among them?

Local and smaller regional firms such as athletic clubs, manufacturer's outlets of athletic apparel, sports memorabilia shops, and sporting goods chains also provide sports marketing opportunities. However, due to the relatively limited number of positions available and the fact that these positions are not considered "sports marketing" for the purposes of this text, they are not further discussed here. However, work experience in these areas can be invaluable to the individual who hopes to work his way into the mainstream of the sports marketing business.

FINANCIAL MANAGEMENT AND
BUSINESS CONSULTING INTERESTS

The final group of sports management firms which offers services to athletes and other sports related entities provides consulting and financial management. These companies handle the personal financial affairs of athletes, teams, and sports organizations, as well as more "traditional" clientele.

The first type of company within this group is the business management and/or accounting firm. Since many of the services offered by these two entities overlap, they are considered jointly in this discussion. However, the quantity and scope of the services provided by each firm may differ, much like the diversity in the previously mentioned sports management firms.

The phrase "full business management" is really a synonym for monitoring day-to-day personal business activity. Examples of this include the reconciliation of individual bank statements, the preparation of personal checks for bill paying purposes, and general ledger preparation which enables the financial manager to more easily summarize quarter-end financial data. These activities are assumed by the financial manager in order to provide the athlete or entity with an accurate and timely accounting of the over-all financial position. This snapshot, if accurate, allows the client to make the best future financial decisions based on his current and projected cash flow. This projection is most often reflected in quarterly or monthly financial reports which highlight one's financial well-being.

Related business management services commonly provided include investment monitoring and risk vs. return analysis. Note that unless licensed to do so, most business management and accounting firms do not sell investments. Rather, they counsel their clients on the ramifications of potential acquisitions. Within this monitoring process, it is likely that the management firm would also provide conservative advice in the areas of retirement and estate planning. Also provided is review and assistance, if necessary, of potential property acquisitions. Included in this would be an analysis of financing alternatives, as well as an economic review of the quality of the investment itself. Related to this, business managers often evaluate business opportunities which customarily "find" their way to especially young, financially liquid, athletes earning mega-salaries.

Finally, these managers conduct a review of the insurance portfolio to ensure adequate coverage at competitive rates. The insurance products which are standard for individual athletes include health, life, and disability among others.

All of these activities are undertaken as part of a larger financial planning framework. In the event that the athlete may have an outside financial planner, the business management group simply acts as an additional check and balance, making sure all financial matters are in order.

As the aforementioned activities are assumed, the most renowned business management firms, especially the accounting firms, are constantly involved in tax planning for their clients. Long before preparation of state and federal returns is required, the managers analyze and review the client's status. This includes corporate and partnership accounts, as well as estate and private foundations. The purpose of this analysis is to ensure the most favorable tax treatment allowed by law.

These sports management firms provide added value to the client in several ways. First, they preserve the capital of the client by advocating conservative financial and tax advice. Business management firms and accountants enable the athlete to build a future by suggesting and monitoring those activities that provide long-term growth with minimal risk. Finally, as with the negotiating agent, financial managers act as the financial shield—protecting the athlete from the inevitable onslaught of financial requests.

In a similar fashion, accounting and business management firms typically act as team members (as discussed in Chapter 4), working in conjunction with an athlete's agent, marketing representative, and attorney. This type of comprehensive business management can cost the star athlete tens of thousands of dollars per year, depending on the number of services provided. Charging either a management fee—a percentage based on some pre-determined criteria—or on an hourly basis, the firm employs the same caliber of business professionals and support common throughout Corporate America.

It is not unusual for the sports management portion of an organization to be a division or even an affiliate or subsidiary of a larger, full service management firm. For instance, one of the "Big 6" accounting firms may have a division dedicated to the development of entertainment clientele. If this is the case, it would usually require the newly hired staff professional "to earn" an opportunity to work on this prestigious staff.

Banks and trust companies are also participants in the sports management business. These financial institutions are structured to handle much more than the traditional retail and investment banking functions. Many of the larger banks and all of the trust companies offer what can generically be called "private banking" or "trust services." This private banking/trust function is comprised of many of the business management services listed above, with one notable exception: these organizations actually build and manage the investment portfolio of the athlete as well. This essentially allows the athlete or organization to have a "one-stop-shop" for financial services. This one-stop-shop is regularly viewed as the major benefit of having this type of management group manage one's financial affairs.

Retail banking services are also a part of the comprehensive financial package offered by these institutions. Customized credit, enhanced personalized service, and other financial perks all accompany this relationship.

It is not unusual for these institutions to also acquire the assets slated to be managed. In short, the bank or trust company plans, implements, and reviews the entire financial status of the client. In terms of compensation, these banks and trust companies charge an asset management fee, usually about 1 percent, in exchange for their expertise. This fee is based on the total assets under management and creates an incentive for the portfolio manager to increase the value of the portfolio. Since the management firm is not paid on a commission basis, there is no incentive to make unnecessary trades or churn the account. Instead, the manager is rewarded with a larger management fee as the value of his athlete's portfolio continues to climb.

As with the accounting firms and business management groups previously mentioned, these organizations add value and retain professionals in much the same manner. As a vital team member, a bank or trust company will have the awesome responsibility of performing multiple roles for the affluent star. Responsibility for this account can become a burden if it is not correctly managed, as fewer checks and balances exist when one, full service firm is handling the entire financial management.

Other service providers, such as brokerage houses and insurance carriers, also participate in specific areas of the sports management industry. These participants, however, usually play a very defined role as a team member either providing products—an insurance policy, for example, or services—the trading of a security, etc. Even in this specified role, they play a very important part as they facilitate the overall financial plan while serving as an integral part of the financial team. However, these companies do not usually offer the type of comprehensive management functions and large scale employment opportunities described throughout this chapter. Accordingly, affiliated financial services are not reviewed in detail.

THE "BIG 3"

Within the last quarter century, three large, full service sports management companies have flourished. These three, namely IMG, ProServ, and Advantage International have developed outstanding corporate identities by concentrating their efforts on quality and hard work—and a little bit good luck and some incredible timing.

It is this type of firm that many of us identify as "sports management" in the United States. That is, these are the headliners in corporate sports management, offering a wide variety of services for their clientele; a clientele that consists of corporations and special events in addition to athletes and entertainers. On the surface, these three may appear very similar. However, a closer look reveals significant differences in both expertise and corporate philosophy.

The first of these three firms to be discussed is International Management Group (IMG), founded by Mark McCormack. A collegiate golf standout from William & Mary, McCormack attended Yale Law School before beginning his law career in Cleveland, Ohio. As an attorney, McCormack initially handled player exhibitions and contracts. This background and experience enabled him to win the trust of a very young Arnold Palmer in 1960. Upon agreeing to represent Palmer, McCormack signed who later became IMG's first client. Gary Player, an unknown at the time, and Jack Nicklaus, a newly turned professional, also signed on with McCormack shortly after Palmer's commitment. From these not so humble beginnings, IMG has become one of the premier firms in athlete representation and event management over the last thirty years.

IMG, whose world headquarters are located in Cleveland, boasts in excess of twenty offices in more than a dozen countries. Employing hundreds of specialists in such fields as marketing, finance, law, broadcasting, tax, publishing, public relations, and arts management, IMG provides a wide array of professional services to its many divisions.

Within client representation, for example, the firm handles career management, financial planning, marketing, long-term career counselling, accounting, and contract negotiation. These services are performed for broadcasters, musicians, fashion models, and authors, as well as athletes, of course. Athletes represented by IMG's over the years include Dennis Conner, Chris Everett, John Madden, and Alain Prost. Additionally the firm has represented such non-athletes as Rolex, the British Open, and the Nobel Foundation by assisting them in the development of sports marketing campaigns.

IMG has also been recognized as a leader in sports event management, television production, rights representation, and financial services. Many athletes and organizations consider the quality of IMG's work and international presence to be unparalleled. However, two of its major competitors beg to differ.

The first, ProServ, is smaller than IMG, but shares many similarities, including an almost identical circumstance regarding its inception. Donald Dell, serving as the Captain of the Davis Cup Team in 1969, founded ProServ by agreeing to represent Arthur Ashe and Stan Smith. Much as McCormack dominated golf, Dell and his company were a tremendous force in the world of tennis—and continue today as an industry leader in sports management.

Headquartered in Arlington, Virginia, ProServ has a staff of approximately 175 which works out of ten offices located in four countries. In addition to representing 150-200 athletes, ProServ also generates revenue from promoting sporting events and representing corporate clients who are looking to cash in on sports sponsorships. Like IMG, ProServ also has television and publication interests and prides itself on a stellar reputation (ProServ).

ProServ's individual sports clients include the likes of Pete Sampras, Stefan Edberg and Gabriella Sabatini in tennis; cyclist Greg Lemond; swimmer Janet Evans; and volleyball great Karch Kiraly. Through an affiliate company, ProServ Basketball and Football, the firm also represents "Dream Team" NBA stars Patrick Ewing and Michael Jordan, as well as recent football superstars Desmond Howard and "Rocket" Ismail.

All in all, ProServ and IMG have much in common: they each offer a very similar array of services to athletes and organizations, both pride themselves on integrity and professionalism and, of course, each has a client list that reads like a "Who's Who" in sports.

Nonetheless, a third sports management firm hoping to provide many of the same sports management functions arrived on the scene in 1983.

Believing their niche to be event marketing, Advantage International has concentrated its efforts on this evolving discipline of sports marketing. Advantage International's current employment statistics mirror those of ProServ—150 employees in ten offices on four continents.

With respect to services offered, Advantage feels it has the competitive edge in the areas of event marketing consultancy, event representation, event management, corporate hospitality, and athlete marketing.

This edge, believes Advantage, is created by its ability as a strategic planner, listening first to the client's needs and then developing an appropriate course of action based on the circumstances and resources available. It is likely, though, that both IMG and ProServ would espouse similar confidence.

Since their specialty is consulting and event marketing, consider some of the companies who have entrusted their event marketing to Advantage: BMW, Compaq, Cadillac, British Petroleum, and General Motors. Needless to say, Advantage has carved out a nice piece of the sports management industry in its first ten years.

While each of these firms promise personal service and a professional commitment, many athletes and organizations do not feel that they will receive *enough* personal attention from larger firms. Most athletes prefer to be the largest fish in a rather small pond rather than a just another big fish in the ocean. This is the primary reason why the types of sports management companies discussed earlier in the chapter can continue to compete with the "Big 3." The "Big 3" apply proven business practices in structured corporate environments. This methodology leads many athletes and other sports entities to pursue smaller groups that are less "corporate" in their appearance.

SPORTS MANAGEMENT COMPANIES: WHAT'S NEXT?

The future of these sports management companies appears bright, provided they remain focused and continue effective strategic planning. The sports marketing/public relations firms will be forced to become even more creative as a globalized sports market creates athlete clutter. Differentiating their respective clientele will become an even larger priority since the opportunity will exist to tap into this international market. Accordingly, an aggressive promotional stance, including community involvement and personal appearances, may make the difference between an average and outstanding marketing career.

Special event management firms will be required to continue providing events that enable sponsors to access very concentrated target markets. These firms must also demonstrate an overall level of financial efficiency as corporate sponsors are becoming, and will remain, very cost conscious. Special event managers are going to be in a position to capitalize on the globalization of sports by increasing the quantity and diversity of events hosted. Creating international events will enable these firms to offer sponsors a more attractive option—captive global audiences. As these captive global audiences arise, special event management firms will be poised to raise additional revenue through the rights acquisition of attractive events.

Managing a more efficient sports complex will continue to be the major challenge for venue management firms. Adding value by reducing overhead and increasing the number of events held at a particular venue is going to be a major priority. Accomplishing this will lead to increased efficiency which will be positively reflected in the management fee they charge.

The large, sports-marketing driven corporations are certain to face the same issues challenging Corporate America as a whole. For example, these firms will devote the appropriate resources necessary to ensure the cost effectiveness of sports related campaigns. This will be accomplished, at least in part, by determining whether current rights fees enable them to purchase desired air time. Along these lines, an added emphasis will be placed on strategic planning, planning that closely scrutinizes the dollars dedicated to the growing global sports market. Any excess "fat" will be eliminated. As many of their campaigns will have an international flavor, sports marketing driven corporations may begin marketing more universal products and services during sports telecasts.

Related to this concept is the likelihood that some of these companies will aggressively pursue becoming "full service" organizations. For example, Nike, desiring full control over its endorsers, has entered the management field by all but assisting in athletes' contract negotiations and by producing sporting events. While many cry "conflict of interest," Nike not-so-quietly continues to build an international sports conglomerate. One must wonder if they will be the exception or the rule as the 21st century approaches.

Finally, financial management and consulting interests may be presented with the greatest opportunity within the sports management business. The increased specialization in the financial community will allow these firms to offer athletes greater investment and managerial alternatives. This unbundling of financial services should serve to increase the size of the athlete's "team" as more specialists will become involved. As more specialists assist the athlete, a more efficient "check & balance" system is created, to the significant benefit of the wealthy sports clientele. As the world economy continues to develop, so too will the sports finance community. This growth will open up new financial markets and increase the number of athletes seeking conservative financial management.

CAUSE AND EFFECT

The sports management business, much like the other four areas encompassing the business side of sports, contributes to the overall success and well being of all industry participants. For example, it is not unusual for sports consulting groups to assist athletic departments in a number of situations. Helping an athletic department run more efficiently by reducing expenses and/or increasing revenue, counseling the department on matters dealing with the NCAA, or providing motivational and leadership advice to the staff are all areas in which sports management companies support the interests of the athletic department.

Agents, when acting as members of a larger, full service representation team, benefit from sports management companies as well. Retaining an appropriate management party can make the agent appear even more professional in the eyes of his client, as this team play highlights an agent's commitment to the best interests of his players. As this management team continues to provide quality services for the player, the agent stands to benefit from this success as he will gain referrals from existing clients and enjoy a strategic advantage when recruiting new athletes.

Sports management firms provide professional sports franchises with a number of services that favor their bottom line. They secure corporate sponsorships which add revenue directly to the team. Sports management firms also reach those message resistant consumers, which leads to increased sales of the products and services targeted toward the sports consumer. As sales increase, the demand for advertising time rises, resulting in a rise in the amount of money demanded for network contracts. As these media related contracts increase, a similar rise in gross revenue is witnessed at the franchise level.

Related to the aforementioned issues are other advantages gained by the media from its relationship to sports management companies. For instance, without the sponsorships developed by these firms, many athletic events could not take place. Therefore, special event marketing plays a vital role in the ultimate profitability of many media interests. This is especially true with respect to cable television, where many "made for TV" events are shown.

12

DOLLARS
AND NONSENSE

*B*ert Geiger, a career minor league baseball player with the Detroit
Tigers, Chicago White Sox and Los Angeles Dodgers, now specializes in
asset allocation and risk management for highly compensated
individuals. It was during this seven year minor league career that
Geiger was able to witness, first hand, the financial needs and concerns
of professional athletes.

Bert has used these personal experiences to build a successful
financial planning firm for high net worth professionals, business owners
and entertainers, especially athletes. Currently, he serves as Vice
President for Financial Planning Network & Securities, Inc. in Atlanta,
Georgia. FPN & Securities, Inc. is a full service financial planning and
investment management firm which currently has approximately twenty
professional baseball players as asset management and financial
planning clients.

There are only two areas in athlete representation that impact the
player for his entire life: the provision of financial services, along with
managing an athlete's financial future, and the providing of conservative,
comprehensive accounting and tax related services.

With respect to financial services, the goal is to make absolutely certain that the athlete maintains his standard of living once he or she has retired from competitive athletics. This can be accomplished through a close working relationship between the financial parties and the athlete. These parties, serving as a check and balance system, can work together to build the solid investment portfolio required for the client to maintain the standard of living to which he has become accustomed.

I often ask my clients a somewhat strange question, "Do you remember Al Capone?" Capone, a gangster by trade, was the guy that neither the FBI nor the Bureau of Alcohol, Tobacco & Firearms was able to prosecute. However, the Internal Revenue Service **was** successful in its attempt to curtail his shady activities. The bottom line: you can run, hide from, and deceive almost everybody—but not the IRS. "Don't mess with the IRS," I tell my clients, "They'll have the last word, every time."

If a mobster like Capone can't dodge the IRS, certainly professional athletes will have even less success. This is why it is imperative that the athlete retain someone who is capable of managing his complex tax situation. Accordingly, financial planners and brokers must work as a team to ensure proper tax planning and compliance. While professional athletes may not hold the same disdain and disregard for the Establishment as the late Mr. Capone, they are likely to suffer similar consequences if they do not adhere to tax laws.

Much like the personal representation process where numerous sports agencies compete for the right to negotiate the athlete's contract, the financial management portion of the sports business is equally competitive and diverse with large brokerage houses such as Merrill Lynch, Shearson Lehman, and Paine Webber competing directly with small companies such as FPN. In between the service firms are a host of mid-sized firms offering similar services. It has always seemed to me that the size of the firm was not nearly as important as the individual relationship one has with his client. Moreover, regardless of size, each firm is always in search of qualified individuals who are in the enviable position of bringing in new business immediately. In this scenario, qualified means that the individual already has any necessary professional licenses, has been in the financial services business for a number of years, and has an established and portable client base.

However (from my vantage point), it is difficult to work for one of these larger brokerages for a couple of reasons. First, most of them have sales quotas where the brokers are instructed or encouraged to sell the firm's own investment product—regardless of whether that particular investment makes sense given the needs of the client. Second, the larger brokerage firms do not have a clear understanding of how much work is involved in the solicitation and management of athletes. Consequently, it may not be time or cost effective for them to pursue athlete accounts. Nonetheless, these firms actively pursue athletes because of the high number of transactions present in most athletes' portfolios. Consider that many athletes regularly invest upward of $1,000,000 in various investments. On the other hand, it may require as many as fifty other individual investors like you and me to achieve this same dollar level of investments. A couple of "big" sports clients and a financial planner or broker can make a steady living.

Whatever the size of the firm, the group's ability to diversify among investments while simultaneously maintaining individual client interest is most important in reaching the athlete's personal financial goals and objectives. Without the proper diversification, an athlete's ability to maintain a high standard of living is significantly reduced.

So, what propelled me into the business of helping athletes secure a sound financial future? For starters, there has been and will continue to be outside influences, such as a teammates, family friends, or even coaches that feel prepared to provide financial advice to the athlete. This can either enhance the athletes position or, more than likely, hinder his ability to maintain his newly acquired wealth. It is because of these "advisors" and their consistently poor advice that I believed my services would be beneficial to the sports community.

The other major reason I entered the business was because I lost *a lot* of money in highly leveraged limited partnerships, as did many athletes in the early eighties, when I was playing. Both my broker and I were consumed by greed. His greed was the result of potentially lucrative commissions; mine was predicated on the guarantee of massive returns and tax write-offs. Having witnessed these losses first-hand, I knew that it was necessary for me to educate and protect other players from falling into the same trap.

Establishing a career in the field of financial services is not without its difficulties. For example, dealing with a player's agent can, at best, be a trying experience. These representatives, along with their firms, in many cases want to manage their client's money. They wish to handle the athletes' money for one very obvious reason: if they manage the financial affairs of their clientele, they can make even more money through both management fees and added commissions. Unfortunately, athletes typically fare very poorly in these situations as conflicts of interest surely exist. For example, some agents set up their own investment deals while others receive referral fees for steering athletes into investments which directly benefit the sports agency.

In the early eighties, the player-agent did everything for the athlete: negotiate the contract, prepare tax returns, and arrange investments. Now, ten years later, the athletes have wised up, handing out the different responsibilities to those for whom he has respect and trust. This establishes an appropriate check-and-balance in the financial services arena and enables the athlete to concentrate on the task at hand, playing professional sports.

Another difficulty exists as many athletes believe, and legitimately so, that financial advisors are going to abscond with their funds— essentially taking advantage of the under-educated and financially unsophisticated athlete. And, believe me, this happens regularly. For instance, in 1991 several NFL players were forced to sue their broker and his firm for the gross mismanagement of their assets. In this particular case, not only did the broker have to make financial restitution for the lost monies but is also serving a prison term of three to five years.

While this unfortunate situation resulted from the athletes granting their advisor(s) power of attorney privileges, it does not excuse the broker's indiscretions or liability. Whenever I hear that an athlete has granted someone power of attorney, I immediately question whose interests the advisor has in mind—his client or his own.

Aside from the financial horror stories, working with the professional athlete can be a very rewarding and lucrative experience. Even though most entry level positions command annual salaries in the low twenty thousand dollar per year range, the upside earnings potential is almost unlimited. Additionally, the more money one manages, the more money one earns. Income derived from the financial services industry is often based on what are called "pay-outs." Pay-outs are a percentage of the fee collected for conducting a transaction; payouts generally range from 30-70 percent of the fee depending on the type of product sold and the size of the firm completing the transaction. Generally speaking, payouts at the larger brokerage firms tend to be less than the small firms due to their ability to capitalize on the volume of transactions completed.

It is extremely satisfying to know that you are in a position to make a comfortable living for yourself while simultaneously enhancing your client's wealth. The specific value I am able to add is financial security—today, tomorrow, and throughout the athlete's retirement years. Helping both you and your client reach long-term financial goals makes everyone involved quite content.

In order to be successful in this financial services area, one must realize that most athletes come from a relatively disadvantaged financial background and, in the case of baseball players (my primary area of interest), many come straight out of high school. Regardless of the potential client's lifestyle or education, one thing remains constant: whether a doctor, lawyer, businessman, or professional athlete, we are taught how to go out and *make* money but not how to *manage* it once we have earned it.

If someone were to ask me today, "Knowing what you know today, what would you have studied in college to prepare for a career as a financial planner for professional athletes?" That's easy: psychology. I mention psychology because of the many outrageous personalities and crazy idiosyncrasies one faces when dealing with athletes. Other, more business oriented disciplines include business and securities law, risk management, and personal finance.

I'm constantly amazed at how little professional athletes save and prepare for their future after sports. I guess they are making up for those lean collegiate and minor league years when they had meager salaries and uncertain futures. You might remember the saying, "The more money you make, the more money you spend"—I often think this was first spoken by one of my athlete-clients.

For example, I handle the financial affairs for one of baseball's highest paid pitchers who described an early minor league experience. It seems that he was supporting his wife and son on only about $500 a month. In order to make ends meet, he was forced to accept financial aid from his family *and* live with three other players. Upon making it to "The Show," he made up for this enormous amount of sacrifice by treating himself and his family to many of the luxuries that we, as working professionals, consider commonplace—a car, home, dishwasher, etc. Fortunately, for both of us, he realized the abbreviated nature of competitive athletics and has built a large, conservative investment portfolio that will carry him throughout his post-career activities—without the fear of living with teammates ever again.

As a concerned financial planner, it is my duty to educate the athlete about the benefits of saving for his financial future. After all, the average length of a player's career is only four years. And while the average career is only a few years, an athlete's financial plan is an on-going, ever-changing strategic plan that addresses changes in salaries, the economy and the alteration of personal goals and objectives. It is up to me, therefore, to begin this education process from the time I first contact a prospective client.

Surprisingly enough, I am seldom in contact with the players' agents or other personal representatives, with the possible exception of the accountant. For the most part, the only time one of these service providers contacts me is when he thinks I may be in an adversarial or competitive position relative to his business interests. Otherwise, my communication is almost entirely with the athlete himself.

When I entered the business in 1985, I had no idea that professional athletes' salaries would escalate to the unconscionable levels of today. How much longer this trend will continue is up to the owners and *their* financial advisors. But I know one thing for sure: as salaries continue to escalate, athletes *should* have larger sums to save and invest. This, it is hoped, will have a very positive affect on my business, as my earnings will grow along side the salary increases enjoyed by the players. Today, for instance, one steady major league player can generate the same amount of income as five or six comparable players did only five years ago.

This being the case, I believe the industry must continue to institute stringent regulations regarding the trading and subsequent management of securities and begin to require an even greater amount of continuing education for those desiring to sell and/or manage investments in the years to come. The sheer number of new products and services being offered every year is unbelievable. Without some type of monitoring system, consumers, and especially athletes, will be placed in a very precarious position, relying on professionals who may not actually be qualified to render the necessary financial services.

The process of prospecting for athlete-clients depends largely on which sport you wish to pursue. One must recall that the most important products being sold are **you** and your **credibility**. You are about to handle one of the most critical phases of an athlete's entire career. Ensuring that his or her (usually high) standard of living will remain long after the playing days have come to an end is an awesome responsibility. Anyway, back to prospecting. I would suggest you review the chapters on how agents secure clients, and apply them in a little more detail. For instance, in baseball, the minor league baseball system is the best place to start developing leads. Subscribing to periodicals such as *The Sporting News* and *Baseball America*, will provide you with the necessary statistics on each player and on every minor league team. In short, the financial manager seeking new clients becomes a "scout" of sorts as he attempts to discover those players with major league potential. The problem arises when the financial advisor is forced to wait for that star minor leaguer to make it to the "Show;" a waiting period that provides the advisor with little income as the minor leaguers are poorly compensated as a rule.

While the legal and ethical requirements for managing an athlete's finances are numerous, I will mention only two. First, one must possess a strong conscience. It is possible to earn large sums of money over a short period of time in the sports business but you will no doubt be out of business in no time if these sums are derived improperly. On the contrary, the conservative professional with long range goals is best suited for industry success over the long haul.

Second, you should obtain your C.F.P. (Certified Financial Planner) certification, a process that usually takes approximately two years. This process is begun by contacting the College of Financial Planning in Denver, Colorado. This institution, which is the only accredited one of its type in the nation, will provide you with the necessary periodicals about the six phases of the certification process. One of the great aspects of this program is that it is possible to achieve certification at either a local school or on your own via independent study.

Additionally, you may want to pursue a Masters of Science Degree in Financial Planning as well as a Series 7 license. The Series 7 license requires diligent study and about $450 in related fees. This license, which results from numerous classes and endless "cramming," focuses on such topics as: mutual funds, stocks, bonds, limited partnerships, and the important rules and regulations associated with the Securities Exchange Commission (S.E.C.) and the National Association of Securities Dealers (N.A.S.D.). Also, bear in mind that one must answer at least 70 percent of the questions correctly on an exam that has 300 questions. Also, a prospective licensee must be sponsored by a broker-dealer.

A Series 7 license allows accredited individuals to sell stock, limited partnerships, bonds, and mutual funds, but does not allow for the sale or purchase of options, commodities, or life insurance products. All things considered, this license is a basic prerequisite for those hoping to actively invest funds on behalf of any other person, including athletes.

None of the above mentioned licenses or professional titles will mean anything, however, unless you have established a trusting relationship with the client in which your credibility and integrity are consistently demonstrated.

Assuming that the necessary prerequisites are met, there are three ways for a financial manager to be compensated for his dealings with professional athletes: A flat fee; a brokerage fee based on products sold; and a combination of the two. The manager who charges a flat fee for his services would likely place the client in what are called "no load mutual funds." In this scenario, neither brokerage fees nor sales commissions are charged. Rather, the fee is derived as a percentage (usually about 1-2 percent) of the total assets invested. On the other hand, those managers who charge a fee based on the products sold generate their income as a commission when products are purchased or sold.

There is yet another area in the field of financial services that requires mention—the potentially lucrative business of arranging insurance policies for athletes. These insurance products typically cover career ending disabilities, life, property, and casualty coverage. Naturally, the sale of these policies mandates that one receive an insurance license. Once again, a week or so of classes is required with an additional couple of weeks needed for the property and casualty component. As usual, a qualifying exam must also be passed. By comparison, however, the insurance exam is nowhere near as difficult as the Series 7 exam.

As the issue of insurance is critical in one's overall financial plan, most financial planners have at least a life insurance license. Potential commissions on these products range from 7-60 percent of the annual premium.

The growth potential of most professional sports is astronomical as both team sports, such as basketball, and individual sports like tennis and golf, continue to enjoy monumental increases in revenue. For example, in baseball, the two newest franchises provide new sources of revenue for each of the professional categories addressed in this book. New teams lead to increased numbers of professional athletes, which increases the likelihood of expanding my financial planning practice.

If you set up your financial services business correctly, you will only need 50 to 75 clients in order to produce a very respectable income for yourself. I say 50 to 75 because this is a service business and each athlete requires individual attention. Maintaining close contact with the client base is critical, as without a keen personal understanding of the financial wants and needs of individual athletes, overall financial success in the industry is virtually impossible.

Occasionally, I wonder where my credentials and personal experiences would lead me if I chose to leave FPN. It appears as though my ongoing desire to work in the financial area of sports management could provide me with the opportunity to work in a similar capacity for a professional franchise or even a sports agency, as both of these employ qualified financial personnel. However, unless a potential endeavor includes working closely with the individual athletes, there is little or no chance that I would aggressively pursue such an option; believe it or not—it's just too enjoyable working daily with professional athletes.

After all is said and done, I wholeheartedly recommend this business to those who would like to be their own boss, enjoy the nuances of the financial services industry, and have a sincere desire to help others plan for a bright and successful financial future. We all have, or at the very least should have, a financial plan. As a result, the field of financial planning will never cease to exist. Granted it may take on a different role in our lives, but it will always be of interest to those of us concerned about long term financial security.

In my opinion, the ideal financial planner must be client-oriented, be in a position to offer a wide variety of products (diversification), and maintain close contact with all parties involved in the development and management of the client's account.

Finally, I'm in business because many people spend more time and energy planning a family vacation than they do their overall financial future. Scary, but true!

OVERTIME

Unlike the other areas described throughout this book, many of the opportunities available in sports management-related companies closely resemble traditional positions within corporate America. For example, structured positions in the areas of accounting, financial analysis, human resource management and, of course, marketing exist with regularity throughout these sports management firms. Accordingly, these positions customarily require an undergraduate degree from a college or university and are compensated in a fashion that reflects the entry level pay scale for positions within most Fortune 500 companies.

Relative to most of the disciplines mentioned earlier in the text, sports management companies tend to adhere more strictly to legal and professional regulations. This is not to say, necessarily, that these individuals are any more or less ethical in their business dealings; simply that a greater degree of personal responsibility is borne by those participating in the business.

Nowhere is this more evident than in the field of personal financial management and business consulting. Strict legislation regulating the financial management of and potential liability to athletes exists throughout this industry. Certification and continuing education is the norm; while the client may not always be aware of unethical or illegal dealings on behalf of his representative, at least a governing body is established to act as a watch-dog in these industries. Again, this was evident in Geiger's description of how one financial manager is now serving time for "managing" athletes' assets.

These reasons contribute significantly to the tangibility of these sports-oriented positions. Prospective employers will have a much better understanding of the personal skills used and duties performed when one is employed by a corporation driven by sports marketing rather than a sports agency or even an athletic department. While the great majority of the skills applied throughout the business side of sports are transferable, most firms maintain a better comprehension of those positions they view as mainstream. This is an important issue as many leave the world of sports in hopes of building successful careers outside the business where tangible experience is heavily favored.

Whether in school or already employed, these more traditional sports organizations offer diverse opportunities. These employment possibilities exist for those who continue to view sports' "big picture." For instance, the point has been made that the five areas described throughout this book are inter-related. In fact, this point can be further defined as the disciplines within sports management companies are similarly inter-related: venue management firms correspond with special event marketers; these marketers work closely with corporate sponsors who, in turn, conduct business regularly with public relations firms. This concept should not be lost by those considering work in the area of sports management, as gaining experience in one will lead to tremendous exposure in each of the others. Again, think big picture.

One cannot begin to assess these big picture opportunities without first considering the consumer. For without the consumer, these sports marketing and management efforts would be for naught. Consumers steer the ship; they are the ones who ultimately decide if and when endorsement opportunities will exist for athletes, if special events will be sponsored by major corporations, and whether venue managers are doing an adequate job packaging their products. While other areas in this book focus on keeping the athlete satisfied and productive, sports management organizations must have a dual focus, paying strict attention to both athletes and end users.

As one might imagine, the total number and scope of positions potentially available in the area of sports management is greater than any other discussed in this text. Specifically, opportunities exist in corporations which produce durable consumer items such as automobiles; within consumer product firms, including those in the soft drink, fast food and brewery businesses, as well as computer manufacturers; and the hospitality businesses which also expend tremendous effort and dollars in the world of sports. The list could go on practically forever but, the point is that once Corporate America is involved, the number of potential jobs swells.

This "swelling" does not even consider the numerous and additional positions found in the public relations or advertising business. Nor does it address possibilities within the areas of venue management, business consulting or the "Big 3."

This being the case, sports management-type companies are perhaps the easiest of the five areas in which to begin gathering work experience. The sheer number of opportunities will provide more practical experience, allow for more latitude in the job search and, most importantly, be perhaps the easiest form of sports-related position available to the recent graduate, especially those with proven academic training in the areas of marketing, finance, and administration.

While the absolute number of positions may be greatest in this area, many devote only a modest percentage of their time to sports-related endeavors. For example, many of the "sports" positions at banks and within advertising agencies only spend about one quarter of their time on sports matters. This can, in fact, be helpful to the job seeker for a number of reasons. Attributing only quarter-time to the sports activities allows one to learn and participate in other areas of the firm, gaining invaluable work experience in the purest form of Corporate America. Spending only a portion of one's time on sports also reduces the stress associated with this high profile position. Since the sports-related activities are only a subset of one's total contribution to the organization, any failure to produce results will hopefully be accounted for by increased productivity in the remaining areas of responsibility. Finally, devoting only a portion of one's work day to sports allows for deliberate and steady growth in the sports business, making it difficult to make that big mistake early on in one's sports career. Once again, it boils down to timing, perseverance, and patience.

Gaining credible work experience in this area is arguably the best way to network within the entire sports industry. As previously mentioned, the areas described throughout this manuscript are inter-related, and this especially holds true with respect to sports management companies. Employees and consultants in this area interact with each of the other factions: with athletic departments in fundraisers and special events; with agents through whom many marketing contracts are finalized; with franchises whose venues and athletes are managed by outside interests; and with the media, without whom, segmenting, targeting, and reaching the consumer would not be possible. In short, one not only works with an athlete and his team but, with the consumer and his team as well. Remember, the big picture always includes athletes and consumers.

Corporations capitalize on the consumers' love affair with sports by spending money in sports as franchise and event sponsors, as well as by retaining athlete spokespersons to promote their products or services. Each and every one of these dollars is invested with one of the following in mind: to advertise a product line or service; to promote a specific event, such as the release of a new product; to position and differentiate the advertiser's product or service from its competition; and/or to generate goodwill. The primary purpose for spending this money and devoting these resources to sports-related campaigns is that Corporate America believes we are watching and, subsequently buying, whatever they are selling—a product, an idea, goodwill, peace of mind, etc.

A successful niche exists for those who apply this principle effectively and uniquely. Find a need and fill it—that's what we've always been told. Carving a niche by designing a successful campaign, packaging an idea a little differently, or creating a superior public service announcement will allow you to shine brightly in this area of sports. Be creative. It's one of the few areas of sports where this is inherently possible. Use your creativity to spend the corporate dollar while simultaneously boosting your credibility and professional profile. Use your love affair with sports because if you don't, someone else will!

Before reviewing each of the specific areas discussed in this chapter, it is important to re-visit the concept on which this book is founded: increase revenue or reduce cost. One's ability to contain expenditures and/or raise incremental revenue is the result of successful strategic planning, efficient marketing, and conservative financial management. These ideas no doubt apply throughout our entire discussion but, they are especially relevant considering that this specific area of sports more closely resembles Corporate America than any of the other four previously highlighted categories.

Much like sports marketing-driven firms and financial management companies, positions within marketing and public relations firms can be found by checking local listings. These local and regional listings, including specialty magazines such as *ADWEEK* and other related publications including *The Daily Variety*, provide insight as to where potential career opportunities may exist.

Unfortunately, however, it is extremely difficult to land a job through a newspaper or magazine "help wanted" advertisement, as many of the positions have either already been filled and/or are being advertised only due to company policy. It is my opinion that browsing through the want ads is a worthwhile activity because it will uncover employment angles not previously considered. It is not to say that sending a resume is not a good idea; on the contrary, any feedback from a prospective employer associated with the business side of sports will help further define the job search and career interests—interests that often lead to the creation of a position, either at a firm or on your own.

Assuming that you have successfully searched out and begun working for a public relations or marketing firm, what should you anticipate? As previously stated, most of these groups devote only partial resources to the area of sports. Use this to your advantage. Don't resist contributing to non-sports accounts; realize that the opportunity to assist on multiple accounts will lead to building numerous and effective networks—networks that may eventually help open even more doors in the sports and entertainment industry.

On the other hand, whether self employed or gainfully employed elsewhere, other equally significant opportunities may present themselves. For example, one can work at his own pace, working as necessary, and when time permits. Additionally, this format allows for the raising of revenue through commissions charged for endorsements secured. The major benefit here is that a prospective athlete will be more willing to allow a marketer, or series of marketers, to work as much as possible on his behalf without concern for mounting marketing expenses.

Under either marketing scenario there are similarities that affect one's ability to prosper. For starters, this type of work requires very long hours relative to the financial return. While it is true that doing the little things will add up over time, this sweat equity will not be adequately reflected in one's compensation. Moreover, the necessary preparation, which includes establishing an athlete's image and the overall positioning of the client, often takes substantial time and patience. All the while, it will be up to the marketer to act as the fall guy, shaping a client's image by refusing those opportunities which are inconsistent with the athlete's newly formed persona, and securing arrangements that enhance his long term marketability.

Throughout this entire process it is necessary to make certain that the time frame for results, whether financial or otherwise, is consistent with the athlete's expectations. Without this communication and basic understanding, the client will likely retain someone whose time frame more closely parallels his own.

Special event marketing and management groups are for those who enjoy a flare for strategic planning or creativity. Solving problems, such as how to reach fragmented consumer markets and differentiating Corporate America's products and services, are extremely important issues facing those in the special event business. In addition to strategic planning, creativity is possible in its purest form. Consider the unlimited ideas and concepts that surround this type of event. Involving charities, corporations, and celebrities provides a formula for the unusual and unique. Recently, for example, in-line skating (roller-blading) has become an extremely popular sport. Consequently, those with ingenuity have begun staging events for the benefit of all parties concerned, not the least of whom includes the special event marketer!

As usual, gaining work experience as a volunteer or intern while still in college would be extremely helpful in establishing a track record in this business. Ten kilometer races, as well as volleyball and golf tournaments, are held regularly throughout the country: get involved, it will look good on the resume and enable you to meet some of the industry participants.

When working at or for a special event, attention to detail is a must. "Nuts and bolts" activities such as the setting up and dismantling of venues is necessary; so is troubleshooting with sponsors the day of the event. One must also be prepared to handle the inevitable glitches that are common place at large events such as these. Nonetheless, the variety associated with special event marketing makes this industry a very attractive one for those interested in addressing critical marketing issues and creating new and exciting events.

As we have discussed, venue management firms perform critical, behind the scenes roles in the world of sports. These roles essentially "make or break" sports because, without the firms' participation, the hosting of a successful sporting or entertainment event would be impossible.

And, not surprisingly, many of us often forget that they offer limited positions; positions which ultimately begin many professionals' careers in sports. This behind the scenes experience is a great way to find out how sports really works, as one is exposed to the nuances of hosting events and dealing with municipalities. Venue management firms also present a terrific vantage point from which one can witness the constant politicking that takes place in the sports marketplace.

Acting as the glue that holds sports together, venue managers customarily perform a thankless job that requires long hours and yes, relatively low pay. As previously stated, virtually everyone enters these firms as event coordinators, responsible for all functions necessary to host a safe and successful event. The event coordinator position is, in many respects, very similar to the entry level sales job available with the professional sports franchises. In fact, venue management firms tend to employ about the same number of professionals, each handling a slightly different function.

In addition to, or instead of, noteworthy academic training in business, a degree or similar academic pursuits in the field(s) of administration and management would be most beneficial. Combining this educational background with the right "connection" such as an influential sponsor or public agency may create the appropriate mix required to land the elusive venue management position.

There are numerous opportunities available to those employed by venue management firms. These professionals may leave the firm for positions with major vendors, on-site professional franchises, and other affiliated firms such as county or state agencies. It is also reasonable to assume that these qualified staffers would be desirable to the entertainment conglomerates which ordinarily own venue management firms as subsidiaries.

Corporations driven by sports marketing represent the closest form of mainstream American business found anywhere in the sports business. These corporations, which include athletic shoe manufacturers, brewing companies, and automobile makers, provide excellent training in the form of teaching fundamental business principles.

Unfortunately, however, these major firms, many of which spend hundreds of millions of dollars per year in sports advertising and promotion, are right-sizing—trimming the corporate fat while reducing many mid-level management positions. This obviously makes for a much more difficult time when searching for an initial opportunity with one of these organizations.

Much like the rest of the sports management business, sports marketing driven firms must pay keen attention to the consumer. Accessing the defined target market is the key and will remain the primary focus for these sports-oriented organizations as they realize that captive, properly segmented, potential consumers with purchasing power hold the key to profitability. Once again, the big picture dictates that these corporations pay close attention to both athletes and consumers.

Have you ever *really* looked at one of the race cars participating in the Indianapolis 500? How about the court-side signage at a professional tennis tournament? Each of these examples provide ample employment leads in sports marketing and management. These mega-sponsors, often Fortune 500 consumer products and durables companies or their subsidiaries retain classically trained marketers from top notch graduate schools or similarly impressive major corporations such as Proctor & Gamble or IBM. Much to the dismay of these over qualified candidates and staffers, they tend to spend much of their time handling other "marketing related opportunities" (read: grunt work); opportunities and daily functions which many people would find neither fulfilling nor challenging.

In the event that you are already employed by one of these companies, conduct some basic internal research to determine who handles the sports business and from which corporate location the business is operated. Remembering that sports likely represents only a fraction of the overall marketing plan, be prepared to ease into any sports-related position. This is especially true for those working in mid-sized corporations which devote a smaller portion of their resources to sports. As previously mentioned, this partial devotion to the sports business may actually work to your advantage by not forcing you to produce tremendous results immediately.

As has been the case with the other sports management opportunities, those with experience in this corporate environment often find positions in related sports-oriented organizations such as advertising agencies, professional franchises, or another major corporate sponsor with a similar presence in the world of sports.

Financial management and business consulting interests offer opportunities that require a fine balance between analytical and interpersonal skills. As Geiger noted, the ability to service and educate clients is a major responsibility for those in the financial services business. Part of this educational process includes demonstrating where financial planners actually add value—in the areas of capital preservation, proper diversification, and long term asset growth. All of this must be accomplished without bowing to the greed factor discussed by the contributor.

These services provide the financial manager with a fee that is somewhat hidden to the client. The fee, included in most transactions, is simply added to the total cost of the product or service. Accordingly, the athlete or consumer doesn't "see" the cost; rather it is simply deducted from what is supposed to be a growing investment pool.

In a broader sense, most of these firms handle only a small to moderate number of athletes; few handle exclusively athlete-clientele. In fact, there are a minimal number of corporate positions available, whether one has an impressive track record in finance or not. It may actually be beneficial to begin as a sole practitioner, calling your own shots, setting your own hours, and targeting the consumer group of your choice.

Regardless of how one's business is structured, it is important to be prepared to interface with the other members of the athlete's representation team. Even though Geiger seldom corresponds with this group of professionals, many participating in the financial management and business consulting business regularly plan and network with one another.

This interaction can be critical given the degree of regulation in the securities business, the ever-changing banking and savings & loan industry, and the overall unbundling of the financial services business. After all, three or four opinions and varied personal experiences can be helpful in addressing specific financial issues.

To borrow a phrase from Bert Geiger, it is an absolute must to spend more time planning your career in sports management than the family vacation. Remember the big picture, maintain your integrity, and prepare to strike a delicate balance between the athletes' needs and the consumers' demands. When this is accomplished, a career in sports management will last far longer, and be much more fun, than that family vacation.

****

PART VII:
Conclusion

****

13

WHAT'S A NICE GUY LIKE ME DOING IN A BUSINESS LIKE THIS?

Jonathan Grossman, Co-founder of Universal Sports Consultants in Miami, has a diverse background in the sports industry that includes both extensive academic and practical experience. Upon graduation from the University of Miami, Jonathan entered the Sports Management Program at St. Thomas University. By 1985, he had received his Masters Degree in Sports Administration and enrolled at the Nova University Law School in Ft. Lauderdale, Florida. Additionally, Grossman has taught "Issues in Sports Negotiation" in the St. Thomas University's Sports Administration Program.

The contributor's practical experience is highlighted by his current position as Vice President of Universal Sports Consultants, a sports management firm specializing in contract negotiation and marketing. Specifically, his duties involve negotiating player contracts and endorsement agreements for both team and individual athletes, as well as radio and television personalities.

What's a nice guy like me doing in a business like this? To be honest with you, I'm not exactly sure, but several thoughts do come to mind. The following is an attempt to share those thoughts and offer a little 'food for thought' to those considering a career in the sports industry.

While one might sense a distinct air of cynicism throughout the following remarks, be aware that this attitude reflects many of my personal experiences in the industry.

For as long as I can remember, my goal in life was to get up every morning and read the sports page as part of my job. This, of course, was after I realized that I was not going to be the next Joe Namath or Tom Seaver. Although that dream died hard (and early), it didn't stop me from working towards this often unrealistic, far-fetched dream of being in the sports biz. The thought of seeing *my clients'* names in the newspaper box scores or buying a pack of trading cards and seeing one of my player's would send chills up my spine.

When I attended a ball game as a kid I often wondered, "Who is that guy on the other side of the fence? How did he get onto the field? And how does he know Rusty Staub for crying out loud?"

Early on, I decided I was going to be that guy "on the other side of the fence"—an agent. After all, life couldn't be any sweeter than attending games, talking to players and receiving free tickets and endless autographed sports memorabilia (and even going out to dinner with the guys after the game). All of these perks—and a paycheck, too? Have you ever thought about how much money these guys must be earning?

Okay, so these are not the only reasons I chose this particular career path, but they were among the first and most memorable. As I became older (but not necessarily wiser), I began to rationalize the so-called 'mature' reasons why I wanted to work in the world of sports.

For starters, I didn't want to wake up one day, at fifty years of age and ask myself, "What if—?" I know too many people who have enough regrets to last a lifetime—and this was not going to be my fate. Generally speaking, I had always maintained a high level of confidence about my abilities and was not afraid to fail. So, what was the worst thing that could happen?

Next, because of my lifelong passion for sports, I felt I could really make a difference. Contrary to the stuffed-shirt lawyer or accountant, I could relate to the athletes because I knew what their lives were like and, therefore, they could trust me. There was no question in my mind that since I was the only person alive that didn't hate Richard Todd after throwing five interceptions in the 1982 Conference Championship Game, he would appreciate my support and allow me to be his agent.

Further, who wants a 9 to 5 job with no future, sense of accomplishment, fame or fortune? I wanted the job that would allow me to live out my fantasies—and there are few such jobs available. I wanted a job that pumped the adrenaline in my body every morning, instead of multiple cups of coffee. I wanted the job that everyone would envy—a job that would be fun!

At the time, these all sounded like educated, well thought out answers as to why to pursue a career in sports. I must have done a pretty good job of convincing myself because these reasons certainly motivated me to do whatever was necessary to embark on a journey that is far from over.

A ROAD TO GLORY?

By the time I was completing my junior year at the University of Miami, my passion for sports was still consuming my very existence. As a maniacal fan, high school basketball coach, and private basketball tutor, it was becoming very clear to me that I would have a permanent place for sports in my life. While my notions of being the next Seaver or Namath had recently passed, my dream of wearing a world championship ring and getting a call from the President of the United States still shined quite brightly.

During my final semester at The University of Miami and while cutting one of my classes, I decided to see what a career counselor would have to say about my future. During my "informational interview" I was asked the infamous question, "If money were not an issue, what would you do with your life?" Without hesitation, I replied, "Why, I would be a big time sports agent of course! After all, how many of these guys could there be? It can't be that tough, can it?" The counselor informed me of a Master's Program in Sports Administration at St. Thomas University—I dashed out the door in search of a pay phone.

After calling twice just to be sure that this program was accredited and acknowledged by the general sports public, I went for a meeting. Upon talking with the director, I learned the program was only a year and a half and that most of the courses were in the evening. They informed me of the invaluable volunteer experiences (i.e. crowd control at a golf tournament and/or ushering at spring training baseball games) and the internship program after the course work was completed. Already, I'm thinking this will be a picnic—I'll get a tan, meet the key players in the business and be working for a top sports agency within a year!

For those of you wondering why one should attend such a school, as I did, let me tell you exactly why I took the plunge. First, I felt it would give me the time necessary to determine if there was a future for me in this business. Second, it would look great on a resume to have a specialized degree in my chosen field (thinking it would open up the job market for me). Finally, I had already considered going to law school and believed the sports management degree could help my application to law school. For the most part, these were legitimate reasons and this portion of my education did in fact achieve those goals.

However, a program such as St. Thomas' allows you the time to network and investigate the profession if one *actually* does the 'nuts and bolts' work. I learned very quickly that the agents were not going to come to me but that I was going to have to knock on their doors, one by one. I had to spend hours on the phone telling everyone how grateful I was to them for spending just a minute or two speaking to me (despite the fact that I was paying for the call) and reminding me that very few jobs existed. The one constant I kept hearing throughout graduate school from each of these 'contacts' was, "Go to law school—if you go, the jobs will come."

So, after completing my master's degree and completing my internship at a local sports marketing firm (by the way, I was happy just to get the rejection letter from IMG at the time) and writing to every agent and organization I could think of, I went right back to school. My folks sure were happy to see that I had regained my sanity by enrolling at Nova Law School in Ft. Lauderdale, Florida. I could hear them saying, "He wasn't really going to do that sports stuff, was he? A law degree, now *that's* a future," Well, at least somebody was happy!

Despite all the hours of hell that the first year of law school brings, I maintained all of my grad school contacts. I remembered all those well wishers telling me how helpful this degree would be in landing a job in sports. The only problem was that their tune had changed to, "Call me when you get out—we can't use a law clerk this summer—see ya in a couple of years." But it was during this period that my first lesson in persistence paid off.

During graduate school I obtained a directory of agents from The Association of Representatives for Professional Athletes (ARPA) which listed representatives from all over the country—this quickly became the primary resource from which my resume campaign began. By the time I was in law school it had been updated three times with the appearance of an occasional new name or two. On Thanksgiving Eve, I contacted one of these "new listings" in California and was able to reach the agent long enough to give him my sales pitch. Although he primarily practiced law and had only a small 'sports practice,' this opportunity represented the crack in the door I was looking for. That one "cold call" led to three summers in Los Angeles working for the firm, bringing two new football clients into the fold and feeling that I was ready to hit the big time.

Before I tell you how it all works out, let me say a few things about the law school experience. In my second and third years I volunteered for a minor league baseball team in Miami. While I was receiving a great background in administration, it was tough driving from the ballpark to the local bank (at midnight) in order to make our nightly cash deposit, get home at 1:00 AM, *and* make it to my class, The Fundamentals of Federal Income Tax, by 8:30 the next morning. To be sure, my classmates could not understand why I wasn't clerking, making real money, and sleeping regular hours.

They also just could not comprehend why I went to meet with the President of the New York Jets a few hours prior to a final exam even though we all knew that I was not going to be offered a job. The funny thing is that you can't explain the passion of this business to "ordinary" people.

Well, I managed to pass my courses, receive my law degree, move to L.A. to work for the firm, take the bar exam (which is a story in and of itself!) and start working in the industry. Unfortunately, after the second day on the job I was informed that there had been a major "shake-up"—and that all bets were off. After calling most of those contacts I had previously developed it dawned on me that finding another job in sports was almost hopeless. Apparently, drastic times required drastic measures. The one thing that all of my academic pursuits taught me was that I was capable of succeeding on my own. Accordingly, I moved back to Miami, rolled the dice and hung out my shingle.

What did this whole process teach me? For starters, the more education you can get, the better—*but* an education is by no means required. The most important element is experience—anywhere, anytime, anyhow and at any level! A law degree will provide you with a broad base of knowledge and some degree of credibility. It will not, however, give you that first client. Further, unlike the real world, your salary *will not* be commensurate with your education.

The process also enabled me to view many aspects of the business from the "ground up;" and it is very important to know (and learn) something about everything. Remember, even if you're just taking tickets or selling programs, you've begun climbing over the other side of that fence.

Finally, I do believe that education and experience go hand-in-hand

and that they compliment rather than compete with one another. Gain as much as you can of both, make the commitment to follow your instincts and your road should lead to glory.

TOOLS OF IGNORANCE

Working in the sports industry is a lot like playing catcher on a baseball team—most people would want to give it a try but very few actually have the guts to get behind the plate. For the most part, this is a hard, nasty, dirty business where the rewards are few and far between. Though I am only a rookie by industry standards, certain constants have become evident. The following "do's" and "don'ts" may not prevent you from becoming battered and bruised, but I hope they will at least give you a chance to play the game. My advice to all of you is to make certain you are wearing your mask, chest protector and shin guards at all times.

There is an old saying among coaches which goes something like this: "Don't get too high after a win and don't get too low after a loss." While this is sound advice to all athletes, it also applies to those seeking employment in the sports industry. We have all felt the rush of excitement when that first response comes in the mail from a potential employer. I can remember thinking, "Wow, an envelope with the New York Jets logo on it addressed to me!" Never mind that it was a standard 'don't call us, we'll call you' letter. The point was that someone actually acknowledged my existence in the world of sports.

Conversely, there is nothing more disappointing than not receiving a response at all, or worse, thinking you may be close to that dream job only to find out that it was given to the owner's nephew. The emotional rollercoaster associated with this ebb and flow of activity must be handled appropriately. The earlier one learns to take one day at a time and to build momentum in your career slowly and steadily, the sooner he will travel down that previously mentioned "road to glory." Remember, those traits we attribute to great athletes such as maturity, composure, patience and confidence also build great sports executives.

The reality is that there are going to be quite a few "close calls," both positive and negative (with a few more on the negative side) throughout your job search and pending career in sports. It is imperative (for your well being) that your colleagues view you as a young 'Bill Walsh' type—calm, cool, collected and always in control! This will certainly distinguish you from the rest of the pack, many of whom are running around like chickens without heads, sending resumes in all directions.

I can easily recall the chill of the goose bumps the first time I entered a professional franchise locker room—shiny helmets, clean jerseys and the crew from NFL Films all right in front of me. The same was also true the first time I stood on the "other side of the fence," or when a client left me a complimentary set of tickets to the ball game. After all the years of wanting this so much, you just want to yell out to everybody, "Look, I did it!" Unfortunately, you can't—remember, you are a professional!

Perhaps the first action that will dash any hopes of landing that first job in sports is that of revealing that you are an avid fan. There are millions of sports fans in search of that dream job in sports, but no one is going to pay you for your firm allegiance to the team. Rather, your approach must be strictly business, as you must distance yourself from the notorious "Monday Morning" quarterbacks who regularly believe they could run the team better than the organization itself.

After growing up as a die-hard New York Mets fan, I had the opportunity to interview with the franchise's Executive Vice President—a dream come true! We discussed my background, how law school was progressing, job opportunities, etc. Instead of listening to his responses and infinite wisdom, I was busy looking at all the "Mets stuff" (i.e. players' pictures, autographed memorabilia, etc.) in his well decorated office. I still could not believe that I was speaking to the guy who helped build the team! Toward the end of the meeting I just had to tell him exactly how much this meeting meant to me because of my life long passion for the club. What a huge mistake! He leaned over the desk and in a most friendly way said, "Jonathan, in the future, never mention the fact that you are a fan. It is great to be enthusiastic, but you must separate yourself from the bleachers and focus on the office." By now, all the blood had rushed from my face and, to this day, I do not remember shaking his hand to complete the appointment. I may have forgotten the hand shake but I will never forget those words. Remember, you want people to think of you as the Bill Walsh type—not the guy with the face painted green yelling, "Joe Must Go!"

On a more personal note, it is very important to just be yourself and trust your instincts. It will be extremely tempting in the business to put on a facade, essentially coming across as 'Joe Cool,' pleasing everyone. Trust me, athletes can see through you in a heartbeat, and will never respect you if they feel they are being patronized. You can't be all things to all people, especially when dealing with the varied personalities found in the business side of sports.

In order to achieve any level of success in this business, we all must make hard personal decisions. Do you take a job for hardly any money just to gain the experience? Do you try to represent a player even though the prospect is talking with the biggest agent in the country? You have to look yourself in the mirror, be firm in your convictions and give it a shot. There are not that many people you can trust in this industry, so you must be able to have inner confidence to go against the grain and see it through to the end.

If there is one great myth about the sports business it's that sports is a huge industry. While it is true that it is a multi-billion dollar business, be mindful that it is made up of a relatively small number of professionals. In fact, no matter which area you experience, you will interact (either directly or indirectly) with the same people day in and day out. Therefore, your reputation, integrity and character (or lack thereof) will be your calling card throughout the industry. Please don't think "I can screw this guy," and move on to someone else. If you take this approach, you will find many people who will not conduct business with you at all because the word on the street travels very fast!

Finally, regardless of how much education you have or how much work experience you can gather, no one knows everything about anything. However, what you should be striving for is to know something about everything. There is a lot of truth to the notion that knowledge is power. Whether you gain the information about the industry through formal education, work experience, informational meetings or books such as this, the critical issue is to absorb as much information as possible. Once this information is gathered, it is important to determine how much of it you believe and to what extent the information facilitates meaningful conversation and reflection.

Flexibility and diversity are important in this business as evidenced by the inter-relationships of the five areas examined in this book. For example, the agent must be knowledgeable about marketing (sports management companies and the media) so he can maximize his clients' worth; a little bit about the N.C.A.A. (athletic departments) in order to recruit; and have an understanding of sports finance (professional franchise management) in an effort to complete the contract negotiation, etc. Without this broad base of knowledge your dream of a sports career will remain just that—a dream.

HUDDLE UP

By now, many of you are probably thinking to yourselves, "Why does this cynical guy stay in the business? If it is that difficult to enter the industry and that frustrating to participate in it, why bother?" While there are no simple answers, I hope my concluding thoughts suggest a few reasons why I continue to work in sports and why all of you should at least give it "that old college try."

Another famous old sports quote states, "An athlete is nothing more than a little kid in a man's body." Once again, this applies all too often in the case of many sports executives—not to mention all those "would-be" sports business professionals. Because sports evokes such great passion and gets in our blood the way it does, we must all admit to the addiction: Face it, we're all suckers, trapped by the fact that we know exactly what we want to do with our lives. Given the limitless sacrifices we make just to get close to the business, why not go all the way? Since you will never be truly at peace with yourself otherwise, make the commitment, work your ass off and last, but not least—don't let anybody tell you can't do something.

How many careers are there in which a person can really make a difference? Where you can change the course of a life (or lives)? You're right. Not many, but, a job in sports can do that in all aspects of sports and at every level of the business. You might be the College Athletic Director who successfully convinces the student-athlete of the importance of education and the need to prepare for a career in the real world. Perhaps you will become the agent who helps teach the athlete the importance of giving something back to the community—to put a smile on a sick child's face simply by shaking a hand. The chance to have that type of reward and personal satisfaction out of one's career makes a career in sports well worth the time and effort.

Contrary to many other professions, sports will not 'box' you into the common trap of the day-to-day drudgery commonly associated with a "regular job." Rather, you will be meeting people from all parts of the country and beyond, travel to many different areas and experience new things practically every day (any resemblance to a military commercial is purely coincidental). Almost every day, and without warning, I am presented with some problem or scenario that I never imagined when I was back in school. Although at times it can be intimidating, being able to confront, analyze and solve these problems makes for a very well-rounded and content person. So, why bother? Is it worth it? You wouldn't be reading this book if you didn't think so! Those people who can't understand what it means to us to work in this business would never have picked up this book in the first place. But you have, and this should tell you something very important. It means that you have the fire necessary to overcome the odds of finding that first job—the real question, though, is what are you going to do about it?

I hope this narrative has opened your eyes to the realities of careers in sports. As long as you understand what you're getting yourself into, enjoy the long and exciting trip. It is full of detours and long, uphill roads but, for those willing to hang in there, the rewards are spectacular!

Finally, I believe the greatest bit of irony about this business goes back to my childhood. Whenever my grandmother would come to visit us, my brother and I could always expect two things: Having to play the piano (and keep practicing) and, depending on the time of the sports year, a new football, basketball, baseball, etc. As she presented the gift to me she would always shake her head in disgust and ask, "Jonathan, what is this game ever going to do for you?" If she could only see me now! Funny thing is, she is probably watching over all this right now and *still* asking that same question!

14

AT THE BUZZER:
When All Else Fails
Remember These
"Championship Points"

*T*he following final thoughts reflect the critical points stressed throughout this book. They are intended to be referred to, reflected upon, and applied to and within the "real world" of sports management.

First off, be persistent. Realize that there are tens of thousands of students completing their academic training, business professionals attempting career changes, and 'rabid' fans trying to break into the business side of sports. Consequently, it is necessary to be prepared for this competition and to accept the fact that "breaking in" is not likely to happen overnight. It is important to devise a strategic plan that accomplishes your personal agenda. For example, is it possible for you to ease into the business over a period of years or does your timetable permit only planning for your immediate future? A keen understanding of one's ability to remain patient and focused is mandatory for eventual and continued success in the industry.

Creativity is equally important when building a career in sports. Researching, studying and learning the business of sports will enable you to uncover the gaps in the products and services provided in the sports marketplace. These niches will likely include the international explosion of sports, the emergence of new forms of communication, and an increased opportunity for those professionals who provide a unique specialty in the industry.

When developing your "angle" on the business side of sports, take your time. Creative ideas do not come to fruition immediately; they are commonly the result of hard work, discipline, and planning. Angles may also change over time and with increased experience. Place yourself in a position to capitalize on the creative idea when it is uncovered. This can be accomplished by securing the required resources as well as developing the personal network and relationships required for the timely implementation of this creative idea.

Next, always remember the importance of adding value to the product or service you are developing, marketing, or managing. Increasing bottom-line revenue in an easily quantifiable manner, or reducing expenses in a similarly tangible fashion will help you land that first job in sports. This will give employers a reason to retain your services, either as an employee, consultant, or volunteer. Getting started in sports is difficult enough already, so don't make the struggle any more difficult by placing yourself in the position of being just another fixed cost.

The underlying message presented throughout this manuscript is that obtaining work experience in the five major areas which comprise the business side of sports can be most helpful in establishing and building your career. The order in which these categories are experienced is not important. What is important, however, is that one witness each of them first hand. Again, this can be as a volunteer, employee, or independent consultant. Receiving compensation throughout this learning process should not be as much of a priority as gaining the actual hands-on experience. After all, it's not always what you *earn* that counts; sometimes it's what you *learn* that proves to be invaluable in the long run.

Studying and experiencing the 'life-cycle' of the athlete is very important, as this exercise will reveal where opportunities exist for earning a living in the business side of sports. Accordingly, this life-cycle includes collegiate athletic departments, athlete representation firms, professional sports franchises, the media, and sports management companies. Each of these broad areas profits by an athlete's participation in sports. Persistence, creativity, and the ability to add value will maximize the opportunities available within these five disciplines.

Furthermore, attend and become involved in every sports-related event possible. Conferences which address sports management and marketing, seminars relating to the legal environment of amateur and professional athletics, and even sports fundraisers such as memorabilia auctions, and other charity events can provide valuable insight into the industry. Participating in these types of activities will benefit you in a number of ways.

While obviously serving as a great personal experience, these events will also allow you to increase your knowledge base. As this base continues to grow, specific areas of personal interest will also develop. It is identifying these areas of interest that will allow you to concentrate on the specific area(s) you enjoy most. This is critical, as without personal enjoyment and satisfaction, potential success in the industry is all but eliminated. It is similarly important to uncover those areas of sports where no personal interest exists, since a lack of interest will stifle any personal progress and significantly limit one's desire.

Involvement in these events simultaneously enables the participant to acquire "hands-on" practical experience, as well as the unparalleled opportunity to meet the industry's "players." Constant industry exposure to both topics and personalities and a commitment to learning the ins-and-outs of the sports business will provide the tools necessary for capitalizing on that first opportunity to participate in the business side of sports.

Closely related to this discussion is that of the need for either formal academic training or personal continuing education. Formal academic training can range from the completion of graduate studies to obtaining a professional credential. If considering this more formal academic environment, it is important to realize that law school is not the only alternative. In fact, a master's degree in sports management, business, or management science may be equally acceptable, depending upon one's primary areas of interest.

Informally, it is equally important to remain well versed about the developments within the sports management community. In addition to (or instead of) obtaining a graduate degree, researching, analyzing, and reading sports-related publications can serve as a major resource to those in search of a niche in the business. Industry trade journals, legal treatises discussing sports and entertainment related matters, historical works on the evolution of sports in America and books such as this, each contribute to a better understanding of the sports business.

A closing point must be made regarding the numerous relationships formed in the sports community. Although sports is a multi-billion dollar business, it remains a fairly small and relatively closed fraternity. Consequently, it is extremely important not to burn bridges unless it is absolutely unavoidable. It has been said that, "what comes around goes around"—and nowhere is this phrase more applicable than in sports.

Accordingly, it is crucial to regularly do the little things while allowing other industry participants the benefit of the doubt whenever possible. Ultimately, remember to maintain a high level of professional courtesy whenever conducting business.

Finally, enjoy the struggle! Securing a career in the business side of sports will be a tremendous challenge and require relentless determination. Throughout this battle, do not be discouraged by the long hours, hard work, and the initial lack of remuneration. As you begin to experience success, reflect upon all those who told you a career in the business side of sports could not be achieved. Take pride in the fact that you overcame the extremely long odds. Remain motivated, focused, and disciplined. Again, enjoy the struggle—it will make your success that much more satisfying!

BIBLIOGRAPHY

Bodley, Hal. "Players Field Average $1 Million," *USA Today*, April 2, 1992, Sec. A, p. 1.

Code of Conduct for NFLPA Member Contract Advisors, prepared by the National Football League Players' Association (Washington D.C., 1990), Exhibit C.

D'Alessandro, Dave. "Cap Fear," *The Sporting News*, March 9, 1992, pp. 28-30.

Dorsey, Valerie Lynn. "White Unhappy with Black Hiring in NL," *USA Today*, May 29, 1992, Sec. C, p. 12.

DuPree, David. "Players Likely to Encourage Lifting of Cap," *USA Today*, August 1, 1991, Sec. C. p.1.

Hiestand, Michael. "Cost for Day at Ballpark Not Increasing as Rapidly," *USA Today*, April 1, 1993.

Hiestand, Michael. "Even Reputations Can Be Insured," *USA Today*, January 15, 1991, Sec. C.

Hiestand, Michael. "Major League Baseball Ticket Prices Outta Here," *USA Today*, March 3, 1992, Sec. A, p.1.

The History of Advantage International, prepared by Advantage International, Washington, D.C., 1992.

The History of International Management Group, prepared by IMG, Cleveland, Ohio, 1987.

The History of ProServ, ProServ, Arlington, Virginia, 1992.

Kahn, Lawrence M. and Peter D. Sherer. "Racial Discrimination in the National Basketball Association," *The Business of Professional Sports*, p. 72.

Klatell, David A. and Norman Marcus. *Sports for Sale*. New York, New York, 1988.

Knoll, Roger. "Professional Basketball Economic and Business Perspectives," *The Business of Professional Sports*, p. 33.

Lapchick, Richard. "Professional Sports Still Don't Make the Grade," *The Sporting News*, August 2, 1993, page 7.

Lieber, Jill. "Fat & Unhealthy," *Sports Illustrated*, April 27, 1992, pp. 30-38.

Martzke, Rudy. "Owners to Feel Squeeze When TV Money Fades," *USA Today*, April 6, 1992, Sec. C, P. 3.

Miller, James Edward. *The Baseball Business*. Chapel Hill, North Carolina, 1990.

Myers, Jim. "Stereotypes Pit Ability vs. Intellect," *USA Today*, December 16, 1991, Sec. C, p. 1.

NCAA Manual, 1993-94. Overland Park, Kansas, 1992.

Newhan, Ross and Larry Stewart. "Pulling the Plug," *The Los Angeles Times*, February 23, 1992, Sec. C, p. 1.

O'Connor, Robert. *A Complete Guide to Sports Agents*. Dubuque, Iowa, 1990.

Ozanian, Michael K. and Stephen Taub. "Big Leagues, Bad Business," *Financial World*, July 7, 1992, pp. 34-51.

Quinn, Dan. "Johnson Finds Long Road Back to Marketability," *The Sporting News*, January, 1991.

Reilly, Rick. "That's Shoe Business," *Sports Illustrated*, April 26, 1993 p. 76.

Rosentiel, Thomas B. "The National Sports Daily Ceases Publication," *The Los Angeles Times*, June 13, 1991, Sec. D. p. 1.

Scully, Gerald W. *The Business of Major League Baseball.* Chicago, Illinois, 1989.

Secter, Bob. "Batting for Bucks," *The Los Angeles Times*, April 17, 1992, Sec. C, p. 1.

Staudohar, Paul D. and James A. Mangan. T*he Business of Professional Sports*. Chicago, Illinois, 1991.

Stogel, Chuck. "NFL Scouting A $25 Million 'Unscientific Study'," *The Sporting News*, April 16, 1990.

Uberstine, Gary A. *Law of Professional and Amateur Sports*. New York, New York, 1990.

USA Today, "Duke's Champs Score Big in Souvenir Field," August 3, 1992, Sec. C.

Whitford, David. *A Payroll to Meet*. New York, New York, 1989.

Yaeger, Don. *Undue Process*. Champagne, Illinois, 1991.

ABOUT THE AUTHOR

David Carter is a graduate of the University of Southern California where he obtained both a Bachelors of Science degree in Marketing and a Masters Degree of Business Administration in Finance. His career in management consulting has explored and addressed a broad and comprehensive range of sports management issues.

He currently resides in Redondo Beach, California, and welcomes any comments or inquiries about this text to: Post Office Box 7000-18, Redondo Beach, California 90277.

INDEX

CAREER
RESOURCES

Contact Impact Publications to receive a free copy of their latest comprehensive and annotated catalog of over 2,000 career resources (books, subscriptions, training programs, videos, audiocassettes, computer software, and CD-ROM).

The following career resources are available directly from Impact Publications. Complete the following form or list the titles, include postage (see formula at the end), enclose payment, and send your order along with your name and mailing address to:

IMPACT PUBLICATIONS
9104-N Manassas Drive
Manassas Park, VA 22111
Tel. 703/361-7300
FAX 703/335-9486

Orders from individuals must be prepaid by check, moneyorder, Visa or MasterCard number. We accept telephone and FAX orders with a Visa or MasterCard number.

Qty.	TITLES	Price	TOTAL

CAREERS IN THE SPORTS INDUSTRY

	Career Opportunities in the Sports Industry	$27.95	
	Careers for Sports Nuts	$12.95	
	Opportunities in Fitness	$13.95	
	Opportunities in Sports and Athletics	$13.95	
	Opportunities in Sports Medicine	$13.95	
	You Can't Play the Game If You Don't Know the Rules	$14.95	

248

JOB SEARCH STRATEGIES AND TACTICS

___ 110 Biggest Mistakes Job Hunters Make $14.95 ___
___ Change Your Job, Change Your Life $14.95 ___
___ Complete Job Finder's Guide to the 90s $13.95 ___
___ Dynamite Tele-Search $10.95 ___
___ Electronic Job Search Revolution $12.95 ___
___ Five Secrets to Finding a Job $12.95 ___
___ How to Get Interviews From Classified Job Ads $14.95 ___
___ Professional's Job Finder $18.95 ___
___ Rites of Passage At $100,000+ $29.95 ___

NETWORKING, INTERVIEWS & SALARY NEGOTIATIONS

___ 60 Seconds and You're Hired! $9.95 ___
___ Dynamite Answers to Interview Questions $10.95 ___
___ Dynamite Salary Negotiation $12.95 ___
___ Great Connections $11.95 ___
___ Interview for Success $11.95 ___
___ New Network Your Way to Job and Career Success $12.95 ___

RESUMES AND LETTERS

___ 200 Letters for Job Hunters $17.95 ___
___ Dynamite Cover Letters $10.95 ___
___ Dynamite Resumes $10.95 ___
___ Electronic Resume Revolution $12.95 ___
___ Electronic Resumes for the New Job Market $11.95 ___
___ High Impact Resumes and Letters $12.95 ___
___ Job Search Letters That Get Results $12.95 ___
___ The Resume Catalog $15.95 ___

SKILLS, TESTING, SELF-ASSESSMENT, EMPOWERMENT

___ 7 Habits of Highly Effective People $11.00 ___
___ Discover the Best Jobs for You $11.95 ___
___ Do What You Are $14.95 ___
___ Do What You Love, the Money Will Follow $10.95 ___
___ What Color Is Your Parachute? $14.95 ___

DRESS, APPEARANCE, IMAGE

___ John Molloy's New Dress for Success (men) $10.95 ___
___ Red Socks Don't Work! (men) $14.95 ___
___ The Winning Image $17.95 ___

BEST JOBS AND EMPLOYERS FOR THE 90s

___ 100 Best Companies to Work for in America $27.95 ___
___ American Almanac of Jobs and Salaries $17.00 ___
___ Best Jobs for the 1990s and Into the 21st Century $12.95 ___
___ Job Seeker's Guide to 1000 Top Employers $22.95 ___

KEY DIRECTORIES

___ American Salaries and Wages Survey	$94.95	___
___ Dictionary of Occupational Titles	$39.95	___
___ Directory of Executive Recruiters (annual)	$39.95	___
___ Government Directory of Addresses and Telephone Numbers	$99.95	___
___ National Directory of Addresses & Telephone Numbers	$129.95	___
___ National Trade and Professional Associations	$79.95	___
___ Occupational Outlook Handbook	$22.95	___
___ Personnel Executives Contactbook	$149.00	___

INTERNATIONAL, OVERSEAS, AND TRAVEL JOBS

___ Almanac of International Jobs and Careers	$19.95	___
___ Complete Guide to International Jobs & Careers	$13.95	___
___ Guide to Careers in World Affairs	$14.95	___
___ Jobs for People Who Love Travel	$12.95	___
___ Jobs in Russia and the Newly Independent States	$15.95	___
___ Teaching English Abroad	$15.95	___

PUBLIC-ORIENTED CAREERS

___ Almanac of American Government Jobs and Careers	$14.95	___
___ Complete Guide to Public Employment	$19.95	___
___ Find a Federal Job Fast!	$13.95	___
___ Government Job Finder	$14.95	___
___ Jobs and Careers With Nonprofit Organizations	$14.95	___
___ How to Get a Federal Job	$15.00	___
___ Non-Profit's Job Finder	$16.95	___
___ The Right SF 171 Writer	$19.95	___

COMPUTER SOFTWARE AND CD-ROM

___ JOBHUNT™ Quick and Easy Employer Contacts	$49.95	___
___ INSTANT™ Job Hunting Letters	$39.95	___
___ Job Power Source (CD-ROM)	$49.95	___
___ ResumeMaker	$49.95	___
___ Ultimate Job Finder	$59.95	___

SUBTOTAL ___

Virginia residents add 4½% sales tax ___

POSTAGE/HANDLING ($4.00 for first title and $1.00 for each additional book) $4.00
Number of additional titles x $1.00 ---------- ___

TOTAL ENCLOSED ----------------___